Australia as an Asia–Pacific Regional Power

During recent years, in its traditional role as an important Asia–Pacific regional power, Australia has had to cope with a rapidly changing external security environment and a series of new challenges, including a rising China, an increasingly assertive United States, and most notably the global 'war on terror'. This book considers the changing nature of Australia's identity and role in the Asia–Pacific, and the forces behind these developments, with particular attention towards security alignments and alliance relationships. It outlines the contours of Australia's traditional role as a key regional middle power and the patterns of its heavy reliance on security alignments and alliances. It goes on to consider Australia's relationships with other regional powers including Japan, China, Indonesia and India, uncovering the underlying purposes and expectations associated with these relationships, their evolving character—particularly in the post-Cold War era—and likely future directions. It discusses the implications for the region of Australia's new 'Pacific doctrine' of intervention, whether Australia's traditional alliance preferences are compatible with the emergence of a new East Asian security mechanism, and the impact of new, transnational and non-traditional security challenges such as terrorism and failed states. Overall, this book provides an incisive examination of Australia's changing role as a regional Asia–Pacific power in an era of great regional and global upheaval.

Brendan Taylor is a lecturer in the Graduate Studies in Strategy and Defence Program at the Australian National University. He is a specialist on Northeast Asian security, American foreign policy, economic statecraft and alliance politics.

Routledge security in Asia Pacific series

Series Editors: Leszek Buszynski *International University of Japan* and William Tow *Australian National University*

Security issues have become more prominent in the Asia Pacific region because of the presence of global players, rising great powers, and confident middle powers, which intersect in complicated ways. This series puts forward important new work on key security issues in the region. It embraces the roles of the major actors, their defense policies and postures and their security interaction over the key issues of the region. It includes coverage of the United States, China, Japan, Russia, the Koreas, as well as the middle powers of ASEAN and South Asia. It also covers issues relating to environmental and economic security as well as transnational actors and regional groupings.

Bush and Asia
America's evolving relations with East Asia
Edited by Mark Beeson

Japan, Australia and Asia–Pacific Security
Edited by Brad Williams and Andrew Newman

Regional Cooperation and its Enemies in Northeast Asia
The impact of domestic forces
Edited by Edward Friedman and Sung Chull Kim

Energy Security in Asia
Edited by Michael Wesley

Australia as an Asia–Pacific Regional Power
Friendships in flux?
Edited by Brendan Taylor

Securing Southeast Asia
The Politics of Security Sector Reform
Mark Beeson and Alex J. Bellamy

Australia as an Asia–Pacific regional power

Friendships in Flux?

Edited by Brendan Taylor

Routledge
Taylor & Francis Group

LONDON AND NEW YORK

First published 2007
by Routledge
2 Park Square, Milton Park, Abingdon, Oxon OX14 4RN

Simultaneously published in the USA and Canada
by Routledge
711 Third Ave, New York, NY 10017

Routledge is an imprint of the Taylor & Francis Group, an informa business

First issued in paperback 2012

Typeset in Times New Roman by Taylor & Francis Books

British Library Cataloguing in Publication Data
A catalogue record for this book is available from the British Library

Library of Congress Cataloging in Publication Data
Australia as an Asia Pacific Regional power : friendships in flux? / edited
by Brendan Taylor.
    p. cm. – (Routledge security in Asia Pacific series; 5)
    Includes bibliographical references and index.
1. Australia – Foreign relations. 2. Regionalism – Asia. 3. Regionalism –
Pacific Area. I. Taylor, Brendan, 1974–
    JZ1990.A9A97 2007
    327.94 – dc22
       2007007575

ISBN 978-0-415-40421-1 (hbk)
ISBN 978-0-415-54092-6 (pbk)
ISBN 978-0-203-94012-9 (ebk)

Contents

Contributors

Robert Ayson is Director of Studies of the Graduate Studies in Strategy and
Defence Program, Australian National University. In addition to several
previous academic appointments, he was also a Special Advisor to the
New Zealand Foreign Affairs, Defence and Trade Select Committee and
an Intelligence Officer at New Zealand's External Assessment's Bureau.
His research interests include strategic theory, nuclear proliferation and
disarmament, and Asia–Pacific regional stability. His book publications
include *Thomas Schelling and the Nuclear Age* (Frank Cass, 2004). His
articles have appeared in such leading international journals as *Asian
Security*, *The Nonproliferation Review*, *Contemporary Southeast Asia*, *The
Journal of Strategic Studies* and *Comparative Strategy*.

Desmond Ball is a 'Special Professor' at the Strategic and Defence Studies
Centre, Australian National University. He is currently the Co-Chair for
the Australian Member Committee of the Council for Security Cooperation in the Asia–Pacific. He was previously Head of the Strategic and
Defence Studies Centre and a Member of the Council of the International Institute for Strategic Studies in London. His primary research
interests are Australian defence, nuclear strategy and Asia–Pacific security. His book publications include *The Boys in Black: The Thahan Phran
(Rangers), Thailand's Para-Military Border Guards* (White Lotus, 2004),
Death in Balibo, Lies in Canberra (co-author, Allen & Unwin, 2000),
Breaking the Codes: The KGB's Network in Australia, 1944–1950 (co-
author, Allen & Unwin, 1998), *Presumptive Engagement—Australia's
Asia–Pacific Security Policy in the 1990s* (co-author, Allen & Unwin,
1996) and *Politics and Force Levels: The Strategic Missile Program of the
Kennedy Administration* (University of California Press, 1980). His arti-
cles have appeared in such leading international relations journals/
monograph series as *IISS Adelphi Papers*, *International Security*, *The
Journal of Strategic Studies*, *The Pacific Review* and *Security Dialogue*.

Coral Bell is a Visiting Fellow at the Strategic and Defence Studies Centre,
Australian National University. She has held numerous postings
during her long and distinguished career, including within the Australian

Diplomatic Service and as Professor of International Politics at the University of Sussex. Her research interests are mainly in crisis management and the interaction of strategic, economic and diplomatic factors in international politics, especially as they affect US and Australian foreign policies. Her articles have appeared in a number of leading international journals, such as *Foreign Affairs*, *The National Interest* and *The American Interest*. Her most recent publications include *Living with Giants: Finding Australia's Place in a More Complex World* (Australian Strategic Policy Institute, 2005) and *A World Out of Balance: American Power and International Politics in the Twenty-First Century* (Longueville Books, 2004).

Christopher Chung is Adjunct Fellow at the Strategic and Defence Studies Centre, Australian National University. He was previously Deputy Director of Studies, Graduate Studies in Strategy Program, Australian National University. His primary research interests are Asia–Pacific Maritime affairs, China–ASEAN relations and non-traditional security. Dr Chung was recently awarded a PhD from the Australian Defence Force Academy, University of New South Wales, for his thesis entitled *The Spratly Islands Dispute: Decision Units and Domestic Politics*, which he is currently reviewing for publication. In his previous posting with the Organization for Economic Cooperation and Development in Paris, he was also a contributor to and editor of numerous OECD books.

Paul Dibb is Emeritus Professor at and Chairman of the Strategic and Defence Studies Centre, Australian National University. He was formerly a Deputy Secretary in the Australian Department of Defence and Director of the Australian Defence Intelligence Organization. His book/monograph publications include *America's Asian Alliances* (co-edited, MIT Press, 2000), *Towards a New Balance of Power in Asia* (Oxford, 1995) and *The Soviet Union—The Incomplete Superpower* (MacMillan, 1986). His articles have appeared in a number of leading international journals, including *Survival*, *Orbis* and *The Washington Quarterly*. He was also the author of the highly influential 1986 *Review of Australia's Defence Capabilities*.

Sandy Gordon was awarded his PhD from Cambridge University in 1976. He joined the Australian Public Service in 1977, subsequently working in the Office of National Assessments, AusAID and as Executive Director of the Asian Studies Council and Australian Literacy Council. In 1990 he became a Fellow at the Strategic and Defence Studies Centre, Australian National University, where he worked on South Asia and the Indian Ocean. In 1997 he was appointed head of intelligence at the Australian Federal Police (AFP), a position he held until 2000. He then became Co-Chair of the Council for Security Cooperation in the Asia–Pacific Transnational Crime Working Group and a member of the National Expert Advisory Committee on Illicit Drugs. Between 2003 and

2005 he lectured on terrorism and transnational crime at the Australian Defence Force Academy, University of New South Wales. He is currently Associate Professor, Centre for Transnational Crime Prevention, University of Wollongong.

Allan Gyngell is Executive Director of the Lowy Institute for International Policy. He has a wide background in international policymaking in Australia. He joined the then Department of External Affairs in 1969 and had postings to Rangoon, Singapore and Washington. He then spent a number of years working for the Office of National Assessments. He also headed the International Division of the Department of the Prime Minister and Cabinet, from where he was appointed in 1993 as foreign policy adviser to the then Australian Prime Minister, Paul Keating. He has worked as a consultant to a number of Australian companies. His recent publications include *Making Australian Foreign Policy* (co-author, Cambridge University Press, 2003). He is a member of both the Australian Government's Foreign Affairs Council and the Defence and National Security Advisory Council.

Ron Huisken is Senior Fellow at the Strategic and Defence Studies Centre, Australian National University. His research interests include East Asian security, alliance politics, arms control, nuclear weapons and missile defence. He has held a number of research and policy positions, including Research Fellow, Stockholm International Peace Research Institute (SIPRI), Political Affairs Officer, UN Department of Disarmament Affairs, positions with the Australian Department of Foreign Affairs and Trade including Deputy Chief of Mission, Australian Embassy, Bonn and Director-General, Alliance Policy, Australian Department of Defence. His recent publications include *Iraq: Why a Strategic Blunder Looked So Attractive* (SDSC, 2006), *We Don't Want the Smoking Gun to be a Mushroom Cloud: Intelligence on Iraq's WMD* (SDSC, 2004) and *North Korea: Power Play or Buying Butter with Guns?* (SDSC, 2004).

Pauline Kerr is Director of Studies at the Asia–Pacific College of Diplomacy, Australian National University. Prior to taking up this position, she worked for the Australian Department of Foreign Affairs and Trade, the Australian Defence College and the Department of International Relations, Australian National University. Her research interests are currently focused on human security issues in the Asia–Pacific and China's 'new diplomacy'. Her book publications include *Presumptive Engagement—Australia's Asia–Pacific Security Policy in the 1990s* (co-author, Allen & Unwin, 1996). Her articles have appeared in such leading international journals as *The Pacific Review* and *The Washington Quarterly*.

Brendan Taylor is a Lecturer in the Graduate Studies in Strategy and Defence Program at the Australian National University. He is a specialist on Northeast Asian security, American foreign policy, economic statecraft and alliance politics, with a PhD from the Australian National University. He lectures to a number of undergraduate and postgraduate classes at the ANU—where he coordinates Masters-level courses on Asia–Pacific security and the US and East Asian security—as well as to various Australian defence colleges and public fora. He is a frequent commentator in the Australian media and a member of the Australian Committee of the Council for Security Cooperation in the Asia–Pacific. His publications have appeared in such leading international journals as *Asian Security*, *Comparative Strategy* and the *Australian Journal of International Affairs*.

Shannon Tow is a PhD candidate in the Department of International Relations, Australian National University. She is currently working on 'hedging' strategies, specifically in terms of their historical and contemporary application to Australian foreign policy behaviour. Prior to commencing her PhD studies at the beginning of 2005, she worked at the National Bureau of Asian Research (NBR), Washington, where she assisted with the production of the NBR's flagship annual publication, *Strategic Asia*. Her recent publications include 'Southeast Asia in the Sino–US Strategic Balance', *Contemporary Southeast Asia*, vol. 26, no. 3, December 2004.

William Tow is Professor in the Department of International Relations, Australian National University. He was previously Professor of International Relations at both the University of Queensland and Griffith University and an Assistant Professor of International Relations at the University of Southern California. He has been a Visiting Fellow at Stanford University and a Visiting Research Associate at the International Institute for Strategic Studies in London. His book publications include *Asia–Pacific Strategic Relations: Seeking Convergent Security* (Cambridge, 2001), *International Relations in the New Century* (co-editor, Oxford, 2000), *Encountering the Dominant Player* (Columbia, 1991) and *The Limits of Alliance* (co-author, The Johns Hopkins University Press, 1990). His articles have appeared in such leading international relations journals/monograph series as *IISS Adelphi Papers*, *Survival*, *The Pacific Review*, *Asian Security*, *Security Studies*, *China Quarterly*, *Contemporary Southeast Asia* and *International Affairs*.

Michael Wesley is Professor and Director of the Griffith Asia Institute at Griffith University, Queensland. He was previously Assistant Director-General for Transnational Issues at the Office of National Assessments, Senior Lecturer in the School of Politics and International Relations at the University of New South Wales and a Research Fellow at the Asia–Australia Institute, also at the University of New South Wales. His research interests include United Nations peacekeeping, Asia–Pacific politics and security, Australian foreign policy and regional organizations. His recent publications include *Making Australian Foreign Policy* (co-author, Cambridge University Press, 2003) and *Regional Organizations of the Asia–Pacific: Exploring Institutional Change* (editor, Palgrave Macmillan, 2003). His articles have appeared in such leading journals as *Ethics and International Affairs, Australian Journal of International Affairs, Pacific Affairs* and the *Australian Journal of Political Science.*

Hugh White is Head of the Strategic and Defence Studies Centre, Australian National University. Before taking up that position, he was the first Director of the Australian Strategic Policy Institute, an independent, non-partisan centre established by the Australian Government to provide fresh choices about Australia's defence and strategic policy options. He has worked in strategic policy and related fields for two decades. He has served as an intelligence analyst in the Office of National Assessments, a journalist with the *Sydney Morning Herald* and as a senior advisor on the staffs of Defence Minister Kim Beazley and Prime Minister Bob Hawke. Between 1995 and 2000 he was also a Deputy Secretary in the Australian Department of Defence. His recent publications include *Strengthening Our Neighbour—Australia and the Future of Papua New Guinea* (co-author, ASPI, 2004) and *Beyond the Defence of Australia* (Lowy, 2006). He is also a Visiting Fellow at the Lowy Institute for International Policy and writes a regular column for the *Sydney Morning Herald.*

Foreword

Coral Bell

The twenty-first century seems likely to be 'Asia's century'. After 500 years of relative eclipse, in which even the greatest powers of Asia, China and India, as well as the middle and minor ones, were objects (sometimes prizes) rather than players in their own hands in the game of nations, they are now reaching their full potential—strategically, diplomatically and economically. That change will transform the society of states.

Indian scholars have called the five centuries from 1492 until the late twentieth century the 'Vasco da Gama era', that notable navigator's name standing for all the factors which allowed Western ascendancy to be established over an Asian world that was, in many ways, more advanced than the West itself at the time. Certainly it was much larger in both territory and population, and at least as skilled in most arts and sciences.

As late as 1820, according to the economic historians, China and India were the largest economies in the world. In a few decades, they may be so again. So what we are seeing in the present redistribution of power in the world is, in some respects, a return to the past. Yet its affects are much more radical and widespread than most people have realized. Almost everyone has probably noticed by now the rise and rise of China and India, but those two vast sovereignties are only the most spectacular instances of the process of transformation.

According to the demographers, by the middle of the twenty-first century 19 of the world's societies will collectively have more than 100 million people. Eight of them will be Asian (headed by India and China with almost three billion people between them)—comprising a third of the then world total. The other six (Japan, Pakistan, Indonesia, Bangladesh, the Philippines, and Vietnam) will between them have more than 1,000 million. So Australia will have more than four billion Asian neighbours, at various stages of economic growth and with various kinds of political structure. Most of them (except Japan) will be aiming at high rates of economic growth, to lift their respective peoples out of the dire poverty in which the majority of them still live.

Population numbers in themselves have not in the past been much indication of economic strength, diplomatic clout or military capacity. But that was then, and this is now, since the countries in what we used to call the Third World have acquired (in just the last 30 years or so) better technological skills and stronger nationalist consensus, along with an understanding of how to achieve rapid economic growth. Nineteen very large, mostly fast-growing economies, with a need for commodities which are in some cases (crucially perhaps oil) going to be in dwindling supply, offer formidable prospects of competition, and potentially friction. So the world will need careful, prudent and resourceful diplomacy if the worst dangers are to be averted.

The society of states has never been a democracy. It has, for the most part, been an oligarchy—the rule of the few by the great powers of the time. The most vital point to note about the group of great and near-great powers who seem to be emerging at the moment is how much wider and more *diverse* they are than their predecessors of the past. Aside from the eight Asian powers mentioned, there are four African states (Nigeria, Congo, Ethiopia and Uganda) in the '100 million plus' club, two Latin American (Brazil and Mexico) and two Middle Eastern (Iran and Turkey). There is only one Western society—the United States. No individual state within the European Union makes it to the 100 million mark, though the group as a whole (depending on how the 'widening' process goes) may reach a population of 600 million, or more if Russia is eventually recruited. The scarcity of Westerners is not a temporary disparity: according to the demographers, they will shrink to 12 per cent of the world's people.

Australia was of course settled in a time when Western ascendancy was at its peak, and was so much taken for granted that it was unconsciously assumed to be natural and eternal. Our 'great and powerful friends', as defined by R. G. Menzies when he was prime minister, were Britain from the time of settlement until December 1941, and the United States thereafter. But Australia must make its future (economically, diplomatically and strategically) in a world where influence is far more widely distributed—a world of six great powers (the United States, the European Union, China, India, Japan and Russia) and several others (Indonesia and Pakistan in particular), whose choices will be vital to the peace of Asia and therefore also to the future of Australia.

I have no doubt that we have the capacity to live securely and prosperously in that new landscape of the society of states. Australia has no sworn enemies, and several natural or well-cultivated friends. The authors represented in this book are all experts in their particular fields, and their analyses offer very useful guidance in this time of transition.

Acknowledgements

'No man is an island' the metaphysical poet John Donne once wrote. Certainly this is a lesson which the most powerful country the world has ever known, the United States, has come to understand all too well in the context of the continuing Iraq imbroglio. Thankfully, my experience during the course of this project has been almost the antithesis of the recent American experience, blest as I have been to be surrounded by such a large and loyal collection of close friends and allies.

First and foremost, I would like to acknowledge the contribution and support of my friend and colleague Rob Ayson. The idea for this project emerged initially during one of our many discussions late in the evening at the Strategic and Defence Studies Centre, Australian National University. His encouragement, advice and scholarly contribution to the project have been indispensable. I would also like to acknowledge the generosity and forbearance of his lifelong ally, Catherine Ayson, for the many times when dinner conversations have drifted onto work-related matters. At so many levels, her enthusiasm and wise counsel have also been indispensable.

The Strategic and Defence Studies Centre has provided a wonderful environment within which to undertake the project. I would particularly like to thank Des Ball, who for more than a decade now has guided me to and through the early stages of my academic career; Paul Dibb, a man of hidden depths whose friendship and counsel I treasure; Coral Bell, who has taught me that true greatness really does know gentleness; and to Hugh White, who has accomplished the near impossible by inspiring a New Zealander to acquire a genuine interest in Australian strategic and defence matters.

I would like to thank the series editors Leszek Buszynski and Bill Tow for their substantial input into the project and for the confidence they have shown in me. On both a personal and professional level, Bill's scholarly advice and generosity of spirit have been indispensable. The fresh perspectives which Leszek's intermittent visits to Canberra from Japan have injected into the project have also been most valuable. Similarly, I would like to thank Peter Sowden, Tom Bates and Paola Celli at Routledge, who have been a joy to work with; Jennifer Harding for her wonderfully meticulous copy-edit of the manuscript; as well as the Australian National University's Publications Committee who provided generous financial support for the project.

A very special thanks is due to Meredith Thatcher, publications editor and research assistant in the Strategic and Defence Studies Centre, whose dedication in preparing the manuscript went far beyond the call of duty. I also remain particularly indebted to Meredith for her active encouragement of the project during an early period of potential 'strategic drift'. Likewise, to the many friends who have shown an interest and provided support during its course including Sarah Flint, Evelyn Goh, Ron Huisken, Hiau Joo Kee, Josh Straub, Maya Salleh and Ping Yu. I would particularly like to single out the unconditional patience and understanding of Chiraporn Roochitawiwat who, with incredible resilience and always with a cheerful smile, accepted the often unreasonable demands which this project imposed upon the time we were able to spend together.

Last, but not least, to my family. To my sister Rebecca, who has been a stabilizing influence throughout my life and who now, in the form of my valued friend Cameron Crouch, has found the happiness she truly deserves. Finally, to my parents Marie and Gerry, while mounting work demands have both increased the geographical distance between us while reducing the amount of time we have spent together in recent years, I trust you know that you are both never far from my thoughts. I really could not have wished for two more loving, understanding and dedicated parents.

Despite the extensive and various forms of assistance I have received from all of the above, there are undoubtedly errors and shortcomings in this volume. For these, I alone am responsible.

Brendan Taylor
Canberra
December 2006

Acronyms and abbreviations

ADF	Australian Defence Force
AFP	Australian Federal Police
ALP	Australian Labor Party
ANZAC	Australia and New Zealand Army Corps
ANZUS	Australia, New Zealand and the United States (Treaty)
APEC	Asia–Pacific Economic Cooperation
ARF	ASEAN Regional Forum
ASEAN	Association of Southeast Asian nations
AUSFTA	Australia–United States Free Trade Agreement
AusAID	Australian Agency for International Development
BMD	ballistic missile defence
CDR	Closer Defence Relations
CER	Closer Economic Relations
CINCPAC	Commander in Chief Pacific
DCP	Defence Cooperation Program
DIFF	Development Import Finance Facility
DLP	Democratic Labor Party
DOTARS	Department of Transport and Regional Services
DSD	Defence Signals Directorate
EAS	East Asia Summit
ECP	Enhanced Cooperation Program
EU	European Union
FPDA	Five Power Defence Arrangements
GSDF	Japan Ground Self-Defense Force
IMF	International Monetary Fund
INTERFET	International Force for East Timor
ISPS	International Ship and Port Facility Security
JCLEC	Jakarta Centre for Law Enforcement Cooperation
JDP	Joint Declaration of Principles
JSF	Joint Strike Fighter
MFN	most favoured nation
MOU	Memorandum of Understanding
NATO	North Atlantic Treaty Organization

NEIO	Northeast Indian Ocean
NPT	Nuclear Non-Proliferation Treaty
NZDF	New Zealand Defence Force
OTS	Office of Transport Security
PIC	Pacific Island country
PLA	People's Liberation Army
PNG	Papua New Guinea
PNGDF	Papua New Guinea Defence Force
PSI	Proliferation Security Initiative
RAAF	Royal Australian Air Force
RAMSI	Regional Assistance Mission to Solomon Islands
SAARC	South Asian Association for Regional Cooperation
SAF	Singapore armed forces
SCO	Shanghai Cooperation Organization
SDF	Japan Self-Defense Force
SEATO	Southeast Asian Treaty Organization
SLOCs	sea lines of communication
TAC	Treaty of Amity and Cooperation
TCOG	Trilateral Coordination and Oversight Group
TSD	Trilateral Strategic Dialogue
UNAMET	United Nations Mission in East Timor
UNHRC	United Nations Human Rights Commission
UNSC	United Nations Security Council
VSTOL	vertical short take-off and landing
WMD	weapons of mass destruction

Part 1
Laying the table

1 Introduction

Brendan Taylor

Australia's security alignments and alliance relationships—for so long a key component of Australia's national security and defence policies—are currently experiencing a period of profound upheaval. This change is the product of a combination of factors, including the rise of China; important shifts in Japan's postwar security policies; an increasingly assertive United States; the emergence of a distinctive 'East Asian' identity (that could conceivably manifest itself in some form of new regional security mechanism excluding the United States); the ongoing global 'war on terror' (or recently dubbed 'Long War'); a growing awareness of the potentially broader geopolitical challenges posed by 'failed' and 'failing' states; as well as apparent shifts in Australian public attitudes toward a number of key foreign-policy actors and issues.

The changes taking place in Australia's security alignments and alliance relationships are significant because they are occurring at a time when an increasing number of scholars are questioning the broader relevance and sustainability of formal alliance structures, with some even going so far as to predict their outright disappearance within the next decade. In the Australian case, however, a number of its alliances and alignments have actually strengthened in recent times. By way of example, the fact that Australian Defence Force (ADF) personnel and Japan Self-Defense Force (SDF) soldiers recently completed an unprecedented 'tour of duty' together in Iraq, and that Canberra and Tokyo are now in the process of developing a new security agreement, is symbolic of an increasingly close Australia–Japan strategic partnership that looks set to deepen. Potentially in direct competition to this—but riding on the back of an increasingly indispensable economic relationship—there are signs of a new strategic tie emerging between Australia and China. The imperative to cooperate on a range of 'non-traditional' threats, such as terrorism and maritime security, has also resulted in efforts to breathe new life into the Five Power Defence Arrangements (FPDA). In these instances, therefore, the Australian experience appears to run directly counter to what contemporary thinking on alliance politics would anticipate.

Conversely, however, a majority of Australia's security alliances and alignments (and those which have traditionally been its most important) are coming under increasing strain. Despite being in a healthier position than perhaps at any other time during its history, for instance, Australia's alliance with the United States is being subjected to mounting pressure as Canberra struggles to strike an appropriate balance in its relations with Washington and a 'rising China'; to participate in the East Asia Summit (EAS), which explicitly excludes the sole superpower; and to remain sensitive to a somewhat alarming negative shift in Australian public attitudes toward the United States. Likewise, deep public scepticism, coupled with fundamental cultural and perceptual differences, continues to complicate Australia's often-troubled relationship with Indonesia and is likely to preclude indefinitely the development of any deeper strategic tie between the two. Australia's longstanding security relationship with Papua New Guinea (PNG) is currently in an even more precarious position following the collapse of the Enhanced Cooperation Program (ECP), while many (on the Australian side of the Tasman Sea at least) continue to query the utility of maintaining Closer Defence Relations (CDR) with New Zealand.

Inadequate attention has thus far been given to the above trends, not only in the context of what they might collectively portend for Australia's national security in the twenty-first century, but also in terms of what broader applicability the Australian case may have for policymakers and defence planners in other countries, as well as to broader scholarly debates regarding the changing shape of security alignments and alliance relationships. This book aims to shed light on these issues by reflecting upon where the security alignments and alliance relationships of Australia—a key middle power in the Asia–Pacific region—have come from; by taking stock of where they currently stand; and by contemplating where they might be heading.

The book is divided into four parts, each titled to complement its overarching 'friendships' theme. Part 1 ('Laying the table') is designed to introduce and contextualize the volume. Following on from the Introduction, in Chapter 2 Bill Tow lays much of the groundwork for the remainder of the book. Tow's contribution provides a theoretical treatment of how traditional security arrangements (alliances, alignments and coalitions) are adapting and evolving to the demands of what many commentators regard as a new strategic age. Tow begins by contemplating how well traditional theories of alliance politics relate to these changing security dynamics, before adopting a more region-specific focus and considering which theoretical perspectives might best explain ongoing challenges to organizing security in the Asia–Pacific. Tow's basic argument is that, while state-centric security partnerships continue to be germane to the current strategic environment, from a theoretical standpoint these must be explained and validated quite differently from their Cold War predecessors. The broad and varied range of security partnerships in which Australia is currently engaged—and which, indeed, provide the focus for this volume—certainly appears consistent with the incredibly complex and increasingly demanding strategic context to which Tow refers. However, he also goes on to acknowledge that this 'somewhat controversial' security posture that Canberra has adopted—allying and coalescing with great powers that could easily become rivals while simultaneously aligning with an emerging Asia–Pacific community—is by no means a risk-free one. This is a theme, of course, which re-emerges throughout the course of the volume.

Part 2 of the book ('Dining with giants') examines Australia's security relationships with each of the region's great powers—the United States, China, India and Japan. Paul Dibb begins his chapter on the Australia–US alliance by observing that, for more than five decades now, this relationship has weathered and adapted to situations of great strategic change—a resilience which he attributes to Australia's penchant for securing 'a great and powerful friend', in addition to the increased regional influence, intelligence access, defence science and technology collaboration, and provision of advanced US military weapons which the relationship bestows to its junior partner. However, he goes on to address the difficult question of whether these obvious alliance benefits will continue to indefinitely outweigh the costs. Dibb identifies five issues which could potentially put this all-important strategic relationship under immense strain in the coming years. These issues include differences between Canberra and Washington over the (re)emergence of China; the relative decline of Australia's regional strategic weight; the persistence of a revolutionary mindset in Washington that is intent on using America's superior military power to reshape the world; a conflict between the United States and China over Taiwan; and the rise of anti-American sentiment in Australia. While acknowledging that Canberra and Washington currently have close commonality of views when it comes to fighting the 'war on terror', and while concluding that an Asia–Pacific region without the United States would be a dangerous place for Australia, Dibb goes on to question whether the 'war on terror' will ultimately be able to overcome these potential differences and thereby unite the United States and Australia to the same extent as previous wars.

In Chapter 4, Brendan Taylor and Des Ball then examine the 'transformation' which is underway in security relations between Washington's two closest regional allies: Australia and Japan. They demonstrate how this transformation has taken the form of increased security collaboration in the 'war on terror', peacekeeping operations, humanitarian assistance efforts and military exercises, and observe that it has also been reflected in a number of significant policy pronouncements. Ball and Taylor attribute this intensification in Australia–Japan security relations to a range of factors, including their converging threat perceptions in relation to weapons of mass destruction (WMD) proliferation and international terrorism; many of the political and ideological commonalities between the two countries; the fact that both Australia and Japan are in some respects 'outsiders' in East Asia; as well as to the dynamics of their respective bilateral alliance relationships with the United States. While Ball and Taylor suggest that these factors collectively point toward a gradual strengthening of the Australia–Japan security relationship, however, they also conclude that the potential impediments to any further advancement of strategic collaboration—including resource disparities in the military sphere, fundamentally different strategic interests and diverging perceptions of China's (re)emergence—should not be underestimated.

Michael Wesley, in the subsequent chapter, discusses the related, though perhaps more enduring dilemma that Australian policymakers have faced of how to chart their own independent course through the Asian regional order in a manner that remains consistent with this country's commitments under the Australia–US alliance. During recent years, this seeming contradiction has come into sharper relief around the issue of China's (re)emergence. In approaching Sino–Australian relations, Wesley suggests that Canberra has developed two distinct (though clearly interrelated) strategies for reconciling this cognitive dissonance. The first has been to bind China into the existing Asia–Pacific order of institutions and norms with a view to 'socializing' Beijing's behaviour. The second has been to endeavour to quarantine or 'decouple' the management of Sino–Australian ties from the often turbulent US–Sino relationship. While this dual-track strategy presently appears to be enjoying considerable success, Wesley concludes that the volatile nature of the US–Sino relationship and its susceptibility to future crises should provide reason for pause. While it would clearly therefore be premature to celebrate any definitive end to the cognitive dissonance between Australia's regional and alliance prerogatives, Wesley goes on to observe that China's growing level of resource dependence upon Australia, coupled with Canberra's increasing strategic value to Washington (particularly in the Southeast Asian and South Pacific subregions), means that Australia is currently in a better position that at almost any time previously to manage this dissonance in its relations with China and the United States. However the true test of whether Canberra is able to adjust to and maximize the potential benefits of these new material realities will, in Wesley's view, come in the form of a future US–Sino confrontation. In the event of such, he concludes, there is much for Canberra to gain in following the 'studied silence' practised by many of its Southeast Asian neighbours.

In Chapter 6, Sandy Gordon analyzes Australia's sometimes troubled, and often insubstantial security relationship with Asia's other rising power— India. As Gordon suggests, however, with India's economic and military rise continuing apace, and as the strategic interests of Canberra and New Delhi become increasingly coincident, this relatively well-entrenched pattern of passing antagonism and persistent neglect seems almost certain to change. Gordon identifies significant Australian and Indian interests in the Indian Ocean and beyond, suggesting that the greatest commonality is likely to be found in relation to transnational security issues—as opposed to more traditional, state-centric concerns—with energy security, international terrorism, natural disasters and maritime security coming near or at the top of that list. In order to build upon those common interests so as to construct a more solid and realistic platform for the relationship, Gordon suggests that most progress is likely to be made on those issues of joint interest to India and Australia which fall outside their respective bilateral security relationships with the United States. Only in this context, he contends, will New Delhi genuinely come to view Canberra as an independent and legitimate partner in the Indian Ocean. The other key variable in the future of the Australian–India security relationship, of course, remains the issue of whether Canberra will ultimately acquiesce to the sale of uranium to India. As Gordon concludes, a decision in the affirmative would do more than any other factor to enhance the current state of this still-hesitant security tie. As he also concedes, however, such a decision would have significant economic, political and strategic implications extending well beyond Australia's security relationship with India.

The focus of the book moves closer to home in Part 3 ('Working the room'), which examines Australia's security relationships with countries in its nearer region—Southeast Asia and the Southwest Pacific. In Chapter 7 Allan Gyngell discusses Australia's security relationship with Indonesia. This is a relationship which, for reasons of strategic geography, is of immense importance from Canberra's perspective, but which has also been historically fraught with difficulty. Gyngell traces the evolution of this delicate relationship from the 1960s and the establishment of a formal Defence Cooperation Program in 1968, through the troubles of the 1970s associated with the Indonesian invasion of East Timor, the subsequent mismanagement of the territory and the deaths of five Australian journalists at Balibo. He describes the revitalization of the Australia–Indonesian security relationship which occurred during the Keating years, as embodied in the 1995 'Agreement on Maintaining Security'. Consistent with the overarching ebb and flow in relations between Canberra and Jakarta, however, he also describes how the 1997 Asian financial crisis and the Australia-led East Timor intervention of 1999 led to the abrogation of this agreement. Gyngell goes on to describe how the relationship has recovered in the period since 2001, however, with the two countries responding to a range of 'new' security challenges such as people smuggling, illegal fishing and terrorism. This broadening in Australian–Indonesian security relations was formalized in November 2006 with a new framework for security cooperation. While concluding that Australian and Indonesian strategic objectives appear likely to remain broadly convergent and, therefore, on this relatively positive trajectory into the foreseeable future, Gyngell also suggests that we should not underestimate the potential for border issues (particularly over PNG and East Timor) as well as deep-seated societal antipathies in both countries to continue to unsettle the relationship.

In Chapter 8, Hugh White then examines Australia's security relationships with—and perceived strategic responsibilities towards—the small islands of its immediate neighbourhood in the Southwest Pacific. Notwithstanding the useful contributions which New Zealand has made toward managing problems in this part of the world (and which are discussed at greater length by Robert Ayson in Chapter 9), this is very much a part of the world where Australia is essentially a 'lonely superpower' facing immense political and strategic challenges. White's contribution analyzes the more engaged and muscular approach toward this region which has become one, if not *the* defining feature of the Howard years. He considers the evolution of this approach which, as White demonstrates, actually reflects deep and enduring Australian strategic interests. He also examines the problems this approach has encountered thus far and the future prospects for this so-called 'Howard Doctrine'. Reflecting upon the lessons that might be gleaned from what he considers a necessary policy shift towards recognizing Australia's key interests and responsibilities in the stability of its small near neighbours, White contends that this particular 'work in progress' still has a long way to go if Australia is to develop the requisite comprehensive approach to meeting the goals it has identified under the Howard government. Consistent with this, White also concludes that the sheer scope of the task at hand, coupled with the length of time which will be needed to accomplish it, suggests that Canberra will need to act more efficiently and effectively than it has done thus far in developing new forms of closer interaction with its nearest neighbours, if it is indeed to help them overcome their deep-seated problems.

It seems likely that Australia will continue to work closely with another near neighbour—New Zealand—in striving to realize this optimal approach that White advocates. It is this trans-Tasman connection that Robert Ayson dissects in Chapter 9. As Ayson notes, this is a relationship which has historically exhibited an unusual mix—particularly for two such 'natural' alliance partners—of competitive and collaborative elements. Notwithstanding the close historical and cultural ties between the two—forged, not least, on the battlefields of Gallipoli—he begins by observing that the Australia–New Zealand alliance is one that was initially shaped by their common involvement in a range of other multilateral relationships, such as ANZUS. While it took the ANZUS crisis of the mid-1980s, somewhat ironically, to provide the impetus for more direct collaboration between Canberra and Wellington, Ayson details how the Australia–New Zealand security relationship itself almost went into terminal decline during the late 1990s in response to the radical defence reforms introduced by the Clark government in New Zealand. In yet another peculiar twist of fate, however, New Zealand's contribution to the Australian-led East Timor intervention of 1999 breathed new life into the relationship. Notwithstanding sharp differences between Canberra and Washington over the US-led invasion of Iraq, Ayson also suggests that a case can be made that the 'war on terror' has had a similar effect on Australia–New Zealand security ties. With further disturbances in the so-called 'arc of instability' continuing to focus the minds of policymakers in both Canberra and Wellington, and with a range of other non-traditional security challenges requiring trans-Tasman collaboration, Ayson optimistically concludes that Australia and New Zealand may actually be heading towards a new era of closer security relations. This, in turn, he suggests might serve as a model for the development of Australia's relations with other regional partners as alliance relationships, more generally, expand from their traditional defence and intelligence foundations.

One such relationship to which Ayson's findings might well apply is the Australian–Singapore connection. As Ron Huisken suggests in Chapter 10, this is a highly complex, but often underplayed security relationship. Indeed, like so many of the partnerships examined in this volume, he observes that this particular tie has deep historical roots forged during times of conflict. Huisken observes that the Australia–Singapore relationship has developed a surprising level of intimacy in the period since the latter achieved full independence in 1965. This level of intimacy is currently reflected in the military training, exercising and intelligence collaboration (albeit at times troubled) which occurs between the two nations. Huisken attributes this close cooperation to a clear case of mutual interest. For Singapore, collaboration with Australia reflects its longstanding aim to forge security connections beyond its immediate neighbourhood—a tendency most evident in its security relationship with the United States and its strong support for the FPDA. For Australia, defence engagement with Singapore has formed a critical element of its broader strategy to achieve security 'with' countries in the Southeast Asian subregion, as opposed to against them. As reflected in the further intensification of cooperation between Australia and Singapore (which is currently occurring in the 'war on terror') and through regional security initiatives (such as the Proliferation Security Initiative (PSI) and the EAS), Huisken concludes that the upward trend in defence cooperation between these two countries—which has spanned the better part of the past six decades—looks set not only to continue, but to strengthen still further.

The volume's two concluding chapters are contained in Part 4 ('Washing up'). These contributions are each forward-looking in their orientation, focusing particularly on the future viability of Australia's security arrangements and the approach(es) which Canberra has historically adopted in relation to these. In Chapter 11, Christopher Chung examines the continued suitability of Australia's Asia–Pacific alliances and alignments (the majority of which were concluded to deal primarily with conventional, state-based security threats), given the increased prominence of so-called 'new' or non-traditional security challenges. Taking Southeast Asia as his analytical focus, Chung argues that the increased prominence of non-traditional security threats—such as drug trafficking, international terrorism and illegal people movements—in this part of the world has prompted a shift in the form and content of Australia's Asia–Pacific security arrangements. On the one hand, activities encompassed by traditional security arrangements such as the FPDA have broadened, thereby demonstrating that the adaptation of existing security arrangements is viable. At the same time, however, Chung also describes how a number of new frameworks have been developed that are less formal in structure, more expansive in scope and broader in participation than traditional security arrangements. While this leaves Australian policymakers in the relatively advantageous position of having a rather broad 'toolbox' of security arrangements from which to draw, Chung concludes that differing perceptions and prioritization of non-traditional security threats between Australia and its Southeast Asian neighbours will still need to be addressed if these mechanisms are to yield meaningful benefits at the political and operational levels.

The final chapter in the volume, by Pauline Kerr and Shannon Tow, also considers the continued viability of Australia's approach to its traditional Asia–Pacific security relationships, but this time in the context of trends toward greater regional integration. Kerr and Tow describe how Australia is behaving as though a multipolar balance of power already exists in the Asia–Pacific, by both broadening and deepening its bilateral relationships with each of the region's great powers. While acknowledging that this 'diversification' in Australia's approach to its Asia–Pacific security relationships exhibits some merit, Kerr and Tow argue that its essentially bilateral orientation could ultimately undermine this country's ability to establish itself as an influential *regional* player, particularly should the notion of a more 'exclusive' East Asian Community become a reality.

While Canberra has historically proven rather adept at retaining a degree of agency over the management of its Asia–Pacific security relationships by performing what Kerr and Tow characterize as a 'two-step dance' (maintaining close security ties with a 'great and powerful friend' on the one hand while simultaneously engaging with regional partners on the other), they question the continued viability of this 'hedging' strategy. Under a worst-case scenario, Kerr and Tow suggest, Australia's marginalization from the region could also impinge directly upon its alliance relationship with the United States, by undermining Australia's value as a close US ally with intimate knowledge of the Asia–Pacific and with the capacity to shape regional order in a manner consistent with Washington's interests. According to Kerr and Tow, the likelihood of such an outcome remains contingent upon how 'the politics of leadership' amongst the region's great powers ultimately plays out. Kerr and Tow also conclude, however, that Canberra retains a capacity to shape this leadership contest, provided receptivity to Australian diplomatic overtures toward that end can be cultivated effectively with its Asia–Pacific 'dance partners'.

Kerr and Tow's analysis is obviously not only of direct relevance to the Australian case. Indeed, policymakers and defence planners in a number of other Asia–Pacific countries—including the United States, Japan, China, India, South Korea, Singapore, Thailand, New Zealand and the Philippines—presently face a similar set of challenges and are consequently also grappling to understand better their impact upon existing security arrangements. To be sure, Australia's traditionally heavy reliance (some would argue dependence) on security alignments and alliance relationships does make understanding their implications especially pressing. That said, as a key middle power that is currently undergoing major tests regarding both its identity and role in the Asia–Pacific, the Australian experience almost certainly contains lessons of relevance to these other countries, while also promising to reveal a great deal about the major current and future security trends in the region.

2 Alliances and alignments in the twenty-first century

William Tow

More than 15 years since the end of the Cold War, the relevance of alliances remains a highly contentious issue in the study and conduct of international relations. Concerns over how alliances and coalitions relate to global terrorism as, arguably, the major security challenge of our time have intensified. The US Army War College recently published an assessment in its respected journal *Parameters* that concluded that the North Atlantic Treaty Organization's (NATO's) time 'had come and gone' with the demise of the Soviet threat, the building of a viable European regional community and the widening gap between US and European security perceptions.[1] Others argue that postwar alliances in Northeast Asia will fail to withstand the pressures of nationalism that will generate a unified Korea and a more 'normal' Japan less in need of US security guarantees.[2] More expedient and short-term alignments, they insist, will supplant fixed, long-term, bilateral and multilateral alliances when there is a 'convergence of America's interests with those of other states over specific issues and challenges'.[3] Critics of recent trends in US–Australia alliance relations insist that changing Australian interests, including its closer economic ties to China, could render the recent intimacy of the ANZUS alliance obsolete in future years.[4]

Most scholars and analysts of international relations, however, believe that alliances and long-term alignments and coalitions retain an important role in contemporary security politics. In a post-11 September 2001 environment, as John Ikenberry has observed, American unilateralists have often bristled at the constraints imposed on, and limited support extended by, allies for US initiatives to 'democratize' target regimes and eradicate terrorists, but 'the logic of multilateral and alliance-based tools' has nevertheless prevailed.[5] They have proven preferable to *ad hoc* 'coalitions of the willing' because of traditional allies' experience in working with the United States compared to newer, less proven, security collaborators. Moreover, NATO and other traditional allied states' political values are generally more acceptable and reliable to US policy planners than the less stable polities that may be designated as key collaborators in the so-called 'Long War'.

The line between existing alliances which could contribute to an intensifying 'war on terror', and to 'coalitions shaped by missions' (to use the oft-quoted axiom of former US Defense Secretary Donald Rumsfeld) is often a fine one. 'Reliable' allies as preferred coalition partners offer advantages: minimal intra-allied negotiations over mission purposes and constraints, maximum adaptability to addressing the scope of missions required and greater probability that the 'most involved' security partners in a specific, US-led operation would have high levels of force interoperability and greater 'staying power' due to more supportive publics. In the Asia–Pacific, Japan and Australia have emerged as the most conspicuous members of a new 'nuclear family' of a US global counterterrorism coalition that also includes Britain, Israel and parts of Eastern Europe (Poland and the Czech Republic).[6] The Philippines and Thailand have developed into 'non-NATO strategic allies' that already had existing security ties with the United States, but found these to be strengthened in a post-11 September 2001 context (Pakistan and its rival India both represent special and more complicated cases along the peripheries of the Asia–Pacific).

What has united all these states, however, is a shared perception with Washington that the United States alone cannot prevail over those Islamic fundamentalist adversarial forces challenging the liberal values and geopolitical primacy of a US-led order. State-centric security dilemmas may still emerge to blunt this trend (a potential Sino–Japanese rivalry is illustrative), but such has not yet been the case for well over five years since the 11 September 2001 terrorist attacks ushered in a new strategic age. Alliances, alignments and coalitions need to be reconsidered theoretically in terms of how they fit into this new environment. This chapter will provide such an evaluation focusing on three questions. First: How well do major postwar alliance theories relate to the rapidly changing security dynamics of the early twenty-first century? Second: What alliance and alignment/coalition perspectives might explain ongoing challenges to organizing security in the Asia–Pacific region? Third: How does the Australian–US alliance (most commonly known as ANZUS) fit into emerging regional and global security frameworks? The chapter's basic argument is that state-centric security partnerships continue to be germane to the 'Long War' but must be explained and validated quite differently from their Cold War predecessors.

Alliance theory in a post-11 September 2001 era

Writing about alliance theory at the end of the Cold War, Glenn Snyder observed that 'we have no theory about them [alliances] that remotely matches the richness of our theories about war, crisis, deterrence and other manifestations of conflict'. To some degree, he argued, this was due to their 'ubiquity' within the overall study of international relations: alliances and international relations are so intertwined as to be indecipherable. As well, parts of this subject have been studied without full consideration of its entire scope. Collective goods, sociological coalition theory, game theory, structural balancing and rational choice are all components of alliance behaviour that have been investigated. However, they have not been consolidated in a way that any 'grand theory' of alliance and coalitions has emerged.[7] This 'theoretical gap' has become even more pronounced in the post-11 September 2001 timeframe, where the notions of 'threat' and 'adversary' have become blurred by a meshing of state-centric and sub-state levels of conflict and where alliances are increasingly viewed as confidence building mechanisms as well as responses to perceived threats.

Alliances have been traditionally understood as a security commitment between two or more states to support each other against a commonly understood external threat by aggregating their military and other relevant power capabilities.[8] Alliances can also emerge, however, when rival states coalesce to manage their strategic interests, thus compelling them to move beyond capabilities aggregation and power balancing as the sole rationale for alliance. The Molotov–Ribbentrop Pact of 1939 was illustrative of this form of alliance: a non-aggression alliance between natural rivals (Germany and the Soviet Union) that allowed them to demarcate Poland, Finland, Romania and the Baltic States into agreed bipolar spheres of influence. Power balancing, however, dominated the postwar security environment as the United States and the Soviet Union forged alliance networks in Europe and Asia to contain each other. With the demise of the Soviet Union, residual, US-led alliance networks are reconstituting their identity and purpose. Some analysts have argued, for example, that traditional Cold War alliances are shifting to become 'quasi-alliances': alliance behaviour which would not only emanate from threat perceptions but also from promises made by allies in the event specific contingencies unfold.[9] Others assert that alliances are becoming increasingly subject to domestic cultural pressures.[10] Beyond these, alliance politics appears to be yielding to the rise of more informal alignments and coalitions as predominant mechanisms for managing security issues.

Alignments are normally broader, more informal, arrangements than alliances. Coalitions, while also informal, are usually directed more toward achieving a short-term or narrow objective. Alignments are 'expectations' held by policymakers about who will defend whom in various contingencies and the extent to which such a defence will apply.[11] The alignment concept is a quasi-alliance, and threat perceptions may be supplemented by other motives for closer security collaboration such as 'two antagonistic powers being driven together by their shared concern about the behaviour of a common major-power ally'.[12] The probability of states aligning with or against each other varies across different international systems and is shaped by expectations of abandonment and entrapment. States will view security commitments extended by one of the two major powers in a bipolar international system as more credible because that major power's key interest is to prevent capability aggregation against itself from occurring if it abandoned a small power that it deemed significant in global power competition. Alignments tend to be more fluid in a multipolar system, however, due to power being more ambiguous. These are not hard and fast 'rules of alignment' but rather illustrate how expectations can shape alignments in the absence of the formal strategic commitment which usually underwrites an alliance.

Coalitions are less structurally grounded and less predictable than alignments. Rather than being predicated on broad expectations about intentions and commitments of actual or potential security partners as with alignments, coalitions are designed for states to realize immediate security interests. A key objective is to share in the spoils that the strongest coalition power expects (or is expected) to extract over opposing parties or to reduce the risks posed by such parties. This constitutes a form of 'band-wagoning' where smaller states enjoy relative gains through their affiliation with a 'winning coalition', but where the strategic risks of such coalescing can be reduced or limited in an environment where such coalesced groups tend to gain or lose affiliates fairly rapidly. John Mearsheimer has observed, however, that such risks are greater in a multipolar environment 'because the shape of the international order tends to remain in flux', making the size and shape of opposing coalitions difficult to calculate.[13]

In the post-Cold War international security arena, *ad hoc* coalitions have risen to prominence at the expense of alliances and alignments. US-led coalitions have been employed to fight America's two great conflicts in Afghanistan and Iraq. Through such arrangements, Washington has greater freedom to 'pick and choose' those security partners most supportive to the specific geopolitical cause at hand and most able to contribute capabilities that best fit with US military operations. This calculation is reflected in Donald Rumsfeld's now infamous observation that 'generally the mission will determine the coalition; the coalition should not determine the mission'.[14] The exception to this rule appears to be the 'Anglophone' coalition of Australia, Britain and the United States, in which both the Australians and British appear to remain keen to 'punch above their own weight' as acolytes of US strategy.[15] Both of them have converted long-standing bilateral alliances with the United States that were linchpins of Western deterrence strategy during the Cold War into instruments of strategic preemption in the 'Long War'. Both have avoided the pitfalls of alliance dissonance and alignment dissolution plaguing recent US security relations with other traditional NATO partners such as France and Germany and such non-NATO affiliates as Pakistan and South Korea. These partners and affiliates have felt that they acquire too few benefits in return for excessive costs when becoming involved in US-led military interventions, including that they become high-profile targets in their own right for hostile, asymmetrical forces as a result of such involvement. Reacting to such feelings, formal US allies have diminished the value of their relationships with the United States in the eyes of American policy planners, and have elevated the perceived utility of *ad hoc* coalitions involving temporary partners who are willing to fight along with US forces and under US command.

Consumed with axioms of power balancing and other forms of straight-forward state-centric competition, traditional alliance theory could hardly have been expected to anticipate the stark deterioration in the appeal to conventional allies of affiliating with US hegemony, or the growing level of American frustration with managing formal alliance ties in the increasingly amorphous post-11 September 2001 international security milieu. Despite the Bush administration's disillusionment with traditional European (and perhaps South Korean) allies during its first term, however, it has never fully ascribed to the alleged 'primacy' or 'unilateralism' principles that many independent analysts have argued was the case.[16] It has instead sought to identify and implement a judicious mix of alliance and coalition politics to serve what is fundamentally a dual global strategy: responding decisively to intensifying asymmetrical threats such as international terrorism while simultaneously balancing potential state-centric rivals in the three great regions of geopolitical competition: Europe, Asia and the Middle East.

As Rod Lyon has observed, the twenty-first century security environment presents challenges that require both the maintenance of long-term security partnerships (alliances) and informal short-term partnerships (coalitions). 'What is important in choosing the appropriate mechanism is its particular utility in a given instance.'[17] Alliances provide formal guarantees and instruments for intelligence sharing, joint exercising and other aspects of military capacity building that work well against clearly structural threats with state-centric characteristics. Yet these same attributes are often too ponderous and too prone to bargaining between allies before they can be applied to rapidly developing contingencies where coalitions are better suited. The simplicity of coalition organization, and the ease with which they could be formed in response to religious or ethnic forces that show little discrimination in attacking the citizens and interests of diverse states, appeals to those states' elites who are under immense pressure to respond quickly and effectively to such contingencies.

This 'hybridization' of state-centric and asymmetrical security challenges will very likely yield future mechanisms that may not fit the theoretical explanations and rationales for those alliance, alignment or coalition models which are most familiar to us. Such arrangements will be partially shaped by the prioritization of emerging threats to those great powers having the capabilities required to neutralize them. However, they will also be the product of those exercising policy leadership most successfully within both developed and developing polities at intra-state, state-centric, regional and global levels. Theories explaining the future of security partnerships will need to clarify such complexities more effectively than is now the case if the evolution of alliance, alignment and coalition politics is to be adequately understood and applied.

The Asia–Pacific dimension

As has been true for global international security, patterns of security organization in the Asia–Pacific are undergoing a fundamental transformation. The 'San Francisco system' of security alliances has shifted from a containment-based network predicated on the logic of a US 'hub' managing allied 'spokes' in Asia to a more complex web of enduring bilateral and emerging trilateral associations geared toward advancing confidence building, preventative diplomacy and other forms of 'positive security' in the region. The old Soviet alliances with China, North Korea, Vietnam and India are either defunct or diluted beyond recognition. As is the case with Europe, the tight bipolar geopolitical competition that largely dominated the region throughout the Cold War has passed into history. Unlike Europe, however, there is no equivalent of NATO or a European Community in place to shape the Asia–Pacific's future collective security environment.

To be sure, speculation about a 'New Cold War' between the United States and China intensified during the late 1990s and early 2000s, but any 'China threat' that may be evolving cannot be viewed in the same context as the old Soviet–US rivalry. For example, China maintains a formal alliance with North Korea but its commitment to defend Kim Jong II's regime is, at best, ambiguous. Beijing has, instead and illustratively, orchestrated a series of low-key bilateral 'friendship agreements' with Russia, Pakistan and most of the ASEAN states that could be characterized as 'conditional alignments' based on finding common interests around which mutual policy expectations can be shaped.

Beijing has also become a more active multilateral player in the region, differentiating itself from the Soviet Union that was incapable of separating multilateralism in the region from the hierarchical thinking that prompted its ill-fated 'Asian collective security' campaigns of the 1970s—campaigns which were designed to isolate both China and the United States from much of Asia. China has spearheaded a 'new security concept' based on a vision of all Asia–Pacific states attaining politico-economic equality and thus positioning them in opposition to traditional US asymmetrical bilateral security relationships in the region.[18] It has also co-founded with Russia and several Central Asian states the Shanghai Cooperation Organization (SCO)—a coalition that the Chinese regard as an alternative to NATO's expansion of military power into Afghanistan and Central Asia.

US policy analysts who are pessimistic about Chinese intentions argue that Beijing is thus adopting a long-term strategy to organize Asia in a way that positions it in the centre of a new regional order that will marginalize US power.[19] Optimists counter that Chinese leaders were receptive to US Deputy Secretary of State Robert Zoellick's address delivered in September 2005 that invited their country to become a 'responsible stakeholder' in the *existing* international order and developing regional order. Sino–US collaboration on the Six Party Talks regarding North Korea's nuclear weapons capability, and increasing dialogue and cooperation on energy issues, also presage the possible development of a bilateral relationship (between China and the United States in Asia) that is something other than an exclusively competitive one.

In the absence of a 'purely realist' regional security environment that features unmitigated hegemonic competition or unqualified power balancing (which would require the reconstitution of US bilateral alliances back into a containment mode against China) or a complete Sino–US *modus vivendi* leading to a regional security community, what types of alliances, alignments or coalitions might emerge in the Asia–Pacific over the next few decades? How might any such emerging typologies, moreover, relate to Australia's own security priorities?

It is unlikely that the US bilateral alliance system will unravel completely over the short term, but it could be substantially modified. South Korea and the ASEAN states who maintain formal or *de facto* security partnerships with Washington (Thailand, the Philippines and Singapore) are likely to pursue 'hedging' strategies designed to extract benefits from their relations with both China and the United States without falling completely into either powers' sphere of influence for as long as they can.[20] Hedging cannot be pursued credibly, however, without a residual US offshore regional presence sufficiently large to balance China's size, economy and growing military power. If US commitments in the Middle East and Persian Gulf continue to stretch US military power to the limit, then the Philippines, Thailand and even Singapore are more likely to 'bandwagon' toward the Chinese orbit in the absence of an alternative balancer. Neither Japan nor Australia can fulfill the alternative balancer role but, as two of the region's most developed powers, they will remain squarely in the US geopolitical orbit, barring a complete American strategic retraction from the region. So too will Taiwan for it has virtually no other way to turn than towards continued alignment with Washington. US–Indian security relations are strengthening as well. Washington cannot move too close to a self-acclaimed Indian regional power, however, as long as New Delhi remains disposed to challenge China's geopolitical aspirations and hostile to a Pakistan that the US deems to be a critical player in the 'Long War' against global terrorism.

Given this context, recent developments in Northeast Asia are particularly disturbing. China has been unable to prevent the North Koreans from conducting highly provocative missile and nuclear tests. Japanese and South Korean positions over North Korea are sharply divided and, if left unresolved, could permanently erode the US alliance with South Korean political elites that increasingly look to China as a natural economic and security partner. Bilateral tensions between China and Japan have intensified into a major security dilemma, largely fuelled by Chinese fears that unbridled Japanese nationalism is emerging more than sixty years after its wartime defeat in 1945. The December 2005 East Asian Summit in Kuala

Lumpur, originally called to establish greater regional cohesion through financial and institutional collaboration, was thoroughly jettisoned by contending Chinese and Japanese visions of how any such collaborative framework should be organized.

Under these circumstances, prospects for the coexistence of bilateral and multilateral security forums in the Asia–Pacific have at least temporarily declined. This does not mean, however, that the United States and its security allies can revert to the traditional 'hub and spokes' system of alliance management. The benefits of enmeshing China in future regional order building are sufficiently great to avoid, if at all possible, the Chinese reaching the conclusion that a 'containment revisited' posture directed against themselves is being applied by the United States and Japan. In this sense, the February 2005 joint statement of the US–Japan Consultative Committee labelling Taiwan a 'security challenge of concern' was arguably misguided alliance politics.[21] Other approaches to pursuing alliance politics in the region may need to be considered as more appropriately subtle and compatible with the Asia–Pacific's strategically fluid environment.

Both 'virtual alliances' and 'quasi-alliances' have been proposed as intermediate steps to stabilize Northeast Asia's security dilemmas or flashpoints. A virtual alliance is an informal process involving two or more smaller allies who normally do not conduct extensive or formal security relations with each other to upgrade such relations through the coordinative efforts of a common senior ally. The idea is to 'deepen the weakest links' within an existing inter-alliance framework. Ralph Cossa, the key proponent of this concept, delineates three basic characteristics of a virtual alliance: (1) the formation of security consultative mechanisms reflecting common interests and values; (2) the lack of formal treaty or legislative obligations underwriting the parties who are collaborating; and (3) the tendency for such collaborators to diversify their avenues of security cooperation into different regional and global institutions or forums so as to mitigate suspicions by other states that a containment posture is being formulated.[22] The US–Japan–South Korea Trilateral Coordination and Oversight Group (TCOG) was originally formed in 1999 to monitor North Korean nuclear developments; it could be regarded as an example of a 'virtual' alliance. However, apart from running afoul over differences between South Korea and the United States and Japan over how to manage the North Korean threat, the TCOG failed to meet Cossa's third criterion—the associate states diversifying their avenues of security cooperation into different regional and global institutions. Instead, South Korea has gravitated toward China's approach of adopting a softer line toward Pyongyang as the best means to avoid a new war on the Korean Peninsula. Nor has there been visible progress in strengthening the 'weakest link' of the US–Japan–South Korea triad; South Korea's hostility toward Japan actually intensified during the Koizumi government's tenure of office, involving territorial disputes, interpretations of history and the perceived rise of Japanese nationalism. It remains to be seen to what extent a change of governments in Seoul and Tokyo will modify these bilateral tensions.

Victor Cha's quasi-alliance theory has already been cited above but warrants greater discussion. The quasi-alliance explanation acknowledges that inherited animosities can exist between two, unallied, smaller states sharing security guarantees from their common larger ally. However, so long as the larger ally can overcome its smaller partners' mutual fears of strategic abandonment, the antagonisms of the two smaller allies can be subordinated or managed. Both Japan and South Korea have projected their strongest commitment to their respective alliances with the United States when they have individually feared abandonment by Washington to be more probable and have shown less alliance affinity when they have most feared entrapment by Washington's policies. 'The optimal strategy in the alliance game is to maximize one's security from the alliance while minimizing one's obligations to it.'[23] Quasi-alliance ensues because while Japan and South Korea have asymmetrical fears of abandonment and entrapment in regard to each other, US strategic primacy causes those perceptions to be subsumed within the larger framework of each state's ties with the United States.[24]

Consequently, South Korea may resent what it believes to be US lack of respect toward it, relative to what the United States extends to Japan, and may also suffer different types of strain in its relationship with Washington on such issues as nuclear arms control, defence burden-sharing responsibilities and other alliance related issues. From Seoul's perspective, however, the United States must remain engaged in Northeast Asia to 'cap the bottle' of Japanese militarism and to balance Chinese power in addition to deterring the North Korean military threat. Japan continues to view the US alliance as the best hope for avoiding conflict against China, with both Koreas growing more hostile to Japan, and as a legitimizing instrument that should allow it to be part of the world's most prestigious economic and security councils. Such countervailing South Korean and Japanese interests hardly constitute the stuff of converging interests upon which traditional alliance politics is based.

Virtual alliance theory has been criticized because it is focused too narrowly on how changing notions of insecurity over time affect balancing calculations within alliance politics. It has little to say about how disparate alliances involving a major power (for example, the United States) could morph into more enduring mechanisms for cooperative security and regional stability. It appears to some that virtual alliance may be nothing more than coalition theory in different trappings with no logical endgame in sight. Quasi-alliance theory, as Cha has developed it, seems to underplay the economic and technological dimensions of security that have been critical to shaping the strategic perceptions of both Japan and South Korea over recent decades. Such perceptions have engendered collaboration in establishing the Korean Peninsula Energy Development Organization

(KEDO) following the 1994 US–North Korea Agreed Framework, the aforementioned TCOG initiative, and cooperation within the ASEAN-plus-three grouping. Accordingly, as Melvin Gurtov has concluded, quasi-alliance theory, guided by the calculus of 'realpolitik' and the entrapment-abandonment alliance security dilemma, apparently does not provide us with an adequate explanation of Japanese and South Korean policy motives.[25]

If the evolving character of alliances in contemporary Asia–Pacific security politics remains contested, alignment and coalition appear more promising for explaining current patterns of security partnership. If alignment is understood to be expectations of a state about whether it will be supported or opposed by another state (short of a formal alliance commitment) in future interactions related to security behaviour, a thickening web of such understandings is evident in the region.

In the maritime security arena, the trilateral Malaysia–Singapore–Indonesia (Malsindo) program of maritime patrolling commenced in 2004, and has been expanded to include other arrangements such as 'Eyes in the Sky' and has been linked to traditional maritime patrolling alignments such as the Five Power Defence Arrangements (FPDA). Although operating without a formal security treaty, the US–Singapore bilateral relationship has become the most extensive informal security alignment in Southeast Asia. The annual US Naval Cooperation Afloat Readiness and Training (CARAT) series involves all six 'core' ASEAN navies (minus the Indochinese states and Myanmar). Japan, India and South Korea have all likewise raised their maritime profiles in peninsular Southeast Asia over the past few years.[26] China has instigated its own maritime network, often referred to as the 'string of pearls' infrastructure, building up its access to port facilities in Pakistan, Bangladesh, Myanmar, Thailand, Cambodia and the South China Sea that will one day give it greater capabilities to protect its energy supplies transiting from the Persian Gulf.[27]

In the antiterrorism policy sector, the United States has designated Pakistan, the Philippines and Thailand as 'non-NATO allies' to facilitate its military assistance programs (largely counterterrorist in nature) to these countries. The SCO binds Russian and Chinese concerns about Islamic radicalism in Central Asia into institutional collaboration, even as US forces remain deployed in Afghanistan and other Central Asian countries to wage asymmetrical warfare against the same threat. Asia–Pacific anti-terrorism alignments, therefore, are not necessarily evolving in a 'zero-sum' fashion as they are cross-cutting in nature (Thailand relies more on its US treaty ally than on China to support its own maritime security interests, while Pakistan is proving quite capable of separating its antiterrorism cooperation with the United States from its strategic cooperation with China in those geopolitical areas that will maximize its position of strength relative to India). Expectations that underpin both alignments and coalitions are subject to adjustment and change; neither need be sealed by formal accords suggesting eternal strategic fealty.

In the economic security sector, three causal relationships warrant attention. As the economies of Asia–Pacific states have grown, their capacity to support larger national defence budgets and purchase state-of-the-art weapons systems has increased. The 1997 Asian financial crisis partially checked this trend and most Asian states peg their military expenditures to their economic growth. However, defence spending in larger Asian economies such as China, Japan and India has continued to increase, raising the spectre of future arms racing and the intensification of regional security dilemmas. A second factor is the increasing demand for natural resources generated by national economic growth. Safeguarding energy security through source diversification, protection of transit routes and investment in extra-regional fossil fuel exploitation are aspects underwriting intra-regional commercial alignments that can and do spill over into strategic politics. China's deepening ties with Russia in the energy sector, for example, cannot be disassociated from those two countries' recently expanded strategic relations, bilaterally (through the military exercises and intelligence collaboration generated by their Treaty for Good Neighborliness, Friendship and Cooperation signed in Moscow in July 2001) and multilaterally (through the SCO). A third economic dimension affecting regional security politics is the desire of countries like China and India to pursue national wealth and build national infrastructure in a basically conflict-free environment (a posture that has been labelled by Chinese leaders as 'peaceful rise'). To the extent that alignments between Russia and China, China and ASEAN, and the United States and India infuse greater predictability into the region's strategic landscape, the more probable it will be that they will continue to be an important feature within that environment.

Because they have usually formed rapidly in response to specific and often unanticipated contingencies, security coalitions in the Asia–Pacific lack the foundation or durability of formal alliance structures or the pliability of alliances to adjust strategic expectations over long periods of time. Coalitions are theoretically transitory and issue specific: temporary 'force multipliers' that seal transient marriages of convenience to extract immediate gains for their participants in a strategic situation.

In Asia, however, coalitions have proven to be more enduring and to involve far larger numbers of states than is anticipated by traditional coalition theory. Global and regional concerns overlap as rationales for their formation. In Operation *Enduring Freedom*, 27 countries (including all of the US formal treaty allies in the Asia–Pacific) either contributed forces or provided critical offshore logistical support for that US counterterrorist campaign against al Qaeda and the Taliban in Afghanistan. The Four Party Talks and Six Party Talks involving the United States and China brokering the North Korean unification issue and nuclear disputes with the two Koreas, and (subsequently) with both Russia and Japan, have functioned for nearly a decade. The multinational combined support force of military units that coordinated massive rescue efforts in the aftermath of the

December 2004 Indian Ocean tsunami, however, exemplifies the classic modern Asia–Pacific security coalition reacting to a specific critical issue and contingency.

Nuclear non-proliferation and continuing disaster relief and humanitarian intervention all have worldwide ramifications that go far beyond the application of temporary issue-directed coalitions in the Asia–Pacific. In addressing the advantages of a 'broader tent' at the 2006 Shangri La Dialogue in Singapore, Donald Rumsfeld levelled what might be considered the ultimate *coup de grâce* to traditional coalition politics, portraying it as too parochial and too narrow for the times:

> Individual countries or groups of countries can arrange themselves anyway they see appropriate ... [but] ... the kinds of problems we face today, it strikes me, are in many instances, not the kinds of problems that can be dealt with by one country—any country—or even with relatively small numbers of countries. The problems we face today are in large measure global.[28]

The Australian dimension

Reconciling the 'global/regional nexus' in alliance politics has been a major challenge for Australian policymakers over the past two decades. Prime Minister John Howard ascended to power in early 1996 arguing that his Labor government predecessors had neglected the alliance by assigning too much weight to linking with regional economies and polities in ways that belied Australia's geography, culture and history.[29] In his quest to resuscitate ANZUS, Howard pushed for a reaffirmation of alliance purpose and principles. With the Sydney Declaration in July 1996, he moved Australia's defence posture from one emphasizing the so-called 'Defence of Australia' to a more global or 'expeditionary' orientation. He has deployed Australian forces to distant, US-led interventions in Afghanistan and Iraq. Alliance loyalty has clearly paid dividends. By early 2003, one of Australia's pre-eminent defence analysts asserted with high credibility that the United States viewed Australia as its second most important ally (after Britain), creating a dichotomy in Australian foreign policy. Australia's weight as a regional security actor increased by its close affinity with Washington, but that same intimacy worked against Australian diplomacy in the region as the US policies of strategic preemption and other aspects of the 'Bush Doctrine' became increasingly unpopular throughout much of Asia.[30]

Australia has, however, been able to enjoy 'the best of both worlds' during the Howard government's tenure: successfully building closer alliance affiliation by deftly calibrating symbolic deployments of niche military capabilities in support of US global security operations, while solidifying its regional economic and security ties in ways that have overcome previous

Asian propensities to condemn Australia as an American 'deputy sheriff' and as a regional outsider. It has orchestrated this balancing act by pursuing at least key four strategies: (1) capitalizing on its abundant natural resources by exporting its natural gas, coal, iron ore, beef and other commodities to a booming 'China market' (uranium is about to be added to this itinerary), thereby fully integrating itself into the region's economic growth cycle; (2) projecting a clearly independent diplomacy into the region by recognizing North Korea (the United States and Japan do not), engaging in a more 'pragmatic' human-rights relationship with China (devoid of the ideological trappings that impede Sino–US relations in this policy area); (3) fostering a wide array of political-military and military-to-military bilateral dialogues with nearly every state in the region; and (4) sustaining a commitment to confront an emerging 'arc of instability' in various parts of the South and Southwest Pacific by intervening selectively and appropriately in East Timor, in the Solomon Islands and in other subregional flashpoints, thus precluding the possible exploitation of the fragile micro-states that comprise it by rival external powers.

In cultivating these strategic policies, Australia has successfully pursued a strategy of regional alignment, creating positive expectations amongst its neighbours that it will be a reliable and constructive partner in regional order building. It has complemented this posture with one of building closer alliance ties with the United States, by identifying niche areas where it could contribute symbolically and substantively to its superpower partner's global postures as they have evolved since the 11 September 2001 terrorist attacks. Its February 2003 White Paper on foreign policy, *Advancing the National Interest*, clearly designates Australia's foreign policy as global in scope and concludes that 'the security and prosperity of the Australian people depend vitally on the quality and strength of the political, defence and intelligence partnerships and the economic links that we are able to maintain around the world'.[31] Australia continues to sustain an overt alliance relationship with the United States and an intimate, enduring alignment with Britain—a former alliance that became an alignment when Australia and the United States jointly chose not to include the United Kingdom as a formal ANZUS partner at the outset of the Cold War. In this context, the US annual Ministerial Meetings involving foreign affairs and defence officials (commonly known as AUSMIN) have recently been supplemented by the initiation in late March 2006 of an Australian–UK Ministerial Meeting (AUKMIN) process.[32]

Selected regional alignments and coalitions complement Australia's two 'global' security partnerships. They do so in ways that provide Australia with an interlocking web of defence associations that allow it to simultaneously play a role as a global 'niche' player in the international security arena while remaining pertinent to burgeoning regional security arrangements. Evolving relations with Japan are illustrative. In a speech delivered to the Japan Press Club in early August 2006, Foreign Minister Alexander

Downer argued that while Japan and Australia were both 'liberal democratic American allies in the Asia–Pacific', both faced common 'global
security challenges' that demanded closer bilateral security cooperation.[33]
Later that month, Australia and Japan reportedly moved to explore a more
formal bilateral defence relationship in which Japanese and Australian
military forces could, according to Downer, 'play an effective role in the
region and cooperate in relief emergencies or in peacekeeping'.[34] Underlying
this rhetoric is Australia's recognition that assimilating Japan's accelerated normalization as a strategic actor in the region will be a critical challenge for Australian foreign policy—especially since North Korea's nuclear
policy has become increasingly aggressive and China's concern about the
recently formed Trilateral Strategic Dialogue (TSD), as a possible Australian–US–Japanese coalition directed towards containing its own rising
power, remains potentially acute. How well Australia can manage its
security relationship with Japan as a mutual US ally while persisting with its
cultivation of deeper economic and political ties with China will be one of
the key tests for its foreign policy architects over the next decade and
beyond.

The 'global/regional nexus' is also a factor in emerging alignments that
Australia is maintaining or contemplating. For example, Singapore has
been characterized by Australia's Department of Foreign Affairs and
Trade (DFAT) as 'one of the Australian Defence Force's most valuable
combined exercise partners' and the two countries maintain an extensive
set of bilateral arrangements that includes combined training, intelligence
sharing and personnel exchanges.[35] Both countries are members of the
FPDA and work with the United Kingdom, New Zealand and Malaysia
to strengthen collaboration on counterterrorism measures throughout
maritime Southeast Asia. The 'global dimension' of this type of coordination relates to combined antiterrorism and anti-piracy exercises that Singapore and other ASEAN maritime states conduct not only with the
United Kingdom but, beyond the strictly FPDA context, with American
and other NATO European maritime components. Also, illustratively,
after a seven-year hiatus following the increase of Australian–Indonesian
tensions during the 1999 East Timor crisis, Canberra and Jakarta
recently concluded a bilateral Framework Agreement for Security Cooperation to replace the Agreement for Maintaining Security that was jettisoned by Indonesia following that crisis. Australian–Philippines defence
ties have also increased markedly since 11 September 2001, with Canberra offering millions of dollars in counterterrorism assistance to that
country and establishing in August 2005 an inter-agency counterterrorism
mechanism at the senior officials level. Australia is also now an observer
at the annual joint US–Philippines *Balikatan* annual counterterrorism
exercises.

The relationships with Southeast Asia and the South Pacific represent
perhaps the most formidable instance of Australian policymakers being

required to reconcile countervailing policy imperatives when managing their country's alignment policies. In 2003, the Howard government developed the doctrine of 'cooperative intervention' to justify the deployment of Australian forces to restore order in the Solomon Islands and to rationalize a permanent Australian security role of maintaining 'law and order and good governance' throughout the South Pacific to preclude it from either becoming more susceptible to terrorist activities or to external powers' geopolitical rivalries. Growing concerns that China and Taiwan were vying for political influence in Papua New Guinea, Fiji and in other Pacific Island states supplemented already strong Australian apprehensions that terrorist sanctuaries could be easily established in fragile or 'failed state' micro-state policies. The 1987 Declaration of Principles between Australia and PNG is the key alignment relationship underpinning this Australian strategy. It stipulates that in the event PNG were attacked by an outside party, there would be an 'expectation that Australia would be prepared to commit forces to resist external aggression'.[36] In August 2006, reports surfaced that a border clash occurred between PNG troops and Indonesian 'fishermen' who may have been Indonesian military (*Kopassus*) agents in disguise conducting surveillance of West Papuan resistance forces taking refuge in PNG border villages.[37] Australian policymakers may soon confront a major policy dilemma: how to pursue stronger strategic relations with Indonesia without compromising Australia's prerogative to ensure the security of countries such as PNG that are positioned directly in Australia's own 'northern approaches'. Under such circumstances, the politics of alignment may become increasingly difficult to orchestrate.

None of Australia's security relationships with the ASEAN states or with its South Pacific neighbours, however, are intended by Canberra or its Southeast Asian collaborators to mature into formal bilateral alliances. Nor is the TSD with Japan designed to evolve into a mini-NATO for Asia. They are instead responses to specific issue areas. In the ASEAN region, they are predominantly mechanisms for pursuing counterterrorism, but are also targeted at achieving greater coordination in combatting regional and international drug trade, illegal or forced movement of peoples and other non-traditional security concerns. Regarding Northeast Asia, the TSD is primarily targeted toward forging collective strategies against North Korean proliferation, and toward maintaining ties with an increasingly powerful China. These alignments are viewed by their instigators as policy means for responding to the mid-to-long-term mutual security challenges confronting Australia and those states associating with it. They therefore fall in between security coalitions and true alignments. Like coalitions, they focus on specific issue-areas. As with alignments, however, they can be seen as the instruments needed to develop enduring collaborative security relationships without formal, specific, and potentially provocative, threat identification.

Conclusion

Two concurrent and noteworthy trends are emerging in Australian, regional and international security partnerships. On the one hand, alliance politics remains central to the management of global security politics. Contrary to traditional alliance theory, many alliances, including NATO and the US bilateral network in the Asia–Pacific, have adapted to the new conditions and challenges rather than dissolving when the 'general threat' that instigated their creation—a seemingly unified worldwide communist movement—disappeared from the scene. NATO has transformed from a collective defence arrangement to a region-wide and even 'extra-regional' collective security arrangement. ANZUS remains central to Asia's ongoing geopolitics, a complex mix of balancing and institutionalism that is buying time for that region's states and key external players to collaborate in reshaping a stable post-Cold War order.

Yet alliance politics is too cumbersome to effectively respond to an array of short-term crises that are better met through coalition, alignment or a combination of both approaches. A pattern is emerging in which coalitions are initially formed in response to short-term imperatives: removing terrorist elements from weak or failing states; controlling flashpoints of weapons of mass destruction (WMD) proliferation; and achieving short-term maritime security objectives. As the rationales for creating them become more protracted than originally expected, these coalitions are transformed to longer-term alignments, sustained by the knowledge that the interests underlying their existence are still shared, but are reinforced by common expectations that defection of key parties to these arrangements can be avoided without the imposition of formal treaty obligations.

How these three converging trends—alliances, alignments and coalitions—are reconciled with alliance politics (or integrated in a world of asymmetrical threats and ever broadening security challenges) will constitute a large part of the international security story for our times. Australia is projecting a complex and somewhat controversial security posture by allying or coalescing with great powers that could easily become rivals, and by simultaneously aligning with an emerging Asia–Pacific community. To what extent this balancing act will succeed will hinge largely on the ability of Australian policymakers to translate this complex equation into viable regional and international leadership.

Notes

1 S.E. Meyer, 'Carcass of dead policies: the irrelevance of NATO', *Parameters*, Winter 2003–4, pp. 83–97.
2 R. Menon, 'The end of alliances', *World Policy Journal*, vol. 20, no. 2, Summer 2003, pp. 1–20.
3 B. Tertrais, 'The changing nature of military alliances', *Washington Quarterly*, vol. 27, no. 2, Spring 2004, pp. 135–50, insists that there are deep 'historical

forces at work that are forcing permanent alliances to increasingly give way to *ad hoc* coalitions', p. 135.

4 See the recent comments of former Australian Prime Minister Malcolm Fraser reflecting his concern that Australia has become too subservient to US interests relative to its own national interests. 'Just a vassal of the US', *The Age*, 26 July 2006.

5 G.J. Ikenberry, 'American grand strategy in the age of terror', *Survival*, vol. 43, no. 4, Winter 2001–2, p. 28.

6 The term 'nuclear family' of allies was coined by Kurt Campbell in 'The end of alliances? Not so fast', *Washington Quarterly*, vol. 27, no. 2, Spring 2004, pp. 158–9.

7 G.H. Snyder, 'Alliances, balance and stability', *International Organization*, vol. 45, no. 1, Winter 1991, pp. 121–3. Efforts to construct an alliance grand theory, of course, have been made. See, in particular, G. Liska, *Nations in Alliance: The Limits of Interdependence*, Baltimore, MD: Johns Hopkins University Press, 1962; and S.M. Walt, *The Origins of Alliances*, Ithaca, NY: Cornell University Press, 1987.

8 S.M. Walt, 'Why alliances endure or collapse', *Survival*, vol. 39, no. 1, Spring 1997, pp. 156–7.

9 V. Cha, *Alignment Despite Antagonism: The United States–Korea–Japan Security Triangle*, Stanford, CA: Stanford University Press, 1999, p. 4.

10 P.J. Katzenstein and N. Okawara, *Japan's National Security: Structures, Norms and Responses in a Changing World*, Ithaca, NY: Cornell University Press, 1993.

11 Snyder, 'Alliances, balances and stability', pp. 123–4.

12 Cha, *Alignment Despite Antagonism*, p. 4.

13 J. Mearsheimer, 'Why we will soon miss the Cold War,' *The Atlantic Monthly*, vol. 266, no. 2, August 1990, p. 37.

14 Text of a memorandum, 'Guidelines to be considered when committing US forces', written by then Defense Secretary Donald H. Rumsfeld and reprinted as 'In Rumsfeld's words: guidelines for committing forces', *New York Times*, 14 October 2002.

15 P. Bowring, 'What is it about anglophones?' *International Herald Tribune*, 27 March 2003; and Tertrais, 'The changing nature of military alliances', p. 138.

16 See, for example, S. Walt, *Taming American Power: The Global Response to US Primacy*, New York: W.W. Norton, 2005.

17 R. Lyon, *Alliance Unleashed: Australia and the US in a New Strategic Age*, Canberra: Australian Strategic Policy Institute, June 2005, p. 30.

18 Ministry of Foreign Affairs of the People's Republic of China, 'China's position paper on the new security concept', 6 August 2002.

19 See, for example, F. Fukuyama, 'All quiet on the Eastern Front?', *Wall Street Journal*, 1 March 2005.

20 E. Goh, 'The US–China relationship and Asian security: negotiating change', *Asian Security*, vol. 1, no. 3, December 2005, p. 226.

21 See Ministry of Foreign Affairs, Japan, 'Joint Statement—US–Japan Security Consultative Committee', 19 February 2005; and a critical Chinese response, 'FM: US–Japan statement on Taiwan wrong', *China Daily*, 21 February 2005.

22 R. Cossa, 'US Asia policy: does an alliance based policy still makes sense?', *Issues & Insights*, vol. 3, no. 1, September 2001, pp. 13–14.

23 Cha, *Alignment Despite Antagonism*, p. 45.

24 Ibid., p. 55.

25 M. Gurtov, 'Review of *Alignment Despite Antagonism: The United States–Korea–Japan Security Triangle*', in *American Political Science Review*, vol. 94, no. 2, June 2000, pp. 504–5.

26 International Institute for Strategic Studies, *Military Balance 2006*, London: Routledge, 2006, pp. 258–9.

27 S. Ramachandran, 'China's pearl in Pakistan's waters', *Asia Times Online*, 4 March 2005.
28 'Q&A following Secretary Rumsfeld's address to the 2006 Shangri La Dialogue', 3 June 2006.
29 Conservative Australian columnist Gerard Henderson subsequently described this approach: 'In his early years as prime minister, Howard gave the impression he was too focused on rejecting the policy adopted towards the Asian region by his predecessors Bob Hawke and, especially, Paul Keating. The implication was that Labor had been obsessed with Asia and that, consequently, the Coalition would be less engaged.' See G. Henderson, 'How John Howard has matured as a foreign policy statesman', *The Age*, 5 August 2003.
30 P. Dibb, 'The downside of being too close to the US', *The Age*, 4 April 2003. Also see H. White, 'Australian strategic policy', in A.J. Tellis and M. Wills (eds) *Strategic Asia 2005–06: Military Modernization in an Era of Uncertainty*, Seattle and Washington, DC: The National Bureau of Asian Research, 2005, pp. 305–31 for an in-depth assessment of how these factors played into the evolution of Australia's defence strategy from 1996 onward.
31 Commonwealth of Australia, *Advancing the National Interest: Australia' Foreign and Trade Policy White Paper*, Canberra: National Capital Printing, 2003.
32 G. Sheridan, 'Closer ties with Britain make sense', *The Australian*, 30 March 2006.
33 The Hon. Alexander Downer MP, Minister for Foreign Affairs, Australia, 'Australia–Japan: a global partnership', speech to the Japan Press Club, 1 August 2006.
34 As quoted by P. Kelly, 'Warming up to Tokyo', *The Australian*, 12 August 2006.
35 Australia Department of Foreign Affairs and Trade, 'Singapore Country Brief', July 2006.
36 See P. Daley, 'Caught in the crossfire', *The Bulletin*, 29 August 2006, pp. 16–17.
37 Ibid.

Part 2
Dining with giants

3   Australia–United States

Paul Dibb

Australia's alliance with the United States in many ways underpins its status as an Asia–Pacific power. Without the alliance, Australia would be seen more as a smallish country of 20 million people tucked down at the bottom end of Southeast Asia. As it is, Australia's closeness to America and its influence with Washington transforms Australia's regional status: it allows Australia to punch above its weight in regional and, indeed, international security organizations.

Yet not everything is positive about the alliance. Since the 11 September 2001 terrorist attacks on the United States, Washington has become a very demanding ally and, in some parts of the region at least, Canberra is viewed as the ally that cannot say 'no'. In that sense, Australia differs from Canada and even from the United Kingdom. Some of this, no doubt, reflects the intense personal relationship between Prime Minister Howard and President Bush. It remains to be seen how this relationship will fare if the Democrats come to power in Washington in 2008 and/or the Labor Party gains government in Canberra in 2007.

Except for the Vietnam War, the US–Australia alliance has always received overwhelming support in opinion polls in Australia. Opinion was divided about whether Australia should participate in the Iraq War in 2003, but anti-war demonstrations were nowhere near the size of those in the Vietnam War. Some recent opinion polls, however, show a quite disturbing trend, implying, for example, that Australians like Japan and China (and even France and Malaysia) more than the United States.[1] And what is it about America that Australians do not like? Well, 68 per cent of Australians think Australia takes too much notice of the views of the United States in its foreign policy.[2] Even so, support for the alliance itself remains consistently high: over 70 per cent think the alliance is either 'very important' or 'fairly important'.[3] Australians still tend to see Australia as a vulnerable country and appreciate that a strong US military presence in the Asia–Pacific region adds immeasurably to Australia's own sense of security.

However, there are winds and currents that may take us in a different direction in the future. The absence of a clear and present danger like the Soviet Union had already precipitated a sense of drift in the alliance, and reduced relevance for Australia, in the 1990s. Had it not been for 11 September 2001, the US–Australia alliance might now be in much poorer shape. For the future, America's dominance in a unipolar world is set to be challenged by the rise of China and India and a resurgent Russia. The alliance world of 2015–20 will be not as clear-cut or as uncomplicated as the contemporary era. Moreover, America's attitudes to the need for allies may change.

Where has the relationship come from?

It is important to understand that the US–Australia alliance was born in the crucible of the Cold War. From Australia's perspective, the ANZUS Treaty was bought at the price of America's peace treaty with Japan. Washington needed the latter to create an anti-Soviet, and hopefully democratic, bastion in proximity to the Korean Peninsula and the Soviet Far East. From Australia's perspective, the ANZUS Treaty was an insurance policy against a resurgent Japan.[4] However, Australia's participation in the Korean War and the Vietnam War alongside the United States reflected the fact that the real post-Second World War threat was not a resurgent Japan but aggressive communism. Having narrowly missed being invaded by Japan (at least in the popular view), Australia faced the deep-seated fear (during the 1950s, 1960s and through to the fall of Saigon in 1975) that Asian communism was the new threat.

There was a view, particularly in the 1950s, that homogeneous communism was bent on world dominance. Even after the Sino–Soviet split in the early 1960s, the hand of communist China was seen to be supporting North Vietnam—as well as actively supporting communist insurgency movements throughout Southeast Asia. The domino theory was alive and well and, following North Vietnam's conquest of the South, there was palpable concern in Canberra about the fall of dominoes in Southeast Asia to communist expansionism. One of the reasons that a blind eye was turned to Indonesia's invasion of East Timor in 1975 was the fear of Fretilin (a Marxist-Leninist party) taking over a new state in the Indonesian archipelago to Australia's near north.

Importantly, the Soviet Union had risen from the ashes of the Second World War to become a global superpower. Its occupation of Eastern Europe (and the bloody suppression of uprisings in Hungary and Czechoslovakia), its invasion of Afghanistan (which Australian Prime Minister Malcolm Fraser thought heralded the beginning of a third world war) and the Soviet Union's massive military power, combined to instil deep-seated dread of global nuclear war. Moscow's naval deployments into the Indian Ocean and its acquisition of military bases in Vietnam, as well as its intelligence activities in Canberra, brought the potential threat much closer to home. By the late 1970s, Australia's national intelligence assessments reflected the fact that Australia was a probable Soviet nuclear target. It was accepted, certainly by governments, that this was the price to be paid for the alliance.

In fact, Australia's hosting of crucial US intelligence, early warning and communications facilities at Pine Gap, Nurrungar and Northwest Cape became a much more central part of the alliance relationship in the Cold War than is commonly understood.[5] These facilities were crucial throughout the Cold War to US confidence in monitoring Soviet strategic nuclear-weapon capabilities and warning of nuclear attack. They were amongst the most powerful intelligence collection facilities that the United States had anywhere in the world. The fact that Australia hosted these facilities, and had access to their innermost secrets, opened privileged doors in Washington.

In the 1970s, as head of the National Assessments Staff for the National Intelligence Committee, I was privy to these highly classified matters and participated in what was known as the 'Defense-to-Defense Talks' in Washington. Our mission was to thoroughly quiz our American counterparts about US nuclear targeting of the Soviet Union, so that we could understand what Australia was party to in hosting the joint facilities. The Australian team met the directors of the Central Intelligence Agency (CIA), National Security Agency (NSA) and Defense Intelligence Agency (DIA), as well as deputy secretaries of Defense and State. Our directions were that the Australian government subscribed to the concept of 'mutually assured destruction' (MAD), but not any US doctrine of preemptive disarming strikes.

One of the most difficult negotiations that Australia had with the United States was when the Labor government in the 1980s decided that it needed to have 'full knowledge and concurrence' about US operations in the joint facilities. That had not necessarily occurred with any assurance under previous governments of either political party. Long, drawn out and sometimes tense, negotiations with the Americans resulted in agreement that an Australian would always be deputy chief of mission in each of the facilities, and become acting chief if the American chief of mission was absent. We also obtained agreement that Australians would be present 24 hours a day on every operational shift. This was to ensure that we knew precisely what was going on and how the facilities were being used in detail on a day-to-day basis. This was a most unusual arrangement for Americans who were used to the idea that, in countries such as Japan and Germany, the United States treated their intelligence-collection facilities as sovereign American territory with little in the way of involvement by locals.

One needs to understand the nature of the close intelligence relationship that has existed between the United States and Australia for over half a century. Canberra has been a member of the close inner intelligence club of Anglo-Saxon countries that had its beginnings in the Second World War—a club that consisted of the United States, the United Kingdom, Canada, Australia and New Zealand under the UKUSA intelligence-sharing agreement.[6] Only one country has been excluded from that club in its history—

New Zealand, which in the mid-1980s decided not to allow visits by nuclear-powered or nuclear-armed warships. That experience demonstrates the tightly held rules that govern access to some of America's most sensitive intelligence capabilities. In Australia's case, access to American signals and satellite intelligence and assistance with developing our own indigenous intelligence capabilities has been priceless. I mean that in the sense that it is not possible to put a price on how much it would have cost Australia to go it alone and develop such capabilities—it would have simply been beyond Australian indigenous research and development capabilities.

There are, of course, some other crucial areas of security cooperation that have existed from the outset of the alliance relationship. They include defence science cooperation and access to advanced American military equipment. Australia has longstanding defence science and technology cooperation with both its American and British counterparts. Australia's Defence Science and Technology Organisation (DSTO) has the country's second largest concentration of professional research scientists, after the Commonwealth Scientific and Industrial Research Organisation (CSIRO). It carries out highly sensitive practical research into areas such as aeronautics, sonar, advanced radar systems, intelligence (including cryptography), and both offensive and defensive information warfare. There is close cooperation with US defence advanced research agencies in a number of these areas.

Australia's access to US-sourced military equipment is longstanding and has helped to ensure that Australia has maintained a distinct margin of technological superiority in its own region of primary strategic interest.[7] This has been a fundamental defence policy requirement for many decades and it reflects the fact that Australia has a small defence force that needs to operate over vast distances. It can never afford to lose large numbers of personnel or equipment in combat and, therefore, having technological superiority is essential. As the region to Australia's north has become stronger economically over the last decade or so, and has been able to acquire its own more advanced military capabilities, the retention of a margin of technological superiority for Australia has become more demanding.[8]

Of course, Australia has not always purchased its military equipment from the United States. For example, it bought British *Oberon*-class submarines and French *Mirage* aircraft in the 1960s; and continues to buy Swedish designed submarines and, more recently, European helicopters and tanker aircraft. However, the growing dominance of the United States in advanced military research and development and in the international arms trade generally has seen Australia increasingly turn to it for military equipment. So, at present, the Joint Strike Fighter (JSF), airborne early warning and control aircraft and heavy transport aircraft are being—or are likely to be—purchased from the United States. The new combat system for the *Collins*-class submarines is being sourced from a US supplier and the air warfare destroyers will also have a US combat system (the *Aegis* system). The new large amphibious ships (about 25,000 tonnes) may also have American command and control systems, although that is yet to be determined. The new main battle tanks (*Abrams*) are being sourced from the United States, as are some command and control and communications systems and advanced missiles and torpedoes for combat aircraft, submarines and warships. This does not mean that America will become the sole source supplier of advanced military equipment to Australia. Sometimes, the Europeans are not only more cost competitive but more innovative—by necessity—in their design concepts. It is also the case that Washington continues to be resistant—even to such a close ally as Australia—to the release of source code that will enable Australia to modify the performance characteristics of US platforms and weapons.

In summary, Australia's alliance with the United States has weathered a situation of great strategic change from its inception in the early years of the Cold War. It has adapted from the period of global threat to the West from the Soviet Union and regional threats from communist countries such as North Korea and North Vietnam, to the post-Vietnam period when the United States expected allies to be more self-reliant, and the immediate post-Cold War period of drift in the 1990s—when even America's closest allies were not on Washington's radar screen in the same way at all.

For Australia, the core of the ANZUS alliance has always been the need for protection by a great and powerful friend. The United States has reassured Australia in that regard, from providing extended nuclear deterrence through to an expectation that it would defend Australia in the event of a serious threat by a major power. It was not until after the Vietnam War, however, that Australia began to take seriously the requirements spelt out in the Nixon and Guam doctrines for US allies to be able to defend themselves, short of a major threat.

Australia entered the new century with its reputation intact in Washington given that it had fought alongside Americans in every major foreign war involving the United States: the First World War, the Second World War, Korea and Vietnam, and the 1990–1 Persian Gulf War. This commitment carried considerable weight in the corridors of power in Washington. In return, Australia gained quite remarkable access to US sensitive intelligence, cooperation in defence science and technology, and access to advanced US military weapons. Australia's strategic influence in regional affairs and its reputation for military strength were greatly bolstered by its alliance relationship with America.

Where does the relationship currently stand?

So much for past history. The fact is that, since the events of 11 September 2001, Australia's alliance relationship with the United States has become even closer. Australia is now arguably ranked in Washington as America's second closest ally in the world after the United Kingdom. It is not just the superlatives that President Bush lavishes on Prime Minister Howard (for example, he calls him 'a man of steel'). It is not just that Australia willingly contributed combat forces to the invasion of Iraq in 2003 (unlike Canada or New Zealand). Neither is it even because the political parties in government of both the United States and Australia are conservative parties of the right politically (unlike Prime Minister Blair's Labour Party in the United Kingdom). Rather, the unprecedented degree of closeness is explained more by the fact that Prime Minister Howard was actually in Washington on the day of the terrorist attacks on 11 September 2001 and by his government's unquestioning ideological alignment with the new American doctrine on the so-called 'war on terror'. As far as we know, the Howard government has had no significant differences with the United States on such issues as Guantánamo Bay and Abu Ghraib prison (unlike the British government). Nor did it question the American intelligence which allegedly proved that Saddam Hussein was in possession of weapons of mass destruction (WMD).[9]

As a result of the 'war on terror', Australia's defence forces are at an unprecedented level of operational tempo with concurrent military operations in Iraq and Afghanistan, as well as in the Solomon Islands and East Timor. This has once again brought to the surface a debate that is deeply entrenched in the Australian perception of the outside world: should its defence force be structured primarily for the defence of Australia and to operate in its own region or should it be an expeditionary force designed to fight alongside its US ally?

For a quarter of a century, from the fall of Saigon in 1975 to the December 2000 Defence White Paper, successive Australian governments proceeded basically down the former path. But since 11 September 2001 there has been a push by some politicians (particularly the former Minister for Defence Senator Robert Hill) and in certain quarters of the Australian Defence Force (ADF)—particularly the army—to proceed down the expeditionary force path. And there can be little doubt that there are those in the Bush administration who greatly prefer to see Australia construct an expeditionary force designed to operate as a subordinate element of US forces.

Prime Minister John Howard, however, still seems to hew to the concept set out clearly in his 2000 Defence White Paper, namely that the bedrock of Australia's security, and the most fundamental responsibility of government, is to prevent or defeat any armed attack on Australia. The White Paper says Australia's most important long-term strategic objective is to ensure the defence of Australia and its direct approaches. The second strategic objective is to foster the security of Australia's immediate neighbourhood.[10] These have long been the primary drivers of the ADF's force structure and they have generated sufficient options for successive governments to actually use Australian forces further afield—including in coalition operations with our US ally (for example, the government deployed 1,200 troops to Somalia in 1993).

The two official documents issued by Senator Robert Hill when he was Minister for Defence deliberately left a different impression, although they do not directly contradict John Howard's Defence White Paper.[11] These are two quite superficial documents, which are internally inconsistent and do not provide any logical connection between declaratory strategic policy and force structure acquisitions. Instead, there is a heavy emphasis on the so-called 'war on terror' and the primacy of Australia's relations with the United States. The excuse is used that because of increased US strategic dominance, the threat of direct military attack on Australia has diminished and, therefore, Australia's Defence Force can concentrate more on terrorism and the spread thereof—both of which are, of course, also Washington's priorities. There are two problems with this line of reasoning: the first is that the 2000 Defence White Paper did not identify any threat of direct military attack on Australia; and the second is that while fighting terrorists and countering the spread of WMD are clearly important, they are not a primary mission for the ADF—nor should they be.

Senator Hill's view that geography no longer matters in a globalized world, in which terrorism is the primary threat and coalition operations with our US ally are the ADF's main priority, is leading to an unravelling of Australia's force structure priorities.[12] Increasingly, the ADF is taking on the characteristics of an expeditionary force based on a smaller version of the American Marines. Australia is acquiring two of the largest amphibious assault ships in the Asia–Pacific region (bigger than anything China, Japan, India or Russia have) to project a force of some 1,000 troops on each ship equipped with main battle tanks and attack helicopters. Some in the ADF are pressing for the ships to be equipped with the vertical short take-off and landing (VSTOL) version of the JSF, so that once again Australia has an aircraft carrier capability—a capacity which it phased out in the early 1980s. Officials in the Pentagon have indicated that they would be happy if Australia goes in this direction, because it would provide a small but useful force that could slot into an American expeditionary battle group.

The problem with all of this for Australia is that it would leave the nation with 'a one-shot' ADF. By this I mean that it will take almost the total resources of the ADF to protect an embarked amphibious group of this size. It will need air warfare destroyers, submarines, airborne early warning aircraft and fighter aircraft to protect it—unless, of course, the United States can guarantee continual protection. If we are not careful, the entire ADF will be focused on developing this limited capacity at the cost of Australia's hard-won capability, for the first time in its history, of being able to defend itself and project credible force in its own region.[13] As it is, some of Australia's conventional combat capabilities have been wound back: they include the decision to pay off the F-111 strike aircraft early, cut the number of operational FFG-7 frigates, reduce Australia's minesweeping forces, and downgrade its anti-submarine warfare capabilities (allegedly, because of the reduced regional submarine threat). If this is the cost of the alliance, it is starting to get fairly expensive in terms of downgrading Australia's own security.

It is never too late to turn things around and the appointment of Dr Brendan Nelson as defence minister holds out the prospect of a much more logical approach to defence planning in Australia, and one that is less subject to the whims of the single Service chiefs. But we should not underestimate the immense damage already inflicted on Australia's defence planning by the combination of a weak former minister and none-too-subtle pressure from Washington. There is a neat contradiction here between Washington's desire for Australia to play more of a global role in coalition warfare alongside it, and the fact that the United States wishes to see allies contribute to a greater share of the cost of their own security and that of their region. The latter is a particularly challenging issue for Australia given the recent crises in East Timor, the Solomon Islands and Bougainville, and the tsunami disaster in Indonesia, all of which have involved demanding deployments of the ADF at a time when it is also on operations in Afghanistan and Iraq. This marks an essential difference between Australia and countries such as the United Kingdom and Canada, which face no crises in their own neighbourhood. It also makes a mockery of Senator Hill's assertion that the Middle East is Australia's most important strategic priority, no doubt echoing voices in Washington.[14]

None of the above contradicts the fact that Australia's alliance with the United States confers major strategic benefits on it. Australia's defence relationship with America remains a substantial force multiplier for Australia's defence and intelligence capabilities. Since 11 September 2001, Australia's access to real-time intelligence has increased significantly and both our forces are working harder to attain greater interoperability. The question now is whether the benefits of the alliance still outweigh the costs, or whether the opposite is becoming true. Are increasing US alliance demands for Australian participation in far-flung coalition operations beginning to undermine our self-reliant defence capabilities? Has the Australian government undermined our long-term war-fighting capacity to respond to possible serious future threats in our own region? As Desmond Ball observed in 2001, the worst case would involve attempts to do too much with the United States in terms of coalition operations far afield, which would fracture the integrity of both Australia's defence posture and the bipartisan political consensus in favour of a strong defence effort—in which case, both the defence of Australia and the US alliance would be losers.[15] There can be no doubt that the bipartisan political consensus in Australia on defence policy is now fractured, which is a great pity.

At the end of the day, it is very difficult to come up with any precise measure of the costs and benefits of something as broad and enduring as the US alliance. Aldo Borgu has noted that some of the alleged costs and benefits can also be contradictory. For example, the 'war on terror' can be seen to have given a new lease of life to the alliance, but it has also highlighted the importance of *ad hoc* coalitions, which may yet come to impact on the durability and the value of formal alliances.[16] Arguably, the Australia–US alliance is at its strongest since 11 September 2001. Yet it is also the case that Australia has yet to face the consequences of major fatalities in any of its distant coalition operations with the United States. It therefore remains to be seen what the popular reaction would be, given that Australia has not experienced any deaths in combat since the Vietnam War. In fact, the Howard government has been rather cautious in the size of ADF forces that it has committed to distant coalition operations with the United States. They have rarely exceeded 2,000 troops and have generally been much smaller: they have been essentially limited to the provision of niche capabilities, which have not yet seriously jeopardized our ability to meet contingencies in our immediate neighbourhood. Australia could probably write the case study on how to gain the greatest possible influence with the United States for the minimal amount of effort.[17]

It is, however, the case that because of how closely Australia is identified with the United States, Australia bears the cost of any failures in its policy—as currently in Iraq. Howard has asserted that he does not believe that we can 'cherry pick' our obligations under the alliance, although that seems to ignore the history of US assistance to Australia in the past—for example, when Australia had problems with Indonesia over the confrontation in the early 1960s (Indonesia then had the third largest communist party in the world and was heavily armed by the Soviet Union). The Australian concept of defence self-reliance is now in jeopardy, and this will become increasingly so if alliance considerations are allowed to become a force structure determinant at the cost of Australia's ability to undertake independent military operations in our own immediate neighbourhood.

Where is the relationship heading?

Smaller powers, such as Australia, have always relied on external aid for the accomplishment of the basic goal of all states: survival. Neutrality and non-alignment have appealed to some other smaller powers, but these alternatives have never appealed to Australians. The policy of a protective alliance 'has always been the most obvious weapon for the small power and the one most employed'.[18] Yet borrowing someone else's strength can have disadvantages as well as advantages, as we have seen.

Of course, alliances are not merely the product of rational calculations of national interest.[19] They involve shared values, belief systems and a history of cooperation—and none more so than the Australia–US alliance. Stephen Walt has argued that 'alliances deteriorate and dissolve for several reasons [but] the most obvious and important cause is a change in the identity or nature of the threat that produced the original association'.[20] Yet that demonstrably has not been the case with Australia: the end of the Cold War certainly heralded a period of drift in the alliance with the United States in the 1990s, but the events of 11 September 2001 were its saviour. It is interesting to speculate what would have happened to the alliance if the terrible attacks on New York and Washington had not occurred and had not Prime Minister John Howard been in Washington that day.[21] The question now is whether Australia's unwavering support for the United States, during a period when some of America's other allies have kept their distance or been openly critical, has become the expected norm in Washington.

As Harries and Switzer have observed, it is a timely reminder that in dealing with a great democratic ally, the same axiom applies as in dealing with any other great power: those who can be taken for granted will be taken for granted.[22] Even so, as they note, two things may be said with confidence about the alliance: first it will endure; but, second, it will change. It will endure not only because the advantages that accrue from it are real and substantial (not least in the intelligence and defence arenas), but because the need for 'great and powerful friends' is deeply embedded in the Australian psyche. Moreover, Washington finds itself relying more on allies when it needs both moral support in its 'war on terror' and physical support because even it realizes that it cannot be everywhere at the same time.

The second reason it will endure is because the US unipolar moment is already fading and the world will likely become increasingly multipolar in terms of power distribution, with Asia likely displacing Europe as the region of greater economic strength and military potential.[23] The key challenge here will be the rise of China to power and America's need to check it, if not challenge it outright. Confronted, as it is, by wide-flung global challenges elsewhere—and not least in the Middle East—the United States will increasingly rely on its allies to both maintain a favourable military balance in Asia and to shoulder a greater share of the regional defence burden. That will include higher expectations of an Australia that, as former Secretary of Defense Donald Rumsfeld has noted, spends less than two per cent of gross domestic product (GDP) on defence—a rate of defence spending that compares unfavourably with some European countries.[24] Australia is a rising second-tier military power and, with American assistance, can improve its high-technology, power-projection capabilities, which would be relevant to maintaining favourable regional power balances. Australia's value as a provider of forward basing facilities may also increase substantially in future as the United States becomes less reliant on traditional fixed forward facilities in Northeast Asia.

However, there is a catch here and it relates to one of the main reasons why the alliance may well change. The spectacular rise of China means quite different things for Australia than for the United States. Australia talks about a strategic economic relationship with China—one which recognizes that China will inevitably be Australia's largest trading partner (it is already the largest source of Australian imports and Australia's second largest export market, after Japan). Prime Minister Howard believes Australia will become an energy superpower (Australia has 40 per cent of the world's uranium deposits) and China is seen as a major market.[25] China's spectacular economic boom in recent years has helped Australia's own economic prosperity greatly. China has achieved great success in converting economic opportunities into regional political influence, and not only with Australia: in many ways, Southeast Asia is becoming a Chinese sphere of influence. Most of Australia's neighbours appear quite comfortable with China's growing power. Howard says there is nothing inevitable about competition, still less conflict, between China and the United States.[26]

However, the United States views matters quite differently: the Pentagon says that, of the major powers, 'China has the greatest potential to compete militarily with the United States and field disruptive military technologies that could over time offset traditional US military advantages absent US counter strategies'.[27] The latest Quadrennial Defense Review also observes that 'the pace and scope of China's military build-up already puts regional military balances at risk',[28] an observation that was directly contradicted by the previous Australian Minister for Defence, Senator Robert Hill. The Pentagon's annual report to Congress on the military power of China notes that long-term trends in China's military capabilities 'have the potential to pose credible threats to modern militaries operating in the region' and that analysis of China's military acquisitions suggests it is generating capabilities that could apply to regional contingencies 'such as conflicts over resources or territory'.[29] Australia sees no such threat: instead, in its Foreign Policy White Paper, the government talks about building a stronger partnership 'with a growing and more influential China' as an important objective in Australian policy. It states that China's rise in economic, political and strategic weight 'is the most important factor shaping Asia's future'.[30] All this points to a radical divergence of views between Canberra and Washington and one that is likely to grow as China becomes more powerful.

There is another issue that may herald change in the alliance. Indonesia is inevitably going to be a stronger country; by 2050 its population will be approaching 300 million whereas that of Australia will level off at about 25 million.[31] This will not matter much if Indonesia continues down the path of democracy, but it will inevitably mean that Indonesia's strategic weight in our neighbourhood will greatly increase. This will become a matter of preoccupation for Australia if the democratic experiment should fail in Indonesia and were an extremist Islamic nationalist government to take over. We would then expect Washington to come to our assistance, particularly were a military threat to emerge. That would depend upon a whole host of factors, including America's priority interests elsewhere. In any event, and short of an Indonesian threat, Australia's relative position in our own region of primary strategic interest seems certain to reduce: economic prosperity and population growth will see the power of our neighbours increase. That will be a matter of strategic concern for us, but not necessarily for the United States.

The third issue that might undermine the alliance is if America continues down the path of being a revolutionary force determined to use its great power—including, conspicuously, its military power—to reshape the world. This has been argued persuasively by Owen Harries, an Australian who was formerly editor of the conservative US journal *The National Interest*.[32] He is concerned about a gathering political hostility that leaves America both dominant and increasingly disliked and isolated—which would be an extremely unhealthy state of affairs, not just for the United States but for its Australian ally. If unilateralism and the use of military force becomes an increasing feature of US behaviour, it is bound to generate not only widespread criticism and hostility towards it, but it is likely to provoke an alignment of other major powers opposed to it. To some extent, we are already seeing this in the creation of the Shanghai Cooperation Organization (SCO), which includes China, Russia and most of the Central Asian states. This is starting to look like the beginnings of a new continental alignment opposed to US hegemony and maritime dominance. For the first time, Australia has joined a nascent regional security organization—the East Asia Summit (EAS)—that does not include the United States. That will not please Washington and will be seen as a ploy by China to exclude the Asia–Pacific region's major power from security discussions. If these trends deepen, it is easy to see how Australia could be torn between its attractions to increasing regional prosperity generated by China and its obligations to the US alliance.

The two most serious challenges that could threaten the very fabric of the alliance are, first, a war between the United States and China over Taiwan and, second, a radical change in the Australian domestic political scene to an anti-US stance. With regard to Taiwan, much would depend upon the circumstances at the time and which country provoked the conflict. However, if it were outright Chinese aggression, an Australian refusal to support the United States militarily in such a conflict could cause serious damage to the alliance—perhaps irreparably so.[33] The reasons for this are quite simple: it is hard to think of any other American ally or friend who would agree to be involved (not Japan or South Korea or any of the ASEAN countries, or indeed any European country). Australia's refusal to support the United States with combat power would therefore have high salience in Washington. Australia's Foreign Minister has questioned whether the ANZUS Treaty would automatically apply in the event of a US war with China over Taiwan.[34] While there is nothing 'automatic' about the treaty, Washington would be correct in invoking it in the event of a Chinese attack on US military forces. Australia would be the only US ally in the entire Asia–Pacific region that Washington felt it could turn to for help with confidence. Understandably, the Howard government's preferred policy option is to hope that it will never be faced with this call on the alliance with the United States. In many ways, it is Canberra's worst nightmare.

The other serious contingency that could terminally damage the alliance is if an ultra left-wing Labor government came to power in Canberra that sought to follow the New Zealand model of the Lange Labour government in the mid-1980s and effectively remove Australia from its alliance with the United States. In the 2004 Australian general election, the then leader of the Opposition, Mark Latham, proclaimed that he would withdraw Australian troops from Iraq before Christmas and, before being made leader, he had made personally insulting remarks about President George W. Bush.[35] The Labor Party was decisively defeated in the 2004 election, and the current leader of the Opposition is noted for his commitment to the alliance and his high-level connections in Washington. So, for the foreseeable future this contingency should not arise.

It is not surprising that academic opinion on the future of Australia's alliance with the United States, and whether it will face major challenges such as those outlined above, is highly contested. Some believe that pressures on the alliance will increase rather than decrease in coming years. One school of thought suggests that we should expect America's security partnerships of the new century to become more expansive and less restrictive in geographic scope, more transnational in their dimensions rather than merely being focused on external threats, and more proactive and less defensive in orientation.[36] Some believe that a reinvention of the traditional bilateral security relationship is taking place—a development which has already tested the boundaries of bipartisan support for security policy within Australia and will continue to do so.[37] In this view, Australian strategic interdependence with the United States is an increasingly sound recipe for the challenges of the twenty-first century, even if this comes at the cost of defence self-reliance.[38]

Others have a more cautious approach, acknowledging the strength of the current relationship but also suggesting a number of foreseeable developments with the potential to place the alliance under severe—and possibly terminal—stress.[39] In this view, Australian public opinion is the most vulnerable element in forecasting why the alliance should not be seen as totally secure. The most obvious challenge arises from the 'war on terror' and the possibility that even small casualties in Afghanistan or Iraq 'would probably have a severe effect' on Australian public opinion towards the alliance.[40] Although it is acknowledged that following New Zealand's example is not likely to gain majority support, this school of thought observes that history offers numerous examples of occasions when difficulties arise simultaneously in domestic and international politics to place the alliance in jeopardy.[41]

Perhaps the final word on this subject lies with Paul Kelly, the doyen of the Australian press corps, who argues that the alliance should not require that Australia supports the United States 'on all issues uniformly'.[42] He argues that, in this context, managing expectations is vital: Australia needs to understand when America expects it to do more and America needs to understand when Australia cannot meet these expectations.[43] He believes that the trend over the past half-century will be maintained and that the relationship will strengthen, but acknowledges that history is not linear and that many would contest his view.[44]

Concluding thoughts

Australia will remain a committed American ally for the foreseeable future. There will be no inclination toward a New Zealand or Canadian defence posture: Australia's defence force will not be structured primarily for peacekeeping or peace enforcement, as distinct from conventional military capabilities. There is no evidence that the Australian polity is moving away from firm support for the ANZUS alliance. And should the Labor Opposition come to power in 2007 under the leadership of Kevin Rudd, there will be no wavering on central alliance issues. But it must be understood that a US war with China over Taiwan would face any Australian government, of whatever political persuasion, with choices it would rather not face. And a Labor government would not be in favour of an Australian combat presence in Iraq, as distinct from engineering reconstruction forces.

Australia and the United States have close commonality of views when it comes to fighting the 'war on terror' and dealing with the spread of WMD. Our common support for the success of democracy, in such places as Indonesia and Iraq, and for preventing the emergence of failed states, in such places as the Solomon Islands and East Timor, establishes the basis of a strong alliance partnership for the twenty-first century. Yet it remains to be seen whether the 'Long War' on terrorism unites US and Australian interests to the same extent that they have been united by previous wars. It also remains to be seen whether crises in Australia's neighbourhood (for example, in Papua New Guinea) become the same preoccupation for Australia as the Middle East is currently for the United States.

There are two areas where drift could set in. Maintaining support for the alliance is contingent upon Washington's success in convincing the Australian public of both the necessity and legitimacy of its policies. Australia should not be seen, or described, in the region as 'a deputy sheriff' of the United States. Such an epithet is damaging. A more apposite label—if one must be used—is that offered by Kurt Campbell: 'Australia has become our Britain in Asia.'[45] Yet even this statement has a certain demeaning quality to it.

The second area of potential difficulty in the alliance is over China. As a regional power, Canberra needs influence in Washington and Beijing. Managing to have good relations with both will take astute diplomacy as China becomes more powerful and poses more of a challenge to the United States. History tells us much about the likelihood of tension and conflict between a rising major power and an established power. The strongly positive views of China that currently are held in Australia may shift in the future if Beijing's growing economic and military influence is felt less benignly across the region. However, at present, the greatest potential threat to the alliance may be the absence of a common approach to Beijing. Canberra must realize that its role is not to mediate between Beijing and Washington, but rather to help ensure that China's rise is indeed peaceful and that the United States maintains its pre-eminence in Asia.[46] In good old 'balance of power' terms, the need for a strong US presence in Asia has not diminished.

Finally, a deeper appreciation is required in Washington that Australia has a significant role to play in securing American interests, as well as its own, in the Asia–Pacific region. Australia has become a more assertive power in supporting alliance interests in Japan, and Canberra now has greater geopolitical clout in Southeast Asia and the South Pacific—both of which are important areas with regard to the fight against terror and failed states. But US policy in both regions has been essentially one-dimensional, emphasising the counterterrorism agenda almost to the exclusion of anything else.[47] This preoccupation has promoted an impression that America does not really care about other important regional interests and is giving China an opportunity, especially in Southeast Asia, to gain influence at America's expense.

In the final analysis, the most critical issue for the security of the entire Asia–Pacific region is the nature of the relationships among the major powers: China, Japan, India, Russia and the United States. Australia relies on a balance of power in Asia in which America continues to play the predominant role. An Asia without America would be a dangerous place for Australia.

Notes

1 I. Cook, *Australians Speak: Public Opinion and Foreign Policy*, Sydney: Lowy Institute for International Policy, 2005, pp. 7–8.
2 Ibid., p. 8.
3 Ibid., pp. 13–14. Ian McAllister, who has monitored public opinion towards the United States longer than anyone else in Australia, gets different results: 90 per cent of Australians think that the ANZUS Treaty is very important or fairly important and 84 per cent trust the United States a great deal or a fair amount. See I. McAllister, *Public and Elite Opinion in Australia Towards Defence Links with the United States*, Canberra: Australian National University, 2005.
4 See R.N. Rosecrance, *Australian Diplomacy and Japan, 1945–1951*, Melbourne: Melbourne University Press, 1962.
5 See D. Ball, 'The US–Australian alliance', in B. Rubin and T. Keaney (eds) *US Allies in a Changing World*, London: Frank Cass, 2001, pp. 255–8. See also D. Ball, *Pine Gap*, Sydney: Allen & Unwin, 1988.
6 J.T. Richelson and D. Ball, *The Ties That Bind: Intelligence Cooperation between the UKUSA Countries*, London and Sydney: Allen & Unwin, 1985.
7 See, for example, *Defence 2000: Our Future Defence Force*, Defence White Paper, Canberra: Defence Publishing Service, 2000, pp. 55–6.
8 Ibid., pp. 24–6.
9 For a detailed analysis of the track record of Australian intelligence agencies on the matter of Iraq's WMD see *Report of the Inquiry into Australian Intelligence*

Agencies (known as the 'Flood Report'), Canberra: Commonwealth of Australia, 2004. It concludes that there was a failure of intelligence on Iraq but with one agency, the Office of National Assessments, more exposed and another, the Defence Intelligence Organisation, more cautious on the subject.

10 *Defence 2000*, pp. x, 29.

11 *Australia's National Security: A Defence Update 2003*, Canberra: Commonwealth of Australia, 2003; and *Australia's National Security: A Defence Update 2005*, Canberra: Commonwealth of Australia, 2005.

12 See P. Dibb, 'Is strategic geography relevant to Australia's current defence policy?', *Australian Journal of International Affairs*, vol. 60, no. 2, June 2006, pp. 247–64.

13 See P. Dibb, *Essays on Australian Defence*, Canberra papers on strategy and defence no. 161, Canberra: Strategic and Defence Studies Centre, 2006.

14 In one of his last Cabinet meetings, Senator Hill tried to get this sentiment accepted. The best he could do in his *Defence Update 2005* was to describe Australia as having vital interest in the Middle East—a description that was not applied to any other part of the world (see p. 8).

15 D. Ball, 'The US–Australian alliance', p. 275.

16 A. Borgu, 'Costs and benefits of the US alliance in an age of terrorism', presentation to the Asia–Pacific College of Diplomacy Conference on The Australian–American Alliance, The Australian National University, Canberra, 1–2 December 2005.

17 Ibid., p. 15.

18 R.L. Rothstein, *Alliances and Small Powers*, New York: Columbia University Press, 1968, p. 45.

19 See S.M. Walt, 'Why alliances endure or collapse', *Survival*, vol. 39, no. 1, Spring 1997, pp. 156–79.

20 Ibid., p. 163.

21 On 12 September 2001 Howard announced that 'Australia will provide all the support that might be requested of us by the United States in relation to any action that might be taken'. Note the unqualified nature of this commitment by the use of the words 'all' and 'any'.

22 O. Harries and T. Switzer, 'Loyal to a fault', *The American Interest*, vol. 1, no. 4, Summer 2006, pp. 57–8.

23 A.F. Krepinevich, *Transforming America's Alliances*, Washington, DC: Centre for Strategic and Budgetary Assessments, February 2000, pp. 21–2.

24 These remarks were made at the Australia–United States Ministerial consultations (AUSMIN) talks in Adelaide in November 2005. France spends 2.6 per cent of GDP on defence, Greece 2.9 per cent, and the United Kingdom 2.4 per cent.

25 See A. Mitchell, 'No certainty in a nuclear future', *Australian Financial Review*, 25 November 2006, p. 42.

26 See, for example, Prime Minister the Hon. John Howard MP, address at the opening of the Lowy Institute for International Policy, Sydney, 31 March 2005.

27 United States Department of Defense, *Quadrennial Defence Review Report*, 6 February 2006, p. 29.

28 Ibid.

29 United States Department of Defense, *Annual Report to Congress: Military Power of the People's Republic of China 2006*, Washington, DC: Department of Defense, 2006, p. 1.

30 Commonwealth of Australia, *Advancing the National Interest: Australia's Foreign and Trade Policy White Paper*, Canberra: National Capital Printing, 2003, p. 79.

31 C. Bell, *Living with Giants: Finding Australia's Place in a More Complex World*, Canberra: Australian Strategic Policy Institute, 2005, p. 5.

32 O. Harries, *Understanding America*, Sydney: The Centre for Independent Studies, 2002, pp. 29–30.
33 P. Dibb, *Australia's Alliance with America*, Melbourne Asia policy papers no. 1, Melbourne: University of Melbourne, March 2003, p. 8.
34 The Hon. Alexander Downer MP, Minister for Foreign Affairs, Australia, media conference transcript, Beijing, 17 August 2004.
35 P. Dibb, 'US–Australia alliance relations: an Australian view', *Strategic Forum* 216, Washington, DC: Institute for National Strategic Studies, National Defense University, 2005, p. 3.
36 See R. Lyon, *Alliance Unleashed: Australia and the US in a New Strategic Age*, Canberra: Australian Strategic Policy Institute, June 2005.
37 See R. Lyon and W.T. Tow, 'The future of the US–Australian security relationship', *Asian Security*, vol. 1, no. 1, January 2005, pp. 25–52.
38 Ibid., p. 48.
39 See P. Edwards, *Permanent Friends? Historical Reflections on the Australian–American Alliance*, Lowy Institute paper 08, Sydney: The Lowy Institute for International Policy, 2005.
40 Ibid., p. 54.
41 Ibid., p. 57.
42 P. Kelly, *Shipwrecked in Arcadia: The Australian Experiment*, Cambridge, MA: Harvard University, 2004, p. 27.
43 Ibid., p. 27.
44 Ibid., p. 18.
45 Cited in P. Hartcher, 'A historic shift in foreign policy', *The Sydney Morning Herald*, 1 April 2005, p. 11.
46 D. Blumenthal, 'Alliance takes diverse China roles', *The Australian*, 2 May 2005, p. 9.
47 P. Dibb, 'America and the Asia–Pacific region', in R. Ayson and D. Ball (eds) *Strategy and Security in the Asia–Pacific Region*, Crows Nest, NSW: Allen & Unwin, 2006, p. 189.

4   Australia–Japan

Brendan Taylor and Desmond Ball

In a speech to the Japan Press Club in August 2006, the Australian Foreign Minister Alexander Downer recalled his recent visit to the Al Muthanna province in Iraq, where Australian Defence Force (ADF) personnel had at that time been working in collaboration with engineers from the Japan Self-Defense Force (SDF). In the speech, Downer reminisced about seeing 'a long line of Japanese jeeps with the Rising Sun emblazoned on the sides'. He evoked images of 'Australian soldiers working hand in glove, day in and day out, with Japanese service personnel', and went on to observe what a 'long way' this strategic relationship had come 'in just a few decades'.[1] The irony of this situation was certainly not lost on one of Australia's leading foreign affairs commentators, Paul Kelly, who recalled that Downer's father—himself an Australian politician—was a prisoner of war of the Japanese during the Second World War and also opposed the postwar Peace Treaty between the Allied powers and Japan.[2]

Speaking later in an interview with Kelly, Downer referred to the Australia–Japan relationship as one that is undergoing 'a complete transformation'.[3] Indeed, this is a security relationship that has now grown to the extent that, if the range of cooperative activities could be summated, Japan would be in the top five of Australia's security partners. From Tokyo's perspective, a strong case could even be made that the Australian connection has reached the point of being Japan's second most important security partnership in the world, next of course to its longstanding alliance relationship with the United States. This chapter reviews the evolution of this rather remarkable transformation. It documents the broad range of cooperative security activities in which Canberra and Tokyo are presently engaged, before identifying the factors which appear to be motivating that collaboration. Finally, the chapter examines the future prospects for the Australia–Japan partnership, concluding that while some progressive strengthening of security links is likely, the challenges associated with any further advancement of significant strategic collaboration between Canberra and Tokyo should not be underestimated.

The evolution of Australia–Japan security cooperation

The idea of greater strategic collaboration between Australia and Japan was first publicly broached in the late 1970s and early 1980s, driven largely by concerns relating to Washington's perceived lack of commitment to the Asia–Pacific region.[4] In actual fact, cooperation between Australia and Japan with respect to 'hard' security matters had already begun, in secret, in the mid-1970s—at the instigation of the Australian Secret Intelligence Service (ASIS)—but was essentially limited to secret intelligence exchanges for more than a decade. However, its purview began to be substantially expanded at the beginning of the 1990s, albeit with very tentative initial steps, to include reciprocal visits by senior defence officials, official dialogues on security matters of mutual concern and modest cooperation in some maritime fields (including joint exercises between elements of the respective Australian and Japanese navies).

Australia–Japan security cooperation was given a critically important public dimension when, in May 1990, Yoso Ishikawa became the first Japanese defence minister to visit Australia, and Senator Robert Ray, the Australian Minister for Defence, visited Tokyo in September 1992. Minister Ishikawa's visit 'had little policy content', but the fact that it 'took place without incident or any negative publicity in Australia ... was extremely reassuring to those who wanted a strategic dialogue and the opening of defence contacts between the two countries'.[5] By the mid-1990s, a fairly comprehensive range of cooperative measures had been institutionalized, including regular reciprocal visits by senior defence officials (including chiefs of the defence forces), annual political-military dialogues, expanded intelligence exchanges, joint naval exercises and reciprocal port visits and some surveillance operations. A number of formal policy pronouncements were made reflecting this steadily increasing level of intimacy, including the August 1997 'Partnership Agenda between Australia and Japan' which built directly upon the May 1995 'Joint Declaration on the Australia–Japan partnership'.

Reflecting the growing intensification of the Australia–Japan security relationship itself, such pronouncements have flowed with even greater regularity during the period since the 11 September 2001 attacks on the World Trade Center and the Pentagon. In May 2002, Prime Ministers John Howard and Junichiro Koizumi issued a joint statement on the 'Australia–Japan Creative Partnership' which 'welcomed the expanding dialogue and cooperation between the two nations on security and defence issues, underpinned by their close strategic interests'. An 'Australia–Japan Joint Statement on Cooperation to Combat International Terrorism' was adopted by the foreign ministries in July 2003, formalizing their countries' 'bilateral consultation and cooperation in the fight against terrorism'. In September of that year, then Minister of Defence Robert Hill travelled to Tokyo to sign a 'Memorandum of Understanding (MOU) on Defence Exchanges between the Japan Defense Agency and the Australian Department of Defence', sometimes called the Australia–Japan Security Agreement. This MOU recognized 'Australia and Japan's common strategic interests in the peace and stability of the Asia–Pacific region'; it affirmed the commitment of both countries 'to strengthening high level exchanges, strategic dialogue and senior visits, as well as a range of working-level contacts, staff college exchanges and regular ship and aircraft visits'; and it committed both the Japan Defense Agency (JDA) and the Australian Department of Defence 'to explore new areas of cooperation for promoting and deepening the defence relationship', including with respect to counterterrorism and countering proliferation of weapons of mass destruction (WMD). Hill said: 'This memorandum signals the strength of the existing bilateral defence and security relationship. It also demonstrates the increasing emphasis that Australia and Japan are placing on security cooperation.'[6]

In March 2006, following a bilateral meeting which took place in the context of the so-called 'Trilateral Strategic Dialogue' (TSD) involving Australia, Japan and the United States, the Australian and Japanese Foreign Ministers (Alexander Downer and Taro Aso) issued a joint ministerial statement which noted 'that Australia and Japan had developed a comprehensive strategic relationship of great significance for both countries'—a partnership which 'they decided ... should be developed further'. This theme was reiterated during Downer's August 2006 visit to Tokyo, during which time he proposed a further strengthening of Australia–Japan security cooperation during his meetings with then Prime Minister Koizumi, then Chief Cabinet Secretary (and now Prime Minister) Shinzo Abe and Foreign Minister Aso. According to a senior diplomat at the Embassy of Japan in Australia, 'the idea was received positively on the Japanese side and there is now a consensus between Canberra and Tokyo on the importance of strengthening bilateral security cooperation'.[7]

Current elements of Australia–Japan security cooperation

Downer has been quite explicit about the fact that the agreement which Australian and Japanese officials are currently exploring will not be a formal treaty alliance, but rather, a 'formal security relationship' somewhat akin to the new framework agreement on security cooperation which Australia recently arrived at with Indonesia.[8] Yet when one examines the substance of current security collaboration between Australia and Japan, it is not altogether surprising that some commentators have already gone so far as to characterize their relationship as a 'shadow alliance'.[9] This security cooperation is occurring across a broad and varied number of areas.

The 11 September 2001 terrorist attacks and the subsequent onset of the US-led global 'war on terror' (recently dubbed the 'Long War'), for instance, has generated a myriad of opportunities for expanded Australia–Japan security cooperation—in US-led 'coalitions of the willing' and regional multilateral forums, including the TSD. On the defence side, this has meant expanding dialogues and intelligence exchanges, intensifying cooperation with regard to maritime surveillance activities, and increasing joint exercise activities. For example, in September 2003, military and law enforcement personnel from Australia, Japan, the United States and France conducted Exercise *Pacific Protector* in the Coral Sea, in which a vessel 'suspected' (for training purposes) of carrying WMD was interdicted, boarded and inspected as part of the Proliferation Security Initiative (PSI). The exercise was widely regarded as being aimed at North Korea. Following its successful completion, Australia hosted a second *Pacific Protector* exercise in early April 2006, again as part of the PSI. Held around Darwin in the far north of Australia, the 2006 exercise focused on an air-interception scenario, coupled with ground-based activities. In addition to the involvement of personnel and assets from Australia and Japan, the United States, New Zealand, Singapore and the United Kingdom also participated.[10]

Cooperation in operational situations between Japan and Australia has also increased during the period in question, not only with respect to the provision of intelligence and logistic support, but also in actual combat operations. Along with South Korea, Australia and Japan were the only countries in the region to provide a military contribution to Operation *Enduring Freedom*, for instance, although only the Australian forces participated in combat operations. Nevertheless, Japan's support for the war in Afghanistan was particularly significant in terms of breaking the constraints on overseas deployments of the SDF.

In the case of the war in Iraq, actual Japanese support for Operation *Iraqi Freedom* was very limited. The *Kirishima*, one of Japan's *Aegis* destroyers, was sent to the Indian Ocean in December 2002 to protect Japanese supply ships which were refuelling US and British naval vessels, and to conduct surveillance activities in the area, in accordance with another special antiterrorist law passed in November 2002.[11] It was widely (if only tacitly) understood that this was an indirect contribution to the forthcoming war in Iraq in that it relieved a US *Aegis* destroyer from Afghanistan operations to move into the Gulf.[12]

Following the declared end of the war in Iraq on 1 May 2003, and the passage by the Diet of the Iraq Humanitarian Reconstruction Support Special Measures Law in July, SDF forces were sent to Iraq to assist the US-led coalition forces 'reconstructing' the country—the first time that SDF units have served abroad outside the UN peacekeeping operations framework.[13] Between January 2004 and June 2006, approximately 5,500 SDF personnel were dispatched to the Iraqi city of Samawah, in the southern Al Muthanna province.[14] As alluded to previously, in February 2005 the Howard government deployed 450 ADF personnel to Iraq (in addition to the 850 already stationed there) specifically to guard the SDF personnel engaged in reconstruction work, as well as to help train new Iraqi army units in Al Muthanna province. The Al Muthanna deployment cost Australia some A\$200 million in the 2005–6 fiscal year, compared to a total of approximately A\$270 million for all ADF activities in Iraq in 2004–5, but was justified in terms of ensuring that the Japanese stayed in Iraq and the strengthening of the Australia–Japan security relationship.[15]

Cooperation between Australia and Japan in Afghanistan and Iraq builds on a recent history of collaboration between the two countries in various peacekeeping operations and humanitarian missions. Japan's first military contribution to a UN peacekeeping operation, for example, was its involvement in the UN Transitional Authority in Cambodia in 1992–3. Australia also played an active role in this mission. The two countries again worked closely together in responding to the East Timor crisis of 1999. Australia led the international intervention and Japan, while initially declining military participation, ultimately decided to send SDF personnel to East Timor in 1999. Along with the United States and India, Australia and Japan were also members of the coalition which coordinated assistance efforts in the immediate aftermath of the December 2004 Indian Ocean tsunami.[16]

The decisions by Australia and Japan in December 2003 to participate in US ballistic missile defence (BMD) programs also raise collaborative possibilities. In June 2002, the United States officially withdrew from the Anti-Ballistic Missile Treaty and embarked on a wide-ranging program to develop and deploy both theatre and strategic/national BMD systems, but this really only codified commitments made by the Bush administration before 11 September 2001. Both Australia and Japan had also been interested in different aspects of missile defence well before the attacks that day. However, the 'war on terror' has provided new justifications, with the United States explaining its need for defences in terms of the proliferation of WMD among 'rogue states', and, potentially, international terrorist organizations—with North Korea being prominent in this milieu.

Explaining Australia–Japan security cooperation

There is no doubt that current and prospective geopolitical trends go a long way toward explaining this intensification of security cooperation between Australia and Japan. Indeed, given the growing probability of their common involvement in the 'Long War', counterproliferation initiatives and peace-keeping operations (with and without UN mandates), as well as their mutual interest in BMD developments, it is becoming increasingly likely that elements of the Australian and Japanese armed forces will serve toge-ther in operational situations, including not only combat support activities but also actual combat. It is not difficult to envisage, for instance, Aus-tralian and Japanese units, which are committed to the same theatre, being embroiled in firefights in which they fight, and survive together.

Australia and Japan are in many respects 'natural allies'. They are both liberal democracies, espousing broadly similar economic and political values. Consistent with this, Australia and Japan maintained robust formal alliance relationships with the United States during the Cold War. These alliances, while ostensibly directed against the ideological and military challenge posed by the Soviet Union, have survived the dissipation of that challenge surprisingly well. Indeed, the cultural, ideological and historical commonalities between them provide one rationale for why these respective bilateral alliances have not only outlasted the Soviet threat but—contrary to the expectations of mainstream theories of alliance politics[17]—have actually attained an even greater level of cohesion and intensity during the period since.

A further commonality between Australia and Japan stems from the fact that they are each regarded—albeit to varying degrees—essentially as 'outsiders' in Asia. This ostracism is not only a product of how the region views these two countries, but also one of how Australians and Japanese perceive themselves and their place in this part of the world. The American political scientist Samuel Huntington, for instance, has described Australia as a 'torn country'—a people who, in his words, are 'divided over whether their society belongs to one civilisation or another'.[18] Despite its geographical location in East Asia, Huntington also describes Japan as 'a society and civilization unique to itself', before proceeding to observe that 'however strong the trade and investment links Japan may develop with other East Asian countries, its cultural differences with these countries inhibit and perhaps preclude its promoting regional economic integration like that in Europe and North America'.[19]

A number of other explanations have been advanced for the continuing intensification in Australia–Japan security relations. Kelly, for instance, observes that 'the proposed security agreement coincides with Australia's push for a free trade agreement between Australia and Japan, a standard part of the Howard government's diplomatic technique'.[20] An alternative rationale might be that increased collaboration between Canberra and Tokyo is the product of pressure from their superpower ally, the United States. To be sure, Washington is in the process of executing a 'transformation' of its Asia–Pacific alliances relationships from originally region-specific mechanisms to increasingly 'global' arrangements, and calls have certainly emanated from the United States calling for a more effective integration of America's Asia–Pacific alliances.[21] Publicly at least, however, the primary impetus for driving forward Australia–Japan security cooperation seems to have come not from Washington, but from Canberra and Tokyo. Instead, therefore, one added incentive for increasing communication and security collaboration between these two capitals could potentially be the improved capacity which a more unified approach to alliance politics affords them in shaping the behaviour of their increasingly assertive (and at times unpredictable) superpower ally.

The prospects

The intensification of the Australia–Japan security relationship, transforming it from one involving limited bilateral activity to one in which both

Australia and Japan now rank each other among their leading security partners, points toward a further progressive strengthening of that relationship. As this chapter has demonstrated, Australia and Japan are in many respects 'natural allies'. They are each liberal democracies, sharing broadly similar economic and political values. They are also building an impressive history of association through their collaborations in the 'war on terror' (in Afghanistan and Iraq), peacekeeping operations (in Cambodia and East Timor), humanitarian assistance efforts (including Indian Ocean tsunami relief) and military exercises (such as PSI).

Despite the likelihood of this strengthening in the Australia–Japan security relationship, however, the challenges associated with any further advancement of significant strategic collaboration between Canberra and Tokyo should not be underestimated. First, while it is true that Australia and Japan do enjoy *some* compatibilities in terms of their military resources—particularly when considered relative to other countries in the region[22]—stark resource inequalities exist which are likely to place real constraints on the expansion of cooperative activity between them. A comparison between the Australian and Japanese defence forces reveals that there are very real constraints to the expansion of cooperative activity on the Australian side. The ADF, for instance, is only a small force—perhaps about a fifth of the size of the SDF. Australia's defence budget (US$17.4 billion in 2005) is about a third of that of Japan (US$44.7 billion). Australia's total active defence force is 52,872, compared to the SDF's 239,900. The Australian Army has 26,035 personnel while the Japan Ground Self-Defence Force (GSDF) has 148,200. The Royal Australian Navy (RAN) has six submarines and only ten principal surface combatants (destroyers and frigates).[23] Australia's annual expenditure on defence cooperation averages about A$230 million (about US$150 million)—covering the costs of combined exercises, training programs, overseas visits and various forms of defence assistance—and is focused mainly on the ASEAN and Southwest Pacific areas. It also includes the cost of regional maritime surveillance operations by Australia's P-3C long-range maritime patrol aircraft.[24] The ADF has been operating at an extraordinary tempo since 1999, with both platforms and personnel fully committed.

Second, although the foregoing analysis illustrates that there is no shortage of common security concerns weighing on the minds of policymakers in Canberra and Tokyo, it is important to bear in mind that Australia and Japan still have very different strategic interests, driven in part by the fact that they are each physically located in parts of the world with very different strategic dynamics. From the point of view of the defence of Australia, for instance, Japan lies far outside Australia's 'sphere of primary strategic interest'.[25] Likewise, despite suggestions that Australia is in the process of becoming (if it has not already become) a truly 'global' ally of the United States,[26] there is a risk that the increasing emphasis being accorded to coalition operations and interoperable capabilities will lead to the diversion of resources and distortions in force structure development. The total cost of the Al Muthanna deployment to guard the SDF personnel in Iraq, for instance, was somewhere in the vicinity of A$300 million.[27] This is roughly equivalent to the cost of two *Wedgetail* airborne warning and control aircraft, or five *Global Hawk* unmanned aerial vehicles, or a dedicated multitransponder geostationary communications satellite for the ADF.

It is in relation to the issue of China's (re)emergence, however, that the divergence in threat perceptions between Canberra and Tokyo is most acute. Canberra is clearly the more sanguine on this issue. For Australia, China is seen as such a commercial opportunity that the Howard government appears to have spent little time (publicly at least) considering, for instance, some of the potential geopolitical implications of Australia's growing energy ties with China.[28] Instead, it has consistently come out with statements such as that issued in January 2006 by the Australian Ambassador to the United States Dennis Richardson: 'The question for Australia is not whether China's growth is innately good or bad; Australia made up its mind long ago that it was a good thing. China's growth is unambiguously good for Asia and the United States.'[29]

Tokyo, on the other hand, feels more acutely threatened by China's economic and military rise. By way of example, Japan's December 2004 National Defence Program Outline, which provides guidelines and sets the direction for future Japanese military capabilities, for the first time explicitly identified China as a significant military threat. Consistent with this, Sino–Japanese tensions have spiked during the period since over a host of historical, economic, resource, political, societal and strategic issues.[30] In many respects this worrisome trend is unsurprising given that, as the two historical great powers of East Asia, both countries have aspirations for leadership and influence over the region. We have seen this most clearly in ongoing debates regarding the notion of an East Asian Community. The dilemma for Canberra is a serious one, of course, bearing in mind that Japan and China remain Australia's number one and number two trading partners respectively. The outbreak of open hostilities between them would clearly be catastrophic from Canberra's perspective.

Finally, however much the Australia–Japan security relationship is strengthened, it will remain heavily conditioned by the respective alliances with the United States. And it will be US strategic policies and defence decisions which will primarily determine the directions, pace and dimensions of the continuing expansion in cooperative activities. For both Australia and Japan, after all, these respective alliances with the United States are fundamental bases of their strategic policies and plans. These alliances, and the US strategic directions, affect their respective strategic priorities, force development planning and acquisition programs, and operational commitments. They also affect the scope and opportunities for important cooperative activities between Australia and Japan. Against that backdrop, the degree of incoherence and unpredictability in US policies at the present time seems likely to impose a layer of considerable uncertainty on the unfolding shape of the Australia–Japan security relationship.

Notes

1 The Hon. Alexander Downer MP, Minister for Foreign Affairs, Australia, 'Australia–Japan: a global partnership', speech to the Japan Press Club, 1 August 2006.
2 P. Kelly, 'Warming up to Tokyo', *The Australian*, 12 August 2006.
3 Ibid.
4 W.T. Tow and R. Trood, 'The "Anchors": collaborative security, substance or smokescreen', in B. Williams and A. Newman (eds) *Japan, Australia and Asia–Pacific Security*, London and New York: Routledge, 2006, p. 71.
5 N. Sajima, *Japan and Australia: A New Security Partnership?*, working paper no. 292, Strategic and Defence Studies Centre, Australian National University, Canberra, January 1996, p. 27.
6 Senator the Hon. Robert Hill, Minister for Defence, 'Australia–Japan defence relationship', media release, Canberra, 29 September 2003.
7 S. Hosono, 'Towards a comprehensive strategic partnership between Australia and Japan: Japan's perspective', *Australian Journal of International Affairs*, vol. 60, no. 4, December 2006, p. 591.
8 Kelly, 'Warming up to Tokyo'.
9 P. Jain and J. Bruni, 'American acolytes: Tokyo, Canberra and Washington's emerging "Pacific Axis"', in B. Williams and A. Newman (eds) *Japan, Australia and Asia–Pacific Security*, p. 95.
10 Australian Department of Defence, 'Exercise Pacific Protector 06 overview'.
11 A. Berkofsky, 'Aid and comfort: Japan's aegis sets sail', *Asia Times Online*, 19 December 2002.
12 Y. Sato, 'The GSDF will go to Iraq without a blue helmet', *PacNet* 31, 31 July 2003.
13 G. Fairclough and C. Hutzler, 'Japan: marching on to a new role', *Far Eastern Economic Review*, 15 January 2004.
14 'GSDF contribution hailed', *Daily Yomiuri*, 21 June 2006.
15 P. Walters, 'Spreading freedom is expensive', *The Australian*, 11 May 2005.
16 T. Huxley, 'The tsunami and security: Asia's 9/11?', *Survival*, vol. 47, no. 1, Spring 2005.
17 See, for example, S.M. Walt, *The Origins of Alliances*, Ithaca, NY: Cornell University Press, 1987.
18 S.P. Huntington, 'The clash of civilizations?', *Foreign Affairs*, vol. 72, no. 3, Summer 1993, p. 42; and S.P. Huntington, *The Clash of Civilizations and the Remaking of World Order*, New York: Simon & Schuster, 1995, pp. 151–4.
19 Ibid, pp. 27–8.
20 Kelly, 'Warming up to Tokyo'.
21 See, for example, R. Blackwill, 'An action agenda to strengthen America's alliances in the Asia–Pacific region', in R. Blackwill and P. Dibb (eds) *America's Asian Alliances*, Cambridge, MA: MIT Press, 2000, pp. 126–34.
22 With the obvious exception of Singapore, Australia and Japan are the only two other countries in the Asia–Pacific with the capacity to meaningfully engage in the US-led 'Revolution in Military Affairs'. The armed forces of Australia and Japan are also relatively interoperable.
23 The International Institute for Strategic Studies, *Military Balance 2005–6*, London: Routledge, 2005, pp. 266–7, 279.
24 D. Ball and P. Kerr, *Presumptive Engagement: Australia's Asia–Pacific Security Policy in the 1990s*, Sydney: Allen & Unwin, 1996, p. 63.

25 P. Dibb, *Review of Australia's Defence Capabilities: Report to the Minister for Defence*, Canberra: Australian Government Printing Service, 1986, pp. 3–4.

26 See, for example, G. Sheridan, 'US sees us as a global ally, a vision well worth sharing', *The Australian*, 29 June 2006.

27 P. Walters, 'Spreading freedom is expensive', *The Australian*, 11 May 2005.

28 For further reading see D. Hale, 'China's growing appetites', *The National Interest*, issue 76, Summer 2004.

29 G. Elliott, 'Stay cool on China, ambassador tells US', *The Australian*, 30 January 2006.

30 For further reading see D. Roy, 'The sources and limits of Sino–Japanese tensions', *Survival*, vol. 47, no. 2, Summer 2005.

5 Australia–China

Michael Wesley

On 24 October 2003, Chinese President Hu Jintao addressed a joint sitting of the Australian parliament, in a much more restrained and positive atmosphere than had greeted his American counterpart the day before, when George W. Bush addressed the same body. Hu stated that it was a 'key component' of China's foreign policy to consolidate and develop its all-round cooperation with Australia, and that the People's Republic of China (China) viewed bilateral ties from a 'strategic and long-term perspective'.[1] The following August, Australian Foreign Minister Alexander Downer, on a visit to Beijing, announced that 'Australia and China would build up a bilateral strategic relationship'.[2] Downer's phraseology shadowed that of the 2003 Australian foreign and trade policy White Paper, which talked of 'building a strategic economic relationship with China' and a 'long-term strategic partnership ... in the energy sector'.[3] 'Strategic' is a word whose meanings have become loose and various through overuse, and it is for this reason that the Howard government has been content to use it in the context of Sino–Australian relations. In the Chinese foreign-policy lexicon, elevating Australia to the level of a 'strategic' relationship has precise meaning and substantial import for how Beijing now views its regional relations. But precisely what Canberra means by a 'strategic relationship' has been left undefined. It is an ambiguity that the Australian government hopes will allow it to signal its intention to build a resilient and positive relationship with China without causing too much nervousness in Washington. Beneath this terminological fudging lies Australia's enduring dilemma, the challenge of navigating its own path through the Asian region's emerging diplomatic order while at the same time reconciling this with its commitment to the ANZUS alliance, and the visions of global and regional order that this entails.

More than any other country, China has always symbolized for Australia the immanent evolution of the Asian regional order. This has been a nagging caveat in this country's deep commitment to, and investment in, the American-guaranteed global and regional orders. Australian governments have over time developed two imperatives for trying to reconcile this cognitive dissonance. One has been to work to tie China and the emerging regional order into the existing institutions and norms of the global and regional orders. China's post-1978 embrace of reform-led development has appeared to Canberra to be a key mechanism for engaging China in the status quo, disciplining its revisionist urges, and perhaps even in transforming it from within. The other imperative for Australia has been to try to decouple the management of the Sino–Australian relationship from the turbulent US–China relationship. The more lucrative and significant the ties between Australia and China become, the more collateral damage Australia stands to suffer in each bout of tension between Beijing and Washington. The first section of this chapter explores the emergence of Australia's cognitive dissonance over its relations with Washington and Beijing since 1949, the second section examines the emergence of its two coping imperatives and the final section assesses the likely effectiveness of each of these imperatives.

Historical dilemmas

China and the United States were the two driving strategic forces that shaped Australia's post-Second World War foreign and security policies. Initially, it had been a fear of a resurgent Japan that was foremost in Australian minds, but this had largely dissipated by the mid-1950s, to be replaced by the 'fear that Communism would outpace nationalism in the race for [Asian] people's allegiance'.[4] In 1949, a localized and apparently more malevolent strain of communism had infected Asia's largest country. By 1950, Chinese communist forces were fighting Australian, British and American forces in Korea with such ferocity that a major reason for their reluctance to commit troops to Indochina in the late 1950s was the fear that such action would trigger a countering Chinese intervention, and thus create another Korean War. Yet, in 1955, Australian committed troops to Malaya, where they soon were doing battle against communist insurgents backed by Beijing. Later, they fought Indonesian troops carrying out President Sukarno's policy of *Konfrontasi* with Malaya, again backed by China. And when Australian soldiers were eventually committed to Vietnam, they did battle with guerrillas and with regular forces supplied and equipped through and by China.

The Chifley government in Canberra had wanted to follow Britain's lead in recognizing the new China in 1949. Yet it had postponed its decision at the request of the Nash Labour government in New Zealand, which was just about to go to the polls and was worried that Australia's recognition of the new Chinese regime would be portrayed as evidence that Labour parties favoured communism. Labour's defeat in New Zealand increased the Chifley government's worries about its own looming election. The decision on recognizing the new China was further postponed, given that the Menzies-led Opposition was campaigning hard on an anti-communist message. Having won the election on such a ticket, the new Liberal–Country Party Coalition government could hardly turn around and recognize the new regime in Beijing: 'Although fully in agreement that [recognition] was wise and necessary, they decided they must act slowly.'[5] The new Foreign Minister, Percy Spender, proposed a two-stage plan, first to withdraw recognition from the nationalist regime that had fled to Taiwan, and then to grant recognition to China. The first step was taken in early 1950, but the second step was suspended following the outbreak of the Korean War later that year. Australia remained without any diplomatic representation with either claimant to the Chinese state until 1966, when the Holt government established an embassy in Taipei.

Both sides of politics in Australia therefore privately agreed that however distasteful they found Mao Zedong's regime, Australia's recognition of it was 'wise and necessary'. Richard Casey, who replaced Spender as foreign minister, believed that Australian foreign policy should work to build a regional association that included Australia, its great power allies, and the newly independent Asian states. Because important Asian players such as India and Indonesia were sympathetic to the new Chinese regime, the normalization of Australia's relations with Beijing was an obvious prerequisite for Casey's design. These views, however, never left the realm of private opinions in deference to the hard line response taken towards China and regional security by the United States. John Foster Dulles, soon to be the new US Secretary of State, visited Canberra in February 1951 to hold discussions on the nascent ANZUS alliance. He told his hosts that Washington was prepared to meet Australian fears over the peace treaty with Japan that was being negotiated, but only if Australia confirmed US policy in the Pacific. This clearly included non-recognition of China. Australia's original intent to include Britain in the ANZUS Treaty was also blocked by Washington, because of London's earlier recognition of Beijing.

Australia was faced with a clear choice that would shape its postwar foreign and security policies, between joining an emerging pan-Asian regional solidarity that gained its ultimate expression at Bandung in 1955, and fitting into a rigid, hub-and-spokes security architecture centred on the United States and firmly committed to containing communism. Under the circumstances, the choice was obvious, particularly since the massive US response to the Korean War reassured Australians that, having faced down the threat from Japan, Washington continued to be willing to invest heavily in countering security threats in the Pacific region. Australia voted at the United Nations to condemn China's aggression in the Korean War in February 1951, at once setting it apart from Commonwealth states such as India, and allowing it to defer the question of recognition of China. Canberra quietly shelved Casey's plan to broaden ANZUS into a regional framework including Asian states and Britain, and in November 1953 Casey told parliament that 'under present circumstances no recognition of Communist China or admission of its representatives to the United Nations would be entertained'.[6] The Labor Party voted at its 1955 National Conference in Hobart to extend recognition to China if returned to power, a decision that precipitated it to split into a rump and a new, vigorously anti-communist Democratic Labor Party (DLP). The Labor Party split was to keep Labor in opposition until 1972. Meanwhile, the DLP's manipulation of preferences in marginal seats meant that coalition governments were unable to move away from their policy of non-recognition of Beijing for fear of antagonising the DLP.

Australia had identified its own national security with American definitions and American defences of regional and global order. This was to provide uncomfortable moments for Canberra from time to time. The dilemma over Taiwan occurred early in the 1950s, when the new Eisenhower administration in the United States announced its 'deneutralization' policy of clearly stating its support for the Taipei regime. Emboldened by American support, the regime in Taiwan began making raids on the mainland—provocations that rapidly escalated into the first Formosa crisis. The Australian Cabinet held tense discussions regarding what to do if open war broke out between Beijing and Washington over a regime that Australia had withdrawn recognition from a few years previously. Even more jarring for Australian policymakers was Dulles' statement after the first Formosa crisis that, 'as far as treaty relations are concerned, Formosa is now in the same category as South Korea, the Philippines, New Zealand and Australia'—a clear signal of Washington's expectation that a conflict in the Taiwan Strait would trigger obligations under the ANZUS Treaty. The consolidation of communist power in northern Indochina following the 1954 Geneva Accords led to the Australian government stationing forces in Malaya, and to Canberra's enthusiastic participation in American designs to develop an Asian NATO, which were to take shape in the form of the Southeast Asian Treaty Organization (SEATO). Both moves amounted to a decisive break from the emerging Asian solidarity symbolized by Bandung. The Malayan and SEATO commitments were justified in terms of Western powers assisting newly independent Asian allies to resist the spreading virus of communism, a motivation that Indian Foreign Minister Krishna Menon had repeatedly denounced as patronizing and neocolonial.

By the early 1960s, opinion in Canberra was largely convinced that Australia had chosen correctly. The solidarity of Bandung had proved either ephemeral or malevolent. Two of the leaders of the Non-Aligned Movement—India and China—had fought a vicious border war in 1962, and Sino–Indian relations thereafter descended into a cycle of hostility and intrigue. The host at Bandung, Indonesia's President Sukarno, had turned his relationship with Beijing into Chinese support for his aggressive policy of *Konfrontasi* against neighbouring Malaya. Australian opinion saw both incidents as evidence of the aggressive nature of Chinese communism, the only defence against which was participation in a vigorous, American-led campaign of containment in Asia. China's aggression was regularly used by the Menzies government to justify the intervention of Australian forces in the Vietnam conflict.

The discordant note in Australia's commitment to the Western alliance against Asian communism was trade. Since 1949, and during periods in which Australian troops fought Chinese or Chinese-backed forces, Australia had conducted a brisk commodities trade with a country whose government it refused to recognize. By 1961, China had displaced the United Kingdom as the principal market for Australian wheat, and in the ensuing decade purchased between 30 and 40 per cent of the Australian wheat harvest. In 1967, Australia became the third largest supplier of goods to China, behind Japan and West Germany. Australia's only deference to Washington's trading embargo against China was to observe the embargo on 'strategic materials'. The contradictions between Australia's security and trading interests led to tensions within the Liberal–Country Party coalition governments. Those in the Country Party who represented Australian farmers worried about the adverse impact on trade of Australia's antagonistic diplomacy towards China. These tensions increased in 1970 when Canada recognized China, and Beijing began favouring Canadian agricultural imports over those from Australia. The government in Canberra began intensive discussions over whether to recognize the new China in order to shore up the A\$100 million per year wheat trade. That the government continued its policy of non-recognition in deference to US policy in the Pacific added to a growing sense that the long incumbency of the Coalition had resulted in sclerosis and a dearth of new ideas.

By the early 1970s, the ideological rigidities of the Cold War stand-off in Asia had given way to a complex balance of power. In Hedley Bull's words, 'the ideological professions of each [of the great powers] provided less and less of an inhibition to its mobility in foreign policy'.[7] China, which during the height of the Cultural Revolution between 1966 and 1968 had lapsed into almost total introversion, had re-emerged as a vigorous campaigner for the end to its diplomatic isolation. In 1970, Australia found itself and its allies outvoted on an Albanian resolution in the UN General Assembly calling for admission of China and the expulsion of the nationalist regime resident in Taiwan. On 25 October 1971, the same chamber rejected an American contention that the question of admission to the United Nations constituted an 'important question' requiring a two-thirds majority, and China entered the United Nations and took up its seat as a permanent member of the UN Security Council at the expense of its Taipei-based rival. Growing numbers of Western governments began to recognize Beijing, but Canberra refused to acknowledge the turning of the tide. By early 1970, Opposition leader Gough Whitlam was arguing that even Washington had 'moved ahead' of Canberra on the question of China, and in July 1971 took the politically risky decision to lead an Australian Labor Party (ALP) delegation to China. The announcement that same month that US National Security Adviser Henry Kissinger had also visited China and had laid plans for President Nixon's visit pulled the carpet from under the government in Canberra. Whitlam led the ALP to victory in the 1972 elections after 23 years in opposition. One of the new government's first actions was to establish full diplomatic relations with China and remove diplomatic recognition from Taiwan.

Sino–Australian relations developed quickly after the establishment of diplomatic ties. For China, Australia became a significant member of the 'second intermediate zone' of its foreign policy schema—a member of the Western alliance with which it had full diplomatic relations and significant trading relations that was also close to the countries of non-communist Southeast Asia, with which China still had no diplomatic relations. From the Australian side, Prime Minister Whitlam assumed full carriage of the relationship with China. His trusted foreign policy confidante Stephen FitzGerald was sent to Beijing as ambassador, and reported directly to the prime minister as well as through the usual channels back to the Department of Foreign Affairs. Whitlam's carriage of the China relationship has been emulated by each of his successors: Prime Ministers Fraser, Hawke, Keating and Howard have each responded to Beijing's sensitivities over hierarchy to personally direct Australia's relationship with China, leaving Foreign Ministers Willesee, Peacock, Hayden, Evans and Downer to manage Australia's other Asian relationships.[8] Australian governments have realized that a strong government-to-government framework is necessary with China before non-state links can flourish. Since at least Bob Hawke, Australian prime ministers have held up the relationship with China as a model for cooperation between countries of different cultures, political systems and levels of development.

For Whitlam, Australia's positive relationship with China symbolized the direction in which he wanted to take Australia's general foreign policy orientation: away from what he saw as a slavish adherence to the positions of the Western alliance towards more of a position of solidarity with the states of the third world. For Whitlam, as for his predecessors and successors, Australia's China policy would always have to be predicated on, and compatible with, the maintenance of the ANZUS alliance. The government of Malcolm Fraser, which succeeded the Whitlam government in 1975, viewed its relationship with China less in terms of solidarity with the third world and more from the perspective of balancing a newly aggressive Soviet Union with a growing presence and interest in the Pacific. The rise of Deng Xiaoping to power in Beijing, and Vietnam's invasion of Cambodia in the late 1970s, established a powerful strategic alignment between China, the ASEAN states, Australia and the United States. Deng's reforms saw Chinese foreign policy turn away from sponsoring revolutionary struggles towards an increasing interest in international stability to underpin economic growth. Common opposition to Hanoi's *de facto* sovereignty over Cambodia resulted in the gradual thawing and establishment of relations between China and the ASEAN states, as well as a strategic imperative that made the forging of close bonds between Australia and China compatible with American strategic goals in the 'Second Cold War'.

Coping with dissonance

The year 1989 marks a watershed in Sino–Australian relations, as well as an end to the era of the easy coexistence of Canberra's relations with Beijing and Washington. That year saw the rapid unravelling of the bipolar stand-off between the United States and the Soviet Union that had provided the strategic context for Australia's relations with China. Also in 1989, Vietnamese troops began to leave Cambodia for good, removing the primary cause for solidarity between Australia's ASEAN neighbours and China. Then, in June 1989, People's Liberation Army (PLA) troops attacked peaceful pro-democracy protesters in Beijing's Tiananmen Square as well as elsewhere across China, leading to widespread loss of life and injury. In the course of a few months, China had lost its strategic attraction and its benign image as a developing country intent on reform. Canberra reacted in harmony with the international chorus of condemnation of China. Prime Minister Bob Hawke wept for the students killed during his address to parliament on the Tiananmen massacre; he might well have wept for the end of an uncompli-cated era in Australia's foreign policy.

Canberra enacted a series of sanctions against China, including a ban on all high-level visits and support for regular resolutions at the UN Human Rights Commission (UNHRC) condemning China's human rights record. But China looms much too large for Australia for such restrictions to last long. Despite one commentator's warning that 'as long as repression per-sists in China, Australians are unlikely to support a return to the close relationship of the pre-1989 period',[9] the Hawke government began quietly normalizing bilateral ties with Beijing, largely unchallenged by significant criticism from within the ALP or from the Opposition. In July 1991 and November 1992, Australian human rights delegations visited China, the first gesture by a Western country in the post-Tiananmen era to begin quar-antining human rights issues from the broader bilateral relationship. Bilat-eral trade continued unabated, and for a period in the early 1990s the economic relationship was regarded by Canberra as the driver of Sino–Australian relations. By 1992, with the visit to Australia of Chinese Vice-Premier Zhu Rongji, official visits had resumed. Prime Minister Paul Keat-ing visited China in June 1993.

A different dynamic had developed in the United States. Sino–American relations have never recovered to their pre-Tiananmen pragmatism. China assumed an almost talismanic role for human rights campaigners and democracy advocates. Taiwan's transition to democracy in the early 1990s both sharpened the contrast with the communist, authoritarian regime in Beijing and served to rally and broaden the ranks of traditional supporters of Taipei in the Congress. Other opponents of China were motivated by their support for Tibetan independence. As the decade wore on, China came to be seen by many in Washington as a strategic threat, a rising power intent on challenging the American-guaranteed regional order in the Asia–

Pacific. Holders of this view cited the rapid growth in China's military budget and its belligerence towards Taiwan and over the South China Sea disputes. Periodic scares over Chinese espionage against American high-technology capabilities further underlined these perceptions. At the same time, China also replaced Japan as the prime economic threat to the United States, courtesy of a steadily widening trade surplus.

As a result of its tentative moves to normalize relations with Beijing after Tiananmen, the first Bush administration soon came under attack from Democratic presidential candidate Bill Clinton for its leniency towards China. China became a stick with which to beat the incumbent in each presidential election in the United States until the 2004 poll. During its first two years in office, the new Clinton administration made the annual granting of most favoured nation (MFN) status to China conditional on progress in its human rights performance. Annual State Department human rights reports were heavily critical of Beijing's record, and Washington was a strong supporter of UNHRC resolutions censuring China. In 1996, the Clinton administration sent two aircraft carrier battle groups to the Taiwan Strait during the crisis over Taiwan's elections. Clinton's successor, George W. Bush, came to office having labelled China a 'strategic competitor'.

Australia found itself buffeted by these tensions in the Sino–American relationship. The Keating government's visions of the growing economic integration and institutionalization of the Asia–Pacific region were threatened by such turbulence. It lobbied strongly for the decoupling of Washington's granting of MFN status to China from Beijing's human rights performance during Secretary of State Warren Christopher's visit to Australia in March 1994. In 1995, Australian Foreign Minister Gareth Evans, concerned about the souring of the Sino–American relationship, urged Washington to stop sending mixed signals to Beijing.

Upon coming to office in March 1996, the Coalition government of John Howard was immediately confronted by the Taiwan Strait crisis, in which China began a series of military exercises and live missile tests off the coast of Taiwan in response to national elections that were predicted to support President Lee Teng-hui's policy of seeking greater international recognition for the Taipei government. Having been elected on a pledge to 'reinvigorate' the Australia–US alliance, the Howard government could hardly act other than to support Washington's sending of two aircraft carrier battle groups to the Taiwan Strait. Beijing reacted by sending bilateral ties into freefall. In June 1996, Chinese Minister for Trade Wu Yi expressed 'strong concern' over the sudden decision to discontinue Australia's Development Import Finance Facility (DIFF) aid program. After Foreign Minister Alexander Downer, under attack in parliament over the DIFF cancellation, stated that 'not one Minister ... has expressed any concern to me about the abolition of the DIFF program',[10] Beijing released the following official statement: 'The Chinese government has, both prior to and after the decision of the Australian government, expressed many times and through various channels its grave concern over the termination of DIFF.'[11] This led to Opposition charges that Downer had misled parliament. Following the declaration of the 'Sydney statement' on closer Australia–US defence cooperation, the *People's Daily* called Australia and Japan 'the claws of a crab' used by the United States to try to contain China.[12] Beijing lodged an official protest at the visit of Primary Industries Minister John Anderson to Taiwan in September 1996, choosing not to honour the unspoken protocol of turning a blind eye to such visits if they were characterised as 'unofficial'.[13] The Chinese government also chose not to be understanding about the Dalai Lama's visit to Australia, and Howard's decision to meet with him; in the face of vociferous denunciations in the Chinese state media, Prime Minister Howard asserted that he would not 'bow to Chinese threats'.[14] Beijing's mood darkened further after Defence Minister Ian McLachlan stated that China was a strategic concern in the region, and after Canberra condemned a June 1996 Chinese nuclear test. Another official Chinese periodical wrote that Australia was 'confused' about whether it wanted to be close to Asia or the United States.[15] The *Guangming Daily* carried an editorial arguing that Australia's embarrassing defeat in its bid for a non-permanent seat on the UN Security Council was because the Howard government had 'altered the direction of [Australia's] foreign policy' away from Asia towards the United States and Europe.[16]

There can be little doubt that China had chosen to send the new Australian government a clear warning about the consequences of actions that displeased China. Canberra's dismay was heightened by the sudden reversal of Beijing's attitudes from those of the early 1990s, which had appeared to bend over backwards to be understanding of incidents not dissimilar to those that had raised China's ire in 1996, and had been characterized by rosy assessments of bilateral relations from the Chinese side. It was a pattern that was to recur in 2001, when the Howard government moved to establish close relations with the new George W. Bush administration in the United States and endorsed the American position during Washington's stand-off with China over the downing of a United States EP-3 surveillance aircraft. Howard also endorsed Bush's April 2001 vow to defend Taiwan and subsequent announcement of arms sales to Taiwan. Australia once again came under attack in the Chinese media and in official statements. In April 2001, three ships of the Royal Australian Navy were challenged by a PLA Navy vessel as they sailed through the Taiwan Strait, a situation that had never before occurred in the course of numerous Australian naval voyages through that waterway.[17]

The Hawke, Keating and Howard governments recognized that both the United States and China were crucially important for Australia. A commitment to the alliance with the United States sits at the core of Australia's foreign policy. Not only does the alliance yield tangible benefits including military equipment and technology, access to a global intelligence-gathering network and shelter under the American nuclear umbrella, it symbolizes Australia's long commitment to the global and regional orders designed and sponsored first by the British Empire and then by the United States.[18] The United States was also the crucial component—a huge, consuming economy—in the Asia–Pacific 'trade cycle' that saw booming Asian economies establishing evermore lucrative trading relations with Australia. Moreover, during the course of the 1990s, it became clear that the United States was becoming more powerful, across a range of indicators vis-à-vis its closest competitors, rather than less powerful as many had predicted in the 1980s. For 'an Australian maritime trading state that lacks an extensive industrial capacity, substantial population base or independently formidable military capability',[19] existing in a region of potential instability, the alliance with the United States has become almost non-negotiable for both sides of politics.[20]

However, China is also crucial. By 2005, China had become Australia's second largest trade partner, its second largest merchandise export market and the second largest source of its merchandise imports. Australia's trade with China has become steadily more essential to its economic prosperity over the past decade, as Chinese demand for commodities has composed a rising share of Australia's economic growth. To place the importance of Sino–Australian trade in its proper political context, the tax cuts given to Australian taxpayers in 2006 were able to be made because of the tax receipts from booming commodities exports to China. According to one observer, 'China is now as critical for Australia's economic security and prosperity as the US is in terms of Australia's military'.[21] And beyond the direct bilateral economic relationship, China has become more central to the economy of the Asia–Pacific region with which Australia conducts two-thirds of its trade. Over the past decade, a new, China-centred dynamic of regional economic integration has emerged. Currently around 58 per cent of China's exports go to other East Asian states, and about 47 per cent of China's imports come from the region. East Asia supplies 60 per cent of China's foreign direct investment, compared to 20 per cent from the United States and Europe combined. China's growth has been the single greatest driver of the post-Asian crisis economic growth of other East Asian countries. This makes Australia and its regional neighbours vulnerable to China's version of soft power, which—sometimes explicitly but most times implicitly—makes current and future relations, including trading relations, dependent on Beijing's approval of a country's conduct towards China.[22] In 1996 and 2001, it signalled strongly to Australia that it is watching Canberra's relationship with Washington closely. Beijing has repeatedly labelled the Australia–US alliance as 'outdated' and 'dangerous', and accused it of being directed towards the containment of China. China has called for a reduction of the American presence in the region and has urged regional countries, including Australia, to look to new forms of security institutions.

Herein lies the source of dissonance at the heart of Australian foreign policy: arguably this country's two most important relationships are potentially mutually incompatible. There has been extensive commentary in

Australia about a possible future 'choice' having to be made between Washington and Beijing in the event of a Sino–American conflict. According to one close observer, by so greatly strengthening Sino–Australian ties, the Howard government has actually sharpened its dilemma between Beijing and Washington.[23] Others, of course, deny that such a choice—actually or potentially—exists. Many argue that Beijing's relationship with Washington is not a completely antagonistic dynamic. Although they compete on some issues, the United States and China also have a deeply interdependent relationship. Despite an aversion to the American strategic presence in Northeast Asia, China's leaders also realize that the US–Japan alliance plays a crucial role in keeping Japan strategically contained. Increasingly, China's leaders recognize that economic growth and domestic stability rely on a deepening engagement with the global economy. Regional instability could choke off its vital economic growth, and there is an acceptance among many Chinese policymakers that the American strategic presence is a crucial component of regional stability. This is a perspective that John Howard shares:

> Australia does not believe that there is anything inevitable about escalating strategic competition between China and the United States. In recent years, both sides have shown themselves keen to cooperate on common interests and to handle inevitable differences in an atmosphere of mutual respect.[24]

But foreign policymaking is at its core concerned with anticipating and planning for significant risks, however improbable. Indeed, the 2003 foreign policy White Paper observed dryly that 'some tensions between Washington and Beijing were inevitable'.[25] Since 1989, therefore, Australian governments have formulated two approaches to coping with dissonance.

Engaging China

The first is to attempt to engage China in the status quo, disciplining its revisionist urges, and perhaps even in transforming it from within. The pursuit of economic reform to a centrally planned economy has meant that Beijing has become preoccupied with the dilemmas of steady yet fast economic growth: social dislocation, a mushrooming middle-class with expanding expectations, rapid industrialization and urbanization, and severe infrastructure shortfalls. Domestically, the pursuit of sustainable reform and broadly distributed growth have become central to regime tenure and political stability: continuing growth depends on access to international resources and international markets, and the disruption of access to either could choke off economic growth and lead to serious internal instability. Australian policymakers, and their counterparts elsewhere in the region and the Western alliance, have attempted to work with these motivations to shape a

China that is development and stability minded, multilaterally engaged, and committed to the existing global and regional orders. The key mechanism for achieving this is expected to be the steady development of inter-dependent linkages and the forging of regional institutions promoting trade liberalization, regional stability and greater understanding.[26] A corollary more shared by European and North American policymakers than their Australian counterparts is that advancing economic reforms in China, along with the 'demand for new institutions, social welfare structures, and a more predictable legal framework',[27] will lead inevitably to political liberalization and democracy in China. These changes are believed to have the potential to breed a sense of Sino–American common feeling and mutual identification that will see disputes between China and the United States become less and less common,[28] and to forestall confrontation by foregrounding vital interdependent links.

Australia's vigorous promotion of regional institutions in the Asia–Pacific during the Hawke–Keating period had these objectives as one of its fore-most rationales: 'Australia worked to bind China into a complex web of multilateral interaction that would provide a political and strategic safety net, as well as enmeshing it in regional economic arrangements.'[29] The Asia Pacific Economic Cooperation (APEC) forum, founded in Canberra in 1989, worked steadily to include China, Taiwan and Hong Kong. The for-mula for overcoming China's objections to joining any organization that gave Taiwan the barest hint of sovereign diplomatic status was identified from the outset, at the initial Canberra meeting:

> Ministers have noted the importance of the People's Republic of China and the economies of Hong Kong and Taiwan. Taking into account the general principles of cooperation [of APEC], and recognising that APEC is a non-formal forum for consultations among high-level representatives of significant economies in the Asia Pacific region, it has been agreed that it would be desirable to consider further involvement of these three economies in the process of Asia Pacific Economic Co-operation.[30]

Identifying the three as 'economies' whose sovereign status was left inde-terminate became the basis for lobbying Beijing until China, Taiwan and Hong Kong joined APEC in 1992. Australia was also closely involved in establishing another piece of regional architecture, the ASEAN Regional Forum (ARF), a security institution conceived as complementing APEC's economic function. Once again, Australian diplomats faced deep resistance from Beijing to joining this body. However, led by the energy and insistence of Gareth Evans, Beijing was finally persuaded to join. Canberra added bilateral dialogues, on security and human rights, to these regional institu-tional engagements of China.

Over the past decade, Canberra has got the China it wished for at the start of the 1990s: market oriented, development focused, multilateralist and compliant with international norms. Beijing has become a vigorous, almost evangelical convert to multilateralism. China's pursuit of regional integration with Southeast Asia has thrown up new institutional forms, such as the East Asian Summit, which have profoundly altered the diplomatic environment in the region. Yet whether these developments have attenuated or accentuated Canberra's cognitive dissonance between Washington and Beijing remains a crucial question.

Decoupling

The second strategy adopted by foreign policymakers to address Canberra's cognitive dissonance has been to try to decouple the Sino–Australian relationship from the turbulent Sino–American relationship. While the first strategy was more associated with the internationalist Hawke and Keating governments, the second was relied on more heavily by their bilateralist-leaning successor administration. As the Howard government began rebuilding relations with Beijing after the difficulties of 1996, it adopted the objective of constructing a Sino–Australian relationship independent of its ties with the United States and centred on the political and economic interests of Australia and China.[31] Howard, advised early in his prime ministership to take a personal interest in the relationship with China, worked assiduously at the bilateral relationship and built slowly on the solid foundations of China's and Australia's economic complementarities. There were important symbolic gestures also. Slowly but surely, Australia has distanced itself from US public criticisms of China's authoritarian political structures and human rights record. In 1997, Australia ceased supporting the annual resolution at the UNHRC that condemned China's human rights record. From an early stage, Canberra was a vocal supporter of China's entry into the World Trade Organization (WTO), and refused to join Washington in lobbying the European Union (EU) to maintain restrictions on weapons sales to China. In October 2003, the Howard government moved decisively to gain symbolic mileage from a coincidence in the visits of President Bush and Chinese President Hu Jintao, by inviting Hu to address a joint sitting of the Houses of Parliament the day after Bush had done so. Alexander Downer further cemented the message of China's importance to Australia when, during a press conference on a visit to Beijing in August 2004, he implied that the ANZUS Treaty would not necessarily commit Australia to the defence of Taiwan:

> The ANZUS Treaty is invoked in the event of one of our two countries, Australia or the United States, being attacked. So some other military activity elsewhere in the world ... does not automatically invoke the ANZUS Treaty. It is important to remember that we only invoked the ANZUS Treaty once, that is after the events of 9/11, because there was

an attack on the territory of the United States. It is very important to remember that in the context of your question.[32]

The decoupling agenda has been driven by Howard's own approach to framing foreign policy in Asia, which he bases on the formula of 'shared interests and mutual respect':

> The relationship between Australia and China is sound because it is built upon the important principles of mutual respect for each other and a recognition that societies that have different cultures and different histories can nevertheless work together very closely if they understand those differences and they focus on the things that bring their two societies together.[33]

The Howard government believes that speculation that globalization will eventually bring about a values convergence between countries such as China and Australia is fanciful. They must therefore relate to each other on the basis of 'mutual respect', refraining from criticizing or trying to change each other's cultures or commitments. Elevating shared interests to the foreground of bilateral relations means that Australia's and China's alliance and alignment commitments should be able to be quarantined from the substance of bilateral relations. The government benches must therefore have been gratified to hear President Hu state in his 2003 address to the Australian parliament:

> We are of the view that, for the smooth conduct of state-to-state relations and for lasting peace and common prosperity, all countries should act in compliance with the following principles … they should respect each other, seek common ground while putting aside differences and endeavour to expand areas of agreement.[34]

Prime Minister Howard certainly believed that progress with the decoupling agenda had been made, telling one audience in 2004:

> I count it as one of the great successes of this country's foreign relations that we have simultaneously been able to strengthen our longstanding ties with the United States of America, yet at the same time continue to build a very close relationship with China.[35]

Certainly, China's muted reaction to developments such as Canberra's announcement in late 2003 of its formal involvement in the US-sponsored ballistic missile defence system and the May 2005 elevation of the US–Japan–Australia Trilateral Strategic Dialogue to ministerial status, lends support to Howard's view. However, whether such decoupling has really been road-tested at a time of greater Sino–American tension remains a major question.

Prospects for resolving dissonance

A glance at history shows that, since the 1950s, the United States has viewed its relationship with Australia in terms of comprehensive mutual obligations. Dulles' conditions, first stated in 1951, that a security agreement between the two countries would be predicated on Australian support for US policy in the Pacific, have become absorbed into both countries' understandings of the alliance. Canberra's commitments outside of the region during the 1990s, and particularly to the Persian Gulf, Afghanistan and Iraq, show the strong identification of subsequent Australian governments with the US-guaranteed global order. Even Australia's actions in its own region have followed closely evolving order-promoting motivations shared by Washington. The 1999 East Timor intervention was prompted by concerns to stop genocidal carnage, just months after Washington and its NATO allies had intervened with the same intent in Kosovo. Interventions in the Solomon Islands and Papua New Guinea in 2003 were driven by the post-11 September 2001 agenda of strengthening failing states against transnational threats. The seizure of the North Korean vessel *Pong Su* in 2003 was hailed in Washington as according with the United States' new activism against transnational proliferation sponsored by rogue states. Australia, along with Britain, was singled out by the 2006 Quadrennial Defense Review as a model for 'the breadth and depth of cooperation that the United States seeks to foster with other allies and partners around the world'.[36]

China's use of the word 'strategic' to describe its relationship with Australia also has a very precise meaning. As Wang Jisi argues, China's foreign policy is directed by a conceptual framework, in which China's relationships are ordered and adjusted hierarchically.[37] Traditionally, China designated as 'strategic' its relations with those countries it expected would continue or emerge as great powers. Relations with other states, which were regarded as important but not actual or potential great powers, occupied the next rung down, as 'partnerships'.[38] This changed in the late 1990s, when China adopted a new 'neighbour first' policy (*zhoubian shi shouyao*), through which Beijing is trying to build 'not only "an amicable neighbourhood" (*mulin*) but also "a tranquil neighbourhood" (*anlin*) and "a prosperous neighbourhood" (*fulin*)'.[39] As one of Beijing's regional neighbours, Australia is seen not only as a stable and dependable source of minerals and energy for China, but also as a crucial element in an 'amicable', 'tranquil' and 'prosperous' neighbourhood. In other words, Beijing sees its relationship with Australia as part of shaping the sort of regional environment that is regarded as most conducive to Chinese interests.

Australia's recent use of the term 'strategic' to describe its relations with the United States and China has focused around economic relationships. The Howard government used the strategic import of a trade agreement with the sole superpower as a significant factor in its public justification of the Australia–United States Free Trade Agreement (AUSFTA) signed in 2004. It saw the AUSFTA as a symbolic statement of the 'reinvigoration' of the Australia–US relationship since 1996, an economic complement to the half-century old security agreement with America. Similarly, with China, the building of a 'bilateral strategic relationship' has a strong economic connotation. Australian policymakers seem to be inviting Beijing to view Australia as a stable, long-term supplier of energy and commodities, and signalling that Canberra sees China as a dependable, enduring customer for Australia's products. More broadly, it seems to be a statement acknowledging the increasing centrality of the Chinese economy to the Asian region's continuing prosperity and stability.

Whether Australia will be able to continue building strategic relationships with both China and the United States at the same time is one (and perhaps the key) question facing Australian foreign policy. It remains to be seen whether the demands of building each relationship at the strategic level are compatible with or corrosive to the other. Canberra's current strategies, focusing either on trying to make the two strategic relationships compatible by tying China into the current regional order, or quarantining each from the other by decoupling the Sino–Australia and Sino–American relationships, seem at the moment to have been effective. China has become an enthusiastic regionalist and multilateralist, while neither Beijing nor Washington has recently made an issue of Canberra's relations with the other. It may, however, be premature to celebrate the end of dissonance.

While Beijing has indeed become a passionate convert to multilateralism over the past five years, we should be careful about assuming that this has amounted to its socialization into the global and regional orders. As Avery Goldstein argues, Beijing's adoption of multilateralism has been partial and strategic: 'It reflected neither a conversion to supranational values nor a new set of inviolable diplomatic principles ... its pragmatic focus on the presumed benefits and the feared costs [of multilateralism] are never far below the surface.'[40] China is a strong supporter of international institutions that it sees as protecting its prerogatives and upholding its international order preferences—such as the United Nations, with its insistence on sovereignty, the great power veto prerogative, and development. With institutions that are potentially threatening or at odds with its preferences—such as those perceived to be dominated by small groups of Western countries—it is both critical and suspicious:

> All countries, big or small, poor or rich, strong or weak, should have the right of equal participation in international economic affairs; and the formulation and revision of the rules of the game should not be determined by only a small number of countries or groups of countries.[41]

Beijing has refused to allow significant questions it regards as close to its interests, such as the Taiwan Strait or the South China Sea, to be considered within regional bodies such as the ARF. It is therefore doubtful whether such a partial and strategic approach to multilateralism has advanced, to any significant extent, the compatibilities between Australia's strategic relationships with Beijing and Washington.

The Howard government's strategy to decouple Sino–Australian ties from the Sino–American relationship may look less successful in the long term than it does currently. It remains possible that Canberra's current simultaneity of good relations with both Washington and Beijing are the product of the first period of genuine strategic alignment between China and the United States since 1989. The 'war on terror' has inaugurated a period of reduced Sino–American tensions, bringing about a convergence of Chinese, American and Australian interests in fighting terrorism, which Beijing lists as one of the 'five poisons' confronting China. It is certainly reasonable to expect that this period of strategic alignment will last for some years—as long as the United States continues to focus on transnational threats and state functionality as its primary international order concerns, and as long as Beijing prioritises economic development and stability. Yet such an alignment will always be vulnerable to incidents that trigger the underlying strategic competition between the United States and China. In such circumstances, dissonance will once again become problematic for Australia. In past confrontations, Washington has signalled that it expects Australian support. Most recently, in 1999 soon-to-be Deputy Secretary of State Richard Armitage stated: 'If Washington found itself in conflict with China over Taiwan it would expect Australia's support. If it didn't get that support, that would mean the end of the US–Australia alliance.'[42] In 1996 and 2001, Beijing signalled that it expects Australian neutrality in the case of Sino–American confrontations, by reacting punitively to Canberra's rhetorical support for the American position during the Taiwan Strait and EP-3 stand-offs. The lesson for Canberra here is that the compatibility of its relationships with Beijing and Washington seems to be predominantly determined by the United States and China, and there is little that Canberra can do to permanently change this structural disadvantage.

Conclusion: living with dissonance

In light of the above, is Australia destined to continue to exist in the state of dissonance first experienced by the Chifley and Menzies governments over 50 years ago, whereby the dictates of rational, interests-based policymaking are trumped by broader strategic concerns? Not necessarily. The first decade of the twenty-first century has brought about decisive changes to Australia's strategic position in ways that make its dependence on the United States and China more perceptual and psychological than actual and material. In other words, Australia's material and strategic position vis-à-vis China and the United States has changed in ways that should make it less vulnerable to punitive actions from either.

Since 1999, Australia has fashioned for itself an image in Washington as a self-starting, highly competent ally by ensuring that the global order goals it shares with the United States are upheld in two regions largely below America's radar: Southeast Asia and the South Pacific. There is no other US ally in the region that could conceivably play this role, which is arguably more important to Washington than the marginal legitimacy gains to be made from Canberra's knee-jerk support for controversial American foreign policy actions. It would seem therefore that Canberra has substantially more room for manoeuvre than it imagines in maintaining its silence during Sino–American stand-offs, before it would begin to endanger its access to the American intelligence and material that are crucial to it playing its order-promoting roles in the region.

Similarly, Australia is not as dependent on direct access to the Chinese market as it may appear. For the first time in its history, Australia is experiencing vigorous competition for its commodities and energy exports from within the Asian region. China is now bidding for Australian exports against traditional markets such as Japan and Korea and newer markets such as India. It is China's demand that has had the effect of 'bidding up' the world price for key commodities, as much as China's actual purchases of Australian commodities, that has resulted in Australia's second 'long boom'. As a result, Australia, rather than its customers, has the bargaining power for the first time in its history of trading with Asia. Consequently, Canberra would seem to have much more capacity for calling Beijing's bluff when China implicitly or explicitly threatens to curtail Sino–Australian trade as the cost for incurring its displeasure. As a great deal hangs on China's continuing access to reasonably priced resources, any decision by Beijing to disrupt commodities markets would be a major decision.

The current conditions suggest that Australia is perhaps now better placed than in any period since 1949 to manage the dissonance of its relations with the United States and China. The question will be whether Canberra can grasp the material realities of the situation and adjust its diplomatic pain thresholds accordingly. The key test will be whether Canberra is willing to emulate the studied silence practised by its Southeast Asian neighbours on the occasion of the next Sino–American confrontation.

Notes

1 President Hu Jintao, 'Building a better future together for a China–Australia partnership of all-round cooperation', address to the Federal Parliament of the Commonwealth of Australia, 24 October 2003.
2 The Hon. Alexander Downer MP, Minister for Foreign Affairs, Australia, media conference transcript, Beijing, 17 August 2004.
3 Commonwealth of Australia, *Advancing the National Interest: Australia's Foreign and Trade Policy White Paper*, Canberra: National Capital Printing, 2003, p. 79.
4 C.P. Fitzgerald, 'Australia and Asia', in Gordon Greenwood and Norman Harper (eds) *Australia in World Affairs 1950–1995*, Melbourne: F.W. Cheshire, 1957, p. 201.

5 Ibid., p. 206.
6 Commonwealth Parliamentary Debates, 27 November 1953, vol. 2, p. 664.
7 Hedley Bull, 'Australia and the great powers in Asia', in G. Greenwood and N. Harper (eds) *Australia in World Affairs 1966–1970*, Melbourne: Cheshire, 1974, p. 325.
8 Interestingly, the other relationship that Australian prime ministers have assumed primary carriage of, for obvious reasons, is that with the United States.
9 E.S.K. Fung, 'Australia and China', in P.J. Boyce and J.R. Angel (eds) *Diplomacy in the Marketplace: Australia in World Affairs 1981–1990*, Melbourne: Longman Cheshire, 1992, p. 291.
10 Commonwealth of Australia, *House of Representatives Official Hansard*, Wednesday, 18 June 1996, p. 2065.
11 Quoted in R. Bridge, 'Downer under siege for aid "u-turn"', *South China Morning Post*, 24 July 1996.
12 M. Baker, 'China launches double attack', *Sydney Morning Herald*, 8 August 1996.
13 'US, Australia play down criticism on Taiwan links', *South China Morning Post*, 9 August 1996.
14 T. Plafker, 'Dalai Lama hails "positive" Howard talks', *South China Morning Post*, 27 September 1996.
15 S. Hutcheon, 'Australia under fire over policy on Asia', *Sydney Morning Herald*, 30 October 1996.
16 S. Hutcheon, 'UN vote blamed on poor links to Asia', *Sydney Morning Herald*, 5 November 1996.
17 I. Henderson, 'Navy row threatens China ties', *The Australian*, 30 April 2001.
18 M. Wesley and T. Warren, 'Wild colonial ploys: currents of thought in Australian foreign policy making' *Australian Journal of Political Science*, vol. 35, no. 1, April 2000, pp. 9–26.
19 W.T. Tow, 'Deputy sheriff or independent ally? Evolving Australian–American ties in an ambiguous world order', *Pacific Review*, vol. 17, no. 2, June 2004, pp. 276–7.
20 Here the case of former Australian Opposition leader Mark Latham is an interesting one. His statements during the 2004 federal election campaign, suggesting that a Latham government would become much more sceptical of the ANZUS alliance, were, according to some commentators, the beginning of a growing conviction in the electorate that he could not be trusted with government—a belief which led to the Howard Government's increased electoral margin.
21 M. Malik, 'Australia and the United States 2004–5: all the way with the U.S.A.?', *Special Assessment Series*, Asia–Pacific Center for Security Studies, Honolulu, HI, February 2005, p. 7.
22 David Shambaugh (ed.) *Power Shift: China and Asia's New Dynamics*, Berkeley, CA: University of California Press, 2005.
23 J. Zhang, 'Australia and China', in J. Cotton and J. Ravenhill (eds) *Trading on Alliance Security: Australia in World Affairs 2001–2005*, Melbourne: Oxford University Press, 2006.
24 Prime Minister the Hon. John Howard MP, address at the opening of the Lowy Institute for International Policy, Sydney, 31 March 2005.
25 Commonwealth of Australia, *Advancing the National Interest: Australia's Foreign and Trade Policy White Paper,* Canberra: National Capital Printing, 2003, p. 80.
26 See for example R. Garnaut, *Open Regionalism and Trade Liberalisation: An Asia–Pacific Contribution to the World Trade System*, Singapore: Institute of Southeast Asian Studies, 1997.
27 Prime Minister the Hon. John Howard MP, address at lunch hosted by Georgetown University, Washington, DC, 13 July 1999.

28 See Senator the Hon. Gareth Evans, Minister for Foreign Affairs, 'Australia in East Asia and the Asia–Pacific: beyond the looking glass', Fourteenth Asia Lecture to Asia–Australia Institute, Sydney, 20 March 1995.
29 A. Kent, 'Australia and China, 1991–95: asymmetry and congruence in the post-cold war era', in J. Cotton and J. Ravenhill (eds) *Seeking Asian Engagement: Australia in World Affairs, 1991–1995*, Melbourne: Oxford University Press, 1997, p. 172.
30 Asia–Pacific Economic Cooperation, 'Chairman's summary statement', First APEC Ministerial Meeting, Canberra, Australia, 6–7 November, 1989.
31 G. Klintworth, 'Australian interests in the region', in W.T. Tow (ed.) *Australian–American Relations: Looking Towards the Next Century*, Melbourne: Macmillan, 1998, p. 153.
32 The Hon. Alexander Downer MP, Minister for Foreign Affairs, Australia, media conference transcript, Beijing, 17 August 2004.
33 Prime Minister the Hon John. Howard MP, address to the dinner in honour of His Excellency Mr Li Peng, Chairman of the Standing Committee of the National People's Congress of China and Madame Zhu Lin, Hyatt Hotel, Canberra, 17 September 2002.
34 Commonwealth of Australia, Official Hansard, 24 October 2003, p. 21698.
35 Prime Minister the Hon. John Howard MP, 'Australia's engagement with Asia: a new paradigm', address to the Asialink–ANU National Forum, 13 August 2004.
36 United States Department of Defense, *Quadrennial Defense Review Report*, 6 February 2006, p. 7.
37 W. Jisi, 'International relations theory and the study of Chinese foreign policy: a Chinese perspective', in T.W. Robinson and D. Shambaugh (eds) *Chinese Foreign Policy: Theory and Practice*, Oxford: Clarendon Press, 1994, pp. 481–505.
38 A. Goldstein, *Rising to the Challenge: China's Grand Strategy and International Security*, Stanford, CA: Stanford University Press, 2005, p. 160.
39 Zhang, 'Australia and China'.
40 Goldstein, *Rising to the Challenge*, p. 127.
41 Embassy of the People's Republic of China in the United Kingdom of Great Britain and Northern Ireland, 'China and Globalization', speech by His Excellency Ambassador Zha Peixin at the Chinese Economic Association Annual Conference, 14 April 2003.
42 Quoted in P. Edwards, *Permanent Friends? Historical Reflections on the Australian–American Alliance*, Lowy Institute paper 08, Sydney: Lowy Institute for International Policy, 2005, p. 45.

6 Australia–India

Sandy Gordon

The end of the Cold War, the incremental Indo–US *rapprochement* consequent upon that event, the liberalization of the Indian economy, a rapidly growing trading relationship and like-minded attitudes on democratic and liberal values should in theory have opened the way for a more substantial relationship between India and Australia. Yet the relationship has been at times difficult, such as following India's nuclear detonations in 1998, and remains relatively low-key—even fickle. Indeed, since the end of the Cold War, the relationship with India has been one 'in search of substance'.[1]

This chapter focuses on the security relationship between India and Australia. It explores Australian and Indian interests in the Indian Ocean and, more generally, analyzes where they might intersect, and assesses how the two countries might build on those common interests to construct a more solid and realistic platform for the relationship.

India as an Indian Ocean power

Although India has ambitions to be a fully fledged Indian Ocean power, it is still not able to project itself into the far recesses of the Indian Ocean. Its power projection capability—as represented by its navy and air force—is currently debilitated by decades of subcontinental focus, approaching block obsolescence and the economic slump of the early 1990s. Yet barring some economic or political catastrophe, India has set a course to take it into the status of a significant pan-Indian Ocean power by 2020, if not before. At the same time, the Indian Ocean itself has risen sharply in salience in the last decade and a half as a location of instability on the one hand and a major conduit for the transport of increasingly vital oil supplies on the other. In light of the above developments, India is bound to be of major strategic significance to Australia in the future.

India's power in the Indian Ocean has two perspectives. First, the increasingly important Indo–US relationship clearly has an Indian Ocean security focus at the broad level of security—securing America's 'west about route' into the Gulf and oil sea lines of communication (SLOCs) out of the Gulf, as well as providing a counterweight to China.

Beneath this broad framework, India is likely to have a growing role in addressing transnational security issues such as piracy and maritime security generally, gun running, people smuggling and trafficking, illicit drug trafficking, terrorism, pandemic disease, climate change and natural disasters (such as tsunamis and cyclones). These issues, along with India's increasingly successful 'Look East' strategy, draw India's strategic gaze to the Northeast Indian Ocean (NEIO) region, which also happens to be a region of major strategic concern for Australia.

The Indian Navy issued a public version of its naval doctrine in 2004.[2] This ambitious document identifies the navy—always the poor cousin of Indian strategy—as the torch-bearer of India's global strategic ambitions. It views the Indian Ocean as India's 'backyard', calling for a blue water capability and 'sea control' in designated areas of the Arabian Sea and the Bay of Bengal. It cites India's 'policing' role in the Indian Ocean and the need to protect far-flung populations of Indian origin. It posits a fully fledged submarine-launched ballistic missile capability as the main plank of India's strategic nuclear capability and suggests India should have at least a two-carrier battle group capacity.

Significantly, the document cites China's current capabilities and alleged goals as the *raison d'être* for such an ambitious program. For example, the document states 'India stands out alone as being devoid of a credible nuclear triad, specially when a *powerful adversary* [emphasis added] like China has massive capability in 14 submarine-launched ballistic missiles'.[3]

India's current and near-term capabilities are insufficient to support such ambitious goals in the Indian Ocean. India's principal surface combatants consist of an ageing aircraft carrier (INS *Viraat*, which fields 15 *Harrier* vertical short take-off and landing (VSTOL) aircraft), five Soviet-era *Kashin*-class destroyers and three indigenously built *Delhi*-class destroyers (the latest allegedly with 'stealth') and a growing fleet of both indigenously built and imported frigates (including the *Talwar*-class Russian 'stealth' frigate). It also has 16 somewhat inadequate submarines, including Soviet-era *Kilo* and *Foxtrot* vessels and four indigenously built T-209/15000s, and a collection of corvettes. Long-range maritime patrol consists of eight recently refitted Soviet *Bear*-class aircraft.

By 2020, however, India is on track to substantially upgrade this inventory. It will acquire the refitted Russian carrier *Admiral Gorshkov* and 18–20 MiG-29K aircraft in 2008. It is building an indigenous air defence ship of 37,500 tonnes, to be commissioned by 2012, and reportedly to carry the indigenously built light combat aircraft. It has ordered a further three *Talwar*-class frigates from Russia, which will take five years to deliver. It is also in the process of developing a submarine-launched ballistic missile capability in the form of its *Sagarika* missile (currently with a range of only 300 km, but reportedly to be extended considerably) and claims to be developing a nuclear-powered submarine, known as the Advanced Technology Vessel Project.[4] It is in the market for a replacement for its *Bear*-class aircraft. It has also placed an order for six French *Scorpene* submarines, to be armed with MBDA SM-39 *Exocet* anti-ship missiles. The *Scorpenes* will be indigenously built and inducted between 2012 and 2017. Significantly, the *BrahMos* supersonic cruise missile, jointly developed and built with Russia, was recently inducted into the navy, to be fitted to the *Delhi*-class destroyers and *Talwar*-class frigates.[5] This formidable, potentially nuclear capable, weapon reportedly travels at mach 2.8 and has a range of up to 290 km (under 300 km to meet Missile Technology Control Regime stipulations). India's new west coast naval base (which will also eventually co-host a comprehensive air force base) was recently opened at Karwar near Goa. It is reportedly the largest in Asia.

The Indian Navy is also planning to extend its presence in the Andaman and Nicobar Islands, which is increasingly seen as a key strategic area. The new facilities, to be known as the Far Eastern Naval Command (FENC), will include: a FENC headquarters based in Port Blair; three major bases; a string of 'anchorages' covering the entire archipelago; a state-of-the-art naval warfare system, presumably with a capacity to monitor vessels passing into and out of the Malacca Strait; basing facilities for submarines; a large ship repair facility; and facilities to maintain a number of Su30 MKI aircraft. Some reports also claim that the United States has encouraged and provided funds for this development.[6]

Even though the navy has set ambitious goals for its Indian Ocean strategy, India is still significantly engaged in its various subcontinental roles—to the detriment of maritime power projection capabilities. Due to ongoing demands in countering insurgencies in Kashmir and the Northeast, added to instability around the border and within India generally, India has to support a paramilitary force of over a million men. This is in addition to the one-million-strong regular army. Moreover, the army and air force still make heavy demands on the capital and equipment account of the defence budget. The army, for example, is in the market for a US$5 billion artillery upgrade and the air force is purchasing 125 *Mirage* fighters, 66 BAE *Hawke* trainer aircraft and the *Phalcon* airborne warning and control system (AWACS).

With all of that, the navy commands only 17 per cent of the military budget (up from 14 per cent in the 1990s). Yet the overall defence budget has grown substantially since 2002. Defence is now allocated over US$20 billion per annum (2006 budget allocation), a rise of 33 per cent since 2002.[7] India's relatively low manpower cost compared to equivalent Western forces, along with its rapidly growing economy and rising overall defence spending, accounts for the fact that naval expansion is still expected to be respectable over the next decade, despite the expected continuing subcontinental focus of Indian defence.

India's economy, built on a decade and a half of incremental, if halting, liberalization, has apparently entered a new growth trajectory of six to eight per cent. Foreign exchange reserves are now over US$145 billion and rising fast. From a defence acquisition point of view, the nature of India's growth—with significant strength in computation and information technology—is supportive of the development of the more sophisticated end of defence technologies. These include ballistic missile, nuclear weapons and guidance systems development. For example, under the arrangement with Russia, India produced the guidance system for the *BrahMos*, while Russia produced the propulsion system. Although the July 2006 test of the *Agni III* failed, the technology will eventually provide India with a comparatively sophisticated intercontinental ballistic missile capacity—one that is far superior to the Scud-type technology widely purveyed through the region by North Korea.[8] India's economic success, along with the approaching block obsolescence of its military, meant that by 2004 the nation had agreed to import more arms than any other developing country, including China. (China, however, topped the ranking between 2001 and 2004).

India and the large powers in the Indian Ocean

The US–Indian relationship has been incrementally developing since the end of the Cold War. It has survived major upheavals such as the Indian detonation of a number of nuclear devices in 1998 and the Indian refusal to support the United States in the second Gulf War. Because the logic driving relations forward has not changed in its fundamentals since 1991, it is worth briefly revisiting the genesis of the revival in the relationship.

Significantly, the relationship was rekindled in 1991 by an overture from Commander in Chief Pacific (CINCPAC)—now United States Pacific Command (USPACOM)—in Hawaii. CINCPAC was responsible for the security of the 'west about route' into the Gulf and its domain covered an enormous stretch of ocean. Given the extremely long lines of access into the Indian Ocean for the external powers, littoral Indian Ocean navies are estimated to have a 'three to one' cruise time advantage over external fleets in Indian Ocean operations.[9] In the context of defence budget cuts in the aftermath of the 1990–1 Persian Gulf War and end of the Cold War, CINCPAC was looking for 'burden sharing' partners. Then as now, India and Australia are the only littoral Indian Ocean powers with navies of that potential.

According to the CINCPAC study associated with the upgrade in relations, India and US foreign policy interests had been steadily converging since the end of the Cold War. The two had common concerns in areas such as international terrorism, the rise of 'Islamic fundamentalism', illegal drug trafficking, support for human rights (and by implication democracy) and 'unrestricted navigation in the Indian Ocean, and adjoining Persian Gulf region'.[10] In addition, even during the George H. W. Bush administration, there was concern about the build-up of China and interest in a possible role for India in countering it. For example, then Senator (now Vice-President) Richard Cheney warned India about China and its global build-up.[11]

Although the Indo–US relationship is still driven by the fundamentals operating in the post-Cold War years, there are important new international concerns providing additional nuance to the relationship. The 'war on terror' or 'Long War' as it is now called, looms much larger in the relationship. In this regard, the new relationship between the United States and Pakistan—necessary to pursue US objectives in Afghanistan—is a recent complicating factor. So far, Washington has been able to balance its interests between India and Pakistan in a way that has been acceptable, if not satisfactory, to both. This balancing requires constant attention. For example, the recent nuclear agreement between the United States and India has been strongly criticized by Pakistan and required a counteragreement by the United States to provide a modern version of the F-16 fighter for Pakistan. This pattern tends to 'up the ante' in Washington's relations with both New Delhi and Islamabad.

Another change is the increasing salience of oil SLOCs out of the Gulf in a world increasingly hungry for, and competitive about, energy. In such a world, China's growing level of activity in the Indian Ocean and surrounding regions is noted with increasing concern.[12] For example, China's assistance in developing a major port at Gwadar in Pakistan—only 400 km from the Strait of Hormuz—has been interpreted as part of a wider strategy to secure oil and gas supplies and SLOCs associated with them by 'gaining a strategic foothold in the Persian Gulf'.[13]

The strategic relationship between India and the United States is now sketched out on a relatively broad canvas. It includes an ongoing program of ever more complex naval exercises, a ten-year defence agreement between the two (signed in June 2005), the decision to make available to India sophisticated weapons such as the latest version of the FA-18 fighter and, most important, the nuclear agreement, which effectively invites India into the nuclear weapons 'club', at least as far as the United States is concerned. According to Secretary of State Condoleezza Rice's policy advisor, this shift in US policy is motivated by the fact that '[The US] goal is to help India become a major world power in the 21st century'. He adds: 'We understand fully the implications, including military implications, of that statement.'[14]

Although Washington might be seen by some as using India as a potential counterweight to China, New Delhi does not unambiguously share this perspective. India does not wish to feel 'manipulated' by the United States for its own self-interest.[15] Indeed, India's behaviour towards China over the last decade can only be described as 'schizophrenic'.

On the one hand, economic, governmental and people-to-people relations between India and China are booming. Two-way trade (currently slightly in India's favour) is set to meet a US$20 billion target by 2008 and the two are discussing a free trade agreement. There are prolific programs of cultural, scientific, technological and political exchange.

On the other hand, leading Indian strategic commentators and some senior government members remain wary of China's growing role in the

Indian Ocean, Central Asia, the Middle East and Africa. Commentators have likened China's interests in the Indian Ocean to a 'string of pearls', meaning a chain of military bases and potential bases stretching from the Malacca Strait to Gwadar near the Strait of Hormuz.[16]

Indian concern about China's naval and other activities in the Indian Ocean goes back to the early 1990s, when India accused China of developing a signals intelligence and telemetry site on Great Coco Island (allegedly leased by China from Burma in 1994), which is proximate to India's Andaman and Nicobar territories. China has also been accused of developing deep-water ports that could potentially be used by the Chinese Navy on Small Coco Island, at Hainggyi, Bassein and a number of other sites. Recently China was accused of conducting joint intelligence exercises with Burma against India's Andaman and Nicobar territories.[17]

Indian and US commentators attribute these Chinese activities to concern over protecting oil SLOCs through the Indian Ocean on the one hand and finding additional trade outlets into the Indian Ocean on the other.[18] In view of this attribution—which would appear to favour a cooperative rather than competitive approach—the level of expressed Indian concern and the view that China is seeking strategically to challenge India in the Indian Ocean is odd, yet in keeping with the overall 'schizophrenic' quality of India's view of China. The situation is not helped by the lack of transparency on the part of both China and Burma. Moves by Beijing that may be innocently focused on a desire to maintain security of vital oil SLOCs, or simply assist Pakistan and Burma with port development for commercial reasons, have been widely interpreted as having a more sinister purpose.

Even senior officials and politicians openly espouse the view that China is a long-term competitor and that any Chinese presence in the Indian Ocean is troubling. This was most candidly expressed in the lead-up to, and aftermath of, the Indian nuclear detonations of May 1998. Then Indian Defence Minister George Fernandez was particularly outspoken about China's threatening role and the fact that China was the main focus of India's nuclear weapons requirements.[19] While this might have been meant as an excuse for India's widely condemned nuclear detonations, concern about China's Indian Ocean role has recently been expressed by the current Defence Minister, Pranab Mukherji, and even in the context of a 'friendly' visit from Chinese naval vessels.[20]

Broad strategic concerns about China's growing role in the Indian Ocean are not the only factors driving both India's security concerns in this part of the world and India's rapprochement with the United States. A host of transnational issues have also plagued security in the region, especially in the NEIO. These were brought into sharp focus by the events of 11 September 2001 and the subsequent 'war on terror'—a development in which India and the United States had strong, shared interests. India's increasingly successful 'Look East' policy, initiated by former Prime Minister Rao in the

early 1990s, has also drawn India's gaze away from its problems to the West
and caused it to focus on the NEIO.

The Northeast Indian Ocean and security

The three main straits connecting the Indian and Pacific oceans are all in
Southeast Asia. These are the Malacca Strait (which carries 600 ships and
11 million barrels of oil a day), the Lombok Strait further east, and the
Sundar Strait, further east again. While closure of the Malacca Strait would
not represent an economic disaster for East Asia (since to bypass it would
add only one-and-a-half days' sailing time), it would be costly—especially
given the already high price of oil.

India's NEIO territories of the Andaman and Nicobar Islands form a 700
km long chain that stretches to within 80 nautical miles of Sumatra and
commands the northern approaches to the Malacca Strait. India thus has a
legitimate role to play in the security of the NEIO. This role has been
brought into focus on several occasions, including the interdiction by the
Indian Navy of a pirated Japanese vessel in 1999 and the tracking by India
and subsequent destruction of a number of Tamil Tiger-controlled vessels
carrying arms to Sri Lanka.

Given concerns in the post-11 September 2001 environment of a possible
merging of pirate and terrorist methods and interests, the United States
asked India early in 2002 to provide escort duty to its supply vessels passing
through the Malacca Strait *en route* to Southwest Asia and the Middle
East. Under this plan, the US Seventh Fleet was to secure the western
approaches, while India was to provide security in the eastern approaches.
India began patrolling on a trial basis in April 2002.

The growing interest on the part of the United States in working with
India is strengthened by the fact that Washington was rebuffed by Indonesia and Malaysia in 2004, when it suggested that Malacca Strait countries
could work with the United States and Japan to protect the security of the
Strait. However, joint action on the part of the Malacca Strait countries to
patrol the Strait has now significantly suppressed piracy activity within the
Strait, but not to the same extent in surrounding NEIO waters.[21]

SLOC security is not the only issue of concern in and around the NEIO.
The region is plagued by a number of transnational problems. These include
terrorism, piracy (as a coastal problem), drug smuggling, gun running, and
people smuggling and trafficking. There is also a range of concerns relating
to the incremental effects of global warming—particularly in relation to sea-
level rise and the potential inundation of heavily populated, low-lying lands
in Bangladesh and India. Moreover, seismic, volcanic and tsunami activity
associated with the fact that the Indo–Australian plate passes up the west
side of Indonesia and the Andaman Sea remain a troubling reality for the
region. Unfortunately, these non-conventional security issues fail to conform to the artificial cooperative mechanisms that reflect the historical basis

of the geostrategic division between Southeast and South Asia—such as ASEAN and the South Asian Association for Regional Cooperation (SAARC).

Most of the above issues deeply affect India's security. For example, the region acts as a conduit for trafficking in arms to fuel separatism and terrorism in India itself, especially the insurgent infested Northeast. The main route for these arms is from Southeast Asia (often originating in Cambodia), through the Thai ports of Ranong and Phuket, into the Andaman Sea and thence to the Bangladeshi ports of Cox's Bazaar and Chittagong. Alternatively, arms pass along this route as far as the Andaman Sea and are then diverted to Sri Lanka to fuel the civil war in that country.

While most of these weapons originate in Southeast Asia, in 2004 a very large shipment of new weapons was interdicted in Chittagong that had apparently originated from China and been delivered via Hong Kong and Singapore. Seized weapons allegedly included 2,000 light and heavy machine guns and semi-automatic rifles, rocket-propelled grenades, mines, 2,500 grenades and a massive quantity of ammunition.[22]

The role of Bangladesh as a major conduit of arms trafficking through the NEIO region also highlights its growing role as a location of convenience for terrorism of the violent jihad variety.[23] On several recent occasions, terrorist acts in India allegedly have included some Bangladeshi involvement.[24] Within Bangladesh, a wide-ranging series of bombings over a number of years has been attributed to, or perpetrated by, Islamic militants.

India is also troubled by temporary and permanent illegal settlement of outsiders, including Chinese fishing families and Bangladeshis, on the 570 islands of the Andaman and Nicobar archipelago. One report cites a figure of 50,000 'foreigners' permanently on the islands—a figure that would be one eighth of the legal population. There is also a continuing threat from visiting fishing folk from China and other regional countries, many of whom establish semi-permanent camps on uninhabited islands.[25]

India was also heavily involved in disaster prevention and mitigation, as witnessed in the aftermath of the December 2004 Indian Ocean tsunami, which severely affected the archipelago. The navy relief effort in India itself involved 32 ships and 21 helicopters. Ships were also sent to assist in the Maldives and Sri Lanka.

In the past five years, both Thailand and China have successively cracked down on the massive flow of drugs from Burma across their respective borders. As a consequence, illicit drugs—now increasingly involving amphetamines as well as heroin—are finding new outlets in and around the NEIO. For example, Bangladesh has emerged as a relatively important conduit for drugs, both from the Golden Crescent and the Golden Triangle. Northeast India has provided an outlet for drugs from Burma for some time, and is consequently the area of India that has been most devastated by HIV/AIDS. With the northern borders of Burma increasingly under pressure from China and Thailand, the Andaman Sea now provides an important means of smuggling drugs out of Burma. These drugs are mostly taken out to fishing boats and then delivered to the west coast of Thailand and beyond including, in several instances, to Australia.[26]

Drugs in Northeast India have become intimately linked with insurgency and are often used by insurgents to finance their activities. For example, the very large seizure of arms at Chittagong in 2004 cited above was valued at between US$4.5 and US$7 million. One view is that only an insurgency group supported by an outside power (Pakistan's Inter-Services Intelligence is often cited by Indian commentators) or by drugs could have afforded such a large importation of arms.[27] According to other accounts, Kuki and Naga activists on both sides of the Indo–Burmese border are involved in drug importations.[28] Other accusations point to a nexus between militant Islamists (although not necessarily violent jihadists) in Bangladesh and drug importations.

This dense interlinking of problems in and around the NEIO illustrates the way in which instability in the region can beget further instability, producing a region of extreme instability and fragility. Such instability is further linked with major power rivalry, as evidenced by the Sino–Indian competition and the way it relates to concern about SLOC security, illegal fishing and the various problems in Burma. All of these developments are likely to ensure that India remains focused on the NEIO as a major security concern.

Australia's strategic interests in the Indian Ocean region

Australia shares India's concerns about security of SLOCs within the Indian Ocean. As India and the United States draw closer, Canberra increasingly also shares India's perceptions of the US role in the Indian Ocean. However, there are subtle yet important differences between the Indian and Australian positions.

As we have seen, India needs to balance a range of interests in relation to the United States, including its self-perception as a large strategic player with a potentially independent role in the Indian Ocean. Australia is a small-to-middle power that will never be a substantial regional player. Australia is, moreover, a signatory to the ANZUS Treaty and reliant upon the US strategic nuclear 'umbrella'. Australia's relationship with the United States is therefore more intense and closer than that of India, notwithstanding the warming relations between New Delhi and Washington.

Furthermore, the very fact of the improvement in the Indo–US relationship—while making closer Indo–Australian relations possible—also ironically somewhat 'queers the pitch' for that relationship. This is because Australia can only appear in New Delhi's eyes as a 'pale shadow' of the United States—a reflection, and a poor one at that, of the US position. So New Delhi might well ask: Why address the servant when you can deal with the master?

Although New Delhi may well perceive Australia to be a pale shadow of the United States in the region, this is not an entirely accurate picture of the actual position. True, Australia shares US (and for that matter Indian) concerns with Gulf oil and SLOC security in the wider Indian Ocean. Its dependence on Middle East oil is growing rapidly, from the current 30 per cent to an expected 70 per cent in 20 years' time. In relation to the role of China, however, Australia's position is somewhat different from the positions of the United States and even India. Australia is not yet ready to enter into any 'strategic' engagement with India of the type that could be construed as being directed against China—not that New Delhi would necessarily welcome that type of engagement. While Washington would also doubtless argue that its position vis-à-vis India and China does not seek to 'balance' China with India, it has been prepared to say openly that it supports India's rise as a major regional power. Australia has been somewhat more cautious. This caution is consonant with Australian policy elsewhere—for example on cross-Strait issues relating to Taiwan. In that context, Australia seeks to avoid being drawn into taking sides between China and the United States since it has powerful interests with both countries and wishes to see a peaceful rise to power by China in Asia. This is presumably why Australian Defence Minister Brendan Nelson, when asked whether the four-power tsunami cooperation involving India, the United States, Japan and Australia, might be formalized as part of a 'core group' for military cooperation, responded to the effect that Australia currently prefers a bilateral approach.[29]

Australia's Indian Ocean focus, moreover, is predominantly to the waters adjacent to Australia and to the NEIO region to the northwest. And in these regions, its sets of relationships have an independent cast well outside its dealings with the United States.

In terms of more direct interests in the Indian Ocean, Australian has territory well out into the Indian Ocean, with the Cocos and Keeling Islands lying 2,700 km from Perth and Christmas Island a mere 400 km from Java. Closer in, Australia's most important gas fields are located off the Northwest Shelf, ranging in extent from Exmouth almost to Darwin. This enormous expanse of sea requires attention in the age of terrorism, and the Australian government has recently purchased two new patrol vessels to assist in that task.

In terms of defence of Australia, the sea–air gap in the area covering the northwest and north is vital to Australia. These are key waters for maritime patrol, submarine operations, maintenance of air superiority, efforts to contain transnational problems such as illegal fishing and illegal migration and the threats such problems can present in terms of the environment and quarantine.

Although the NEIO is somewhat outside these direct interests, Australia will continue to have strong interests in supporting countries at the littoral of the NEIO, especially those of Southeast Asia. Some of this support will be to help address troubling transnational issues. For example, in December 2005, the Australian Foreign Minister, Alexander Downer, met with the Malaysian Deputy Prime Minister, Najib Razak, and subsequently told reporters that Australia was considering sending Royal Australian Air Force (RAAF) P-3C *Orions* for joint patrolling activities in and around the Malacca Strait, presumably to help address maritime security issues in that region.[30] Other supporting arrangements will be of a more overtly 'strategic' nature—for example, those responsibilities accruing under the Five Power Defence Arrangements (FPDA).

If Canberra's aim is indeed to develop a stronger strategic relationship with India—without at the same time appearing to be in any kind of association against China—then it may need to find a way to do so independently of the relationship between India and the United States. Not only does the intensifying Indo–US relationship have a potential anti-China ring about it, but it also effectively trumps the Indo–Australian relationship, for reasons already discussed.

One way of avoiding both the pitfall of being a 'pale shadow' of the United States and of prematurely antagonizing China would be to seek to develop those areas in common that relate to Australia's more independent interests in the Indian Ocean. In particular, Australia's activities—especially those relating to transnational security issues in and around the NEIO— emerge as important in this regard.

For India, Australia's December 2005 offer of *Orion* patrols may once have been redolent of the occasion in the 1990s when *Orions* 'tracked' an Indian destroyer in the NEIO, seen at the time by New Delhi as an unfriendly act. However, times have now changed and such joint patrolling could not only involve Southeast Asian countries but also potentially India. Indeed, Australian strategists have recommended a joint naval approach between India and Australia in the NEIO as a way to take the relationship forward.[31] The March 2006 defence Memorandum of Understanding between India and Australia—signed in the presence of both prime ministers—specifically singles out the NEIO as an area of joint naval activity.

Thus the relationship to date has continued to develop in a somewhat fitful way, but one in which the contours are increasingly defined in terms of joint activity to enhance security—particularly transnational security in the NEIO region. However, there is a serious potential 'wild card' in the relationship—the nuclear issue.

The Australia–India nuclear relationship and its strategic consequences

In the past, India's aspirations as a nuclear weapons power have been a serious impediment in relations with Australia. Following the May 1998 nuclear detonations, Australia (because of time zone factors) was the first country to condemn India. In keeping with Canberra's robust stance on nuclear proliferation issues, that condemnation was framed in strong terms and also involved winding back the military-to-military relationship, such as it then was. Although Washington's reaction was equally strong, Australia (as the smaller power) bore the brunt of New Delhi's adverse response.

However, India's nuclear program focuses on the country's difficult energy situation, as well as the prestige and expected security associated with nuclear weapons. As with most developing economies, economic growth in India is very energy intensive. Yet the country is 70 per cent dependent on foreign oil imports for its liquid energy needs, a figure expected to grow to 91 per cent by 2020. To help meet concerns around energy security, India is planning to generate 40 per cent of its electricity from nuclear sources by 2020.

Although India has substantial supplies of thorium, it is very short of uranium, commanding less than one per cent of global discovered supplies. It is seeking to develop a thorium fuel cycle so that it can eventually overcome its uranium shortage, but this is expected to take many years. Meanwhile, India will depend on uranium to fulfill its ambitious energy program and, at the same time, develop fissionable material for its expanding nuclear weapons arsenal.

One of the factors that has provided an incentive for the Indian government to negotiate a nuclear deal with the United States is the possibility of India being inducted into the global uranium supply market. Australia is developing as a very important potential player in that market. Australia currently commands 40 per cent of global discovered uranium and has little domestic need for the metal. Australia is also rich in natural gas and coal and is already exporting those commodities to India.

In view of the potential importance of uranium in India's energy mix, New Delhi has shown considerable interest in buying uranium from Australia. Pressure was applied on Prime Minister Howard (prior to and during his 2006 visit to New Delhi) to agree to the export of uranium to India.[32]

To date, the Australian government has vacillated on the issue. Howard, after initially appearing negative, seemed to lean to the positive side following consultations with President Bush and his 2006 visit to New Delhi.[33] Since then, however, the Australian position—or at least as expressed by Foreign Minister Downer—appears to have swung back towards the traditional strong stand Canberra has taken against selling uranium to non-signatories of the Nuclear Non-Proliferation Treaty (NPT).[34]

Although there are many considerations at play on the issue of uranium sales to India, nothing would do more to enhance the relationship than a decision to proceed. Failure to do so would be seen in New Delhi as setting a double standard between India and China. Canberra agreed to sell to the latter on the grounds that China is a signatory of the NPT and that the military program would be strictly separated from civil use. From New Delhi's perspective, however, such a position would be inherently unfair. New Delhi would argue that the US–India nuclear agreement would effectively induct India into a global civil nuclear regime that was virtually parallel to the position of nuclear weapons signatories of the NPT like China. India feels, moreover, that its position on non-proliferation has, in fact, been better than that of China, despite its refusal to sign the NPT.[35]

Conclusion

Australia has a strong interest in ensuring that its hitherto fickle relationship with India is placed on a more secure footing. India is not only an important emerging market, but also a future major player in the Indian Ocean. That ocean is, in turn, of considerable importance to Australia—both in terms of broad security considerations and in its role of conduit for a range of debilitating and destabilizing transnational issues.

Australia's strategy in developing a sound security platform for the relationship should involve developing those aspects of Indian Ocean policy that are of joint interest to India and Australia but which fall outside the US alliance. Only then will India come to see Australia as an independent and 'legitimate' player in the Indian Ocean, rather than as a subsidiary to the countries of focus in India's 'Look East' strategy or as a 'pale shadow' of the United States.

There are several ways in which Australia could develop such interests. First, it could focus jointly with India and other regional countries on addressing the range of troubling transnational issues, in turn interlinked with intensifying strategic competition, that trouble the NEIO. Australia has played, and will likely continue to play, a significant regional role in addressing transnational issues such as tsunami and earthquake warning and recovery, as well as counterterrorism law enforcement work. Australia should build on this work in terms of its relationship with India.

Transnational issues in the NEIO do not conform to the boundaries of existing regional organizations. In pursuit of a more coherent structure for cooperation in the NEIO, Australia could use its good offices to encourage greater practical cooperation between ASEAN and SAARC. It could also place greater effort in building an ASEAN Regional Forum (ARF)-like structure around SAARC. It should support India's Asia Pacific Economic Cooperation (APEC) membership. It could also seek to encourage global and Asia-focused organizations like the various UN agencies, Interpol, the World Bank and the Asian Development Bank to pay greater attention in their programming to cross-regional realities like those evidenced by the NEIO.

China's role in the NEIO may simply be a reflection of trading needs and concerns about protecting vital SLOCs rather than a manifestation of any desire to 'challenge' India strategically in the Indian Ocean. Australia could work with India in terms of developing a strategic dialogue in order to clarify China's regional role and to bring greater transparency to China's NEIO activities. At some stage in the future, it may also be possible to introduce China into this dialogue. But the immediate need is for an accurate picture of the extent, nature and motives of China's involvement.

Finally, and most importantly, Australia should also consider presenting itself as a major, and secure, energy supplier to India. However, this would probably involve an eventual decision by Canberra to sell uranium to India on a similar basis to China, provided India's induction into a 'parallel' civil nuclear regime to that of the NPT involves all of the protections offered under the NPT. There will be many considerations at play in Canberra in any such decision, however, that have wide-ranging implications well beyond the relationship with India.

Notes

1 See A. Gordon, 'The search for substance: Australia–India relations into the nineties and beyond', Australian foreign policy papers, Canberra: Department of International Relations, Australian National University, 1993.
2 For a comprehensive description of the document, see 'A maritime doctrine by any other name: the Indian navy's book of reference', *Vayu Aerospace Review*, 2005.
3 Ibid.
4 The reactor for this vessel is being developed at Kalpakkam near Chennai. A prototype has reportedly been operated on land. India also leased a Soviet *Charlie*-class vessel for a number of years. For information on the *Sagarika*, see R.S. Norris and H.M. Kristensen, 'India's nuclear forces, 2005', *Bulletin of the Atomic Scientists*, September/October 2005, pp. 73–5.
5 The *BrahMos* is a derivative of the Russian *Yakhont*. India was responsible for software and guidance and Russia for the propulsion system.
6 R. Maita, 'India bids to rule the waves', *Japan Focus*, no. 424, 18 October 2005. See also S. Ramachandran, *Asia Times Online*, 19 October 2005.
7 This, however, compares the actual figure for 2002 against the estimate for 2006. Typically, Indian defence allocations are underspent.
8 *Agni III* is a solid-fuelled, two-stage ballistic missile capable of delivering a 1.5 tonne payload over a distance of 3,500 km. It is mainly developed from lightweight composites to enable fast re-entry. It will be road and rail mobile and capable of carrying multiple warheads and decoys.
9 'The LM2500 demonstration', *Asia–Pacific Defense Forum*, Winter 1991–2, p. 38.
10 Quoted in S.S. Harrison and G. Kemp, *India and America After the Cold War*, report of the Carnegie Endowment Study Group on US–Indian Relations in a Changing International Environment, Washington, DC: Carnegie Endowment for International Peace, 1993, p. 9.
11 M. Joshi, 'Next door diplomacy', *Frontline*, July 1992, p. 36.
12 A 2004 study by Booz Allen, commissioned by the Pentagon, drew attention to China's Indian Ocean activities, which were ascribed to its desire to protect its oil SLOCS. See B. Gertz, 'China builds up strategic sea lanes', *The Washington Times*, 18 January 2005.
13 S. Ramachandran, 'China's pearl in Pakistan's waters', *Asia Times Online*, 4 March 2005.
14 Quoted in *The Times of India*, 'Arms Americana: US opens military barn door for India', 9 May 2006.
15 See *The Times of India*, 'US using India against China, says Sudarshan', 15 July 2006.
16 Ramachandran, 'China's pearls in Pakistan's waters'.

17 There are numerous articles from Indian commentators to this effect. For a good summary, see S. Ramachandran, 'Myanmar plays off India and China', *Asia Times Online*, 17 August 2005.

18 Ramachandran, 'China's pearls in Pakistan's waters'.

19 D. Bakshian, 'China–Burma–India intelligence', Voice of America background report, New Delhi, 21 May 1998.

20 Ocean Policy Research Foundation (Japan), *Monthly Report*, December 2005, p. 5.

21 See ICC International Maritime Bureau, 'Piracy and armed robbery against ships', Report for 1 January–31 March 2006, April 2006, Table 1, p. 5.

22 The most authoritative account of this seizure is from A. Davis, 'New details emerge on Bangladesh arms haul', *Jane's Intelligence Review*, September 2004.

23 In Bangladesh, many of these attacks are perpetrated using grenades, possibly smuggled through the NEIO route, but possibly also sourced from the Bangladesh military. These include a grenade attack on the leader of the Opposition in 2004, which killed 16 of her entourage, and a 2005 attack, again on Awami League members, in which a former finance minister and four others were killed and 70 wounded. One of the first journalists to draw attention to the escalating terrorism problem in Bangladesh was Bertil Lintner. See 'Bangladesh: extremist Islamist consolidation', *Faultlines*, no. 14, 2001.

24 These include the attacks on Ayodhya, New Delhi and Varanasi.

25 A.B. Mahapatra, 'Andaman faces Kargil-type invasion', *News Insight*, 16 May 2006.

26 Australia's largest ever heroin importation in 1999 was shipped through the Andaman Sea.

27 For the opinion about ISI funding (and also the view of official sponsorship in Bangladesh), see S. Kapila, 'Bangladesh's anti-Indian gun running and insurgent havens persist', South Asia Analysis Group paper no. 987, 29 April 2004.

28 Since 1992 the two activist tribal groups have been contesting the cross-border heroin trade. According to the International Displacement Monitoring Centre, this competition suits the Indian authorities under a 'divide and rule' dictum and they have been encouraging it. See International Displacement Monitoring Centre, 'Manipur: internal displacement due to inter-ethnic strife between the Nagas and Kukis', November 2004.

29 P.S. Suryanarayana, 'Plan to enhance maritime security', *The Hindu*, 7 June 2006.

30 Ocean Policy Research Foundation (Japan), *Monthly Report*, December 2005, pp. 3–4.

31 Australia–India Security Round Table, 'Outcomes statement', Canberra, 11–12 April 2005, p. 2.

32 For a discussion of the Indian position, see K. Kapisthalam, 'India's nuclear quest Down Under', *Asia Times Online*, 20 April 2006.

33 See D. Box and R. Bedi, 'Canberra set to sell uranium to India', *The Australian*, 11 May 2006.

34 'Supplying uranium to India difficult: Australia', *Indian Express*, 2 August 2006.

35 Some of these arguments are expressed in K. Kapisthalam, 'India's nuclear quest Down Under'.

Part 3

Working the room

7 Australia–Indonesia

Allan Gyngell

Geography has determined that Indonesia is a permanent element in Australia's security relationship with Asia. The sprawling archipelago of more than 13,500 islands stretches, as all Australian government strategic appreciations have noted, for 5,000 km across the northern approaches to this country. The strategic implications of this geographical reality were summarized in the famous phrase of the 1986 Dibb *Review of Australia's Defence Capabilities* that Indonesia is the area 'from or through which a military threat to Australia could most easily be posed'.[1] Australia's geography does not, of course, impose itself with the same strategic force on Indonesia, giving an inevitable asymmetry to the security interests each country has in the other.

During the colonial period and after federation, Batavia (now Jakarta) was a regular source of supply and port of call for ships sailing between Britain and its new colonies, and Australia worked comfortably with the government of the Netherlands East Indies. However, with the outbreak of war in the Pacific in late 1941 and the fall of Singapore in early 1942, the defeat and capture of Australian forces fighting in Ambon and Portuguese Timor strongly reinforced the archipelago's place in Australia's new sense of strategic vulnerability.

When the Second World War ended and Indonesian nationalists moved to declare independence from the Netherlands, the Chifley Labor government threw its support behind the revolutionary movement and opposed Dutch efforts to resume colonial control. With India, Australia brought the struggle to the attention of the UN Security Council in July 1947 and represented the new Indonesian state on a 'Good Offices Commission'.

Yet when sovereignty was finally passed to the Indonesian government, one part of the Netherlands East Indies—the territory of West New Guinea—was excluded from the transfer. Indonesia's first president, the charismatic nationalist Sukarno, led an increasingly strong campaign for West New Guinea's return as part of the patrimony of the new state.

The conservative Menzies government, which had replaced Labor in 1949, firmly supported Dutch efforts to hold onto the territory and to reject Indonesia's campaign to incorporate it. A strong reason for this was concern about the implications for the security of the adjoining territories of Papua and New Guinea, which Australia administered under a UN trusteeship. In 1950 the Australian Foreign Minister, Percy Spender, claimed that the interests of the 'inarticulate mass of the native people of Dutch New Guinea' had been fused with the vital strategic interests of Australia.[2] Nevertheless, occasional Dutch soundings about the joint administration of the island of New Guinea were not pursued.

By 1962, however, it was clear that the Dutch and Australian positions on West New Guinea could not be sustained, especially in the absence of support from the United States, where the Kennedy administration was keen to keep Indonesia from drifting further towards the communist side in the Cold War. The territory was finally transferred to Indonesia in May 1963 with the face-saving promise that an 'Act of Free Choice' would be held on its future in 1969. When that carefully stage-managed event was finally held, it hardly met the highest standards of democratic accountability, but it was endorsed by the United Nations and represented the international community's acceptance of the legal inclusion of the territory into the Indonesian Republic. The effect was to give Australia a 'common border' with an Asian country for the first time in its history.

However, this achievement hardly moderated Sukarno's behaviour or restrained the influence of the Communist Party of Indonesia (PKI) on his government as the Americans had hoped. He proceeded to launch a political 'confrontation' struggle against the newly formed country of Malaysia, which brought together the neighbouring British colonies of Malaya, Singapore, Sabah and Sarawak. Australia supported Malaysia politically, and when Indonesia launched military incursions into Malaysia in 1965, militarily as well. Australian troops were stationed in Sabah and Sarawak from mid-February 1965 until confrontation ended in August 1966.[3]

Although skilful diplomacy enabled Australia to maintain effective communications with Jakarta throughout this period, Sukarno's adventurism and incompetent economic policies plunged Indonesia into economic and political crisis. By September 1965 an abortive communist coup attempt and the murder of six senior generals led the military under General Suharto, then the head of the army's Strategic Command, to seize power. A violent nationwide score settling followed, in which hundreds of thousands of people were killed.

Sukarno was finally forced from office in March 1967 and Suharto took over as the head of a 'New Order' government, focused on repairing the economic and international damage of Sukarno's rule. Indonesia turned essentially inwards and in strategic terms abandoned the global, confrontationist focus of Sukarno for a policy of regional economic cooperation, and national and regional 'resilience' building. The most immediate result was the formation of ASEAN in 1967, which gave expression to an emerging idea of a Southeast Asian community.

For Australia, this was largely good news. In the bipolar Cold War structure, Indonesia shifted from a non-alignment which tipped towards the

Soviet Union to one which better suited the West. It helped provide stability in a region which was being shaken by the Vietnam War, in which the United States and Australia were participating, and generated new hopes for the Australia–Indonesia relationship. Gough Whitlam, the leader of the incoming Labor government in 1972, was particularly keen to develop relations with Indonesia despite concerns in corners of his party about the human rights record which had accompanied the New Order's seizure of power.[4]

East Timor

The period of promise was, however, short lived. In April 1974, left-wing Portuguese Army colonels belonging to the underground Armed Forces Movement overthrew the regime of Marcello Caetano, who had replaced the longtime Portuguese dictator Antonio Salazar in 1968. The revolution, which was in large part a response to anger about the wars being fought against independence groups in Portugal's African colonies, was to have dramatic consequences for all Portugal's remaining colonies. An increasingly left-leaning series of provisional governments in Lisbon through 1975 implemented a policy of unilateral withdrawal from its colonies, often in favour of local radical groups. In Portuguese Timor, a small enclave sharing the island of Timor with Indonesia, and badly underdeveloped after nearly 400 years of desultory Portuguese colonial administration, three major political factions emerged: one was committed to continuing association with Portugal, one to independence and one to integration with Indonesia.

By early September the left-leaning *Fretilin* group, which wanted independence, was in charge. As the then Australian Ambassador in Jakarta, Richard Woolcott, later wrote:

> There were real concerns in Indonesia and some other ASEAN countries, fanciful as they may now seem, that a weak, unstable, left-leaning and aid-dependent East Timor could become a 'Southeast Asian Cuba', possibly even with Soviet-supplied missiles directed at Jakarta. This would weaken further the fragile security of the region.[5]

After an intense period of undercover operations by Indonesian forces across the border of the divided island, during which five Australian television journalists were killed at Balibo by Indonesian forces in October, Indonesia openly invaded Portuguese Timor on 7 December 1975.[6]

Australian policy towards the invasion was complex but some clear divisions were apparent between the Department of Defence, which argued for advising the Indonesian government that Australia should be inclined to 'favour the emergence of the territory through self-determination, as an independent state' and the Department of Foreign Affairs, which placed more weight on the advantages of the territory's successful incorporation into Indonesia.[7] The Fraser government, replacing that of Whitlam in November 1975, did not adopt a greatly different position. In January 1978 it recognized the incorporation *de facto* of the territory into Indonesia, and early in 1979 quietly acknowledged (in its negotiations with Indonesia over the delineation of the Timor seabed) Timor's *de jure* incorporation.

The invasion of East Timor, the deaths of the five Australian journalists and the subsequent Indonesian mismanagement of the territory dominated Australia–Indonesia relations for the subsequent two decades. An unusually strong alliance, embracing veterans groups, those suspicious of Indonesia on both the left and the right, the Catholic church, human rights advocates and elements of the broadsheet press, formed a very effective lobby on a number of fronts, while the clumsy and often brutal manner of Indonesian military rule in the colony perpetuated a sense of resentment on the part of the East Timorese. In the public mind, Indonesian behaviour in East Timor cemented a concern about Indonesian expansionism which had first become prominent during Sukarno's campaigns on West New Guinea and Malaysia.

Nevertheless, a consistent theme of defence and foreign affairs analyses was to emphasize the strategic importance of Indonesia. A formal Defence Cooperation Program (DCP) between Australia and Indonesia had begun in 1968. During the following decade this program grew to become Australia's second largest military aid program after that with PNG. The early focus of the program was equipment like the *Nomad* aircraft and attack-class patrol boats, although joint mapping operations were also important. The 1986 Dibb Review reached the conclusion that 'Indonesia has neither the motive ... nor the capacity to threaten Australia with ... potential threats from the North. Were these attitudes to change it would take time for any disputes to develop into major military confrontations.'[8] By the late 1980s there was a shift towards using the DCP to develop capabilities rather than to provide equipment and support. As a result, the focus on training and exchanges grew. The 1993 Strategic Review emphasized: 'Personal contacts are particularly important in developing closer relations with Indonesia. Priority should be given to training and activities that foster long-term personal contact and understanding at all levels, concentrating, where possible, on potential leaders.'[9]

The Keating government

Indonesia did not loom large in the foreign or security policies of Labor Prime Minister Bob Hawke. The word Indonesia appears only once in the 561-page memoir of his eight-year prime ministership, as the destination with Papua New Guinea of his first overseas trip.[10] But the election of Paul Keating (as leader of the Labor Party in 1991) heralded a new approach to Indonesia. Like Whitlam before him, Keating was prepared to spend political capital on the relationship. He had come to office determined to address the problems in the relationship. He subsequently summed up his views this way:

> The coming to power of the New Order government was arguably the event of single greatest strategic benefit to Australia after the Second World War. Without an Indonesian government which was focussed on economic and social development and committed to policies of cooperation with its Southeast Asian neighbours, Australians would have faced three decades of uncertainty, fear, and almost certainly massively greater defence spending. And ASEAN and APEC, the two foundation stones of regional cooperation, could not have developed.[11]

He symbolically chose Indonesia as the destination for his first overseas visit as prime minister in 1992. Suharto was by then clearly in the final period of his power, but Keating built a personal relationship which he used effectively to promote Australian interests—for example by permitting the institutionalization of the APEC leaders meetings, and in the bilateral relationship through the establishment of the Australia–Indonesia Ministerial Forum.

The 1993 Strategic Review subsequently concluded, in quite similar terms to earlier Australian defence planning documents, that 'more than any other regional nation, a sound security relationship with Indonesia would do most for Australia's security. We should seek new opportunities to deepen the relationship in areas that serve both countries' interests.'[12] Keating agreed but thought the suggested ways of achieving this—essentially incremental changes to existing practice—were not ambitious enough. He asked why Australia should not develop a formal security relationship with Indonesia. Australia already had such links with Singapore and Malaysia through the Five Power Defence Arrangements (FPDA), with New Zealand through ANZUS and with PNG through the Joint Declaration of Principles. Why not Indonesia?

The response from officials and Keating's ministerial colleagues was sceptical and cautious, mainly on the grounds that Indonesia, with its long commitment to non-alignment, was unlikely to agree. Despite this, officials commissioned some initial work on the possible shape of such an agreement.

Keating set out his views in a speech in March 1994, saying:

> Changes in Australia and Indonesia and in the world since the end of the Cold War should compel us to take a fresh look at our strategic relationship. I believe great potential exists for further defence cooperation between Australia and Indonesia. ... If we are to turn into reality our policy of seeking defence in and with Asia, instead of against Asia, Indonesia is the most important place it will have to be done.[13]

Keating put the proposal to Suharto during a visit to Jakarta in June 1994 and received a commitment to discuss the matter further. They agreed to nominate emissaries for the job. In Australia's case, this was to be the former Chief of the Australian Defence Force (ADF) General Peter Gration, who had worked hard to develop links between the Indonesian armed forces and the ADF, together with the author, who was Keating's international adviser at the time. A 'non-paper' (prepared by Australia as a basis for discussion in October 1994) set out the rationale for a security agreement:

> Australia and Indonesia share similar strategic concerns. We share an interest in each other's security. Neither is a threat to the other. An agreement or understanding on security cooperation between Australia and Indonesia would benefit us both. It would also strengthen the stability and strategic resilience of the region. An agreement would be consistent with our strong and broadly based bilateral relationship. It would demonstrate the trust and confidence each has in the other. It would have a beneficial impact on public attitudes in both countries. It would provide a formal basis for our more active defence relationship.[14]

When, after a hiatus in the talks from the Indonesian side, negotiations finally got underway (over a year later, in November 1995), it was clear that the main Indonesian problem was not with the content of the agreement so much as with some of the language. Australia had used phrases like 'defence agreement' and 'external threat' which were troubling for the Indonesians given their reservations about military alliances. So, instead of being described as a 'Defence Agreement', it became an 'Agreement on Maintaining Security', while a phrase about external threats was replaced by 'adverse challenges' in order to show that the agreement covered not only military contingencies but the full range of external problems that might affect both countries and benefit from common action.

The Indonesian suggestions strengthened the agreement, making it broader and more relevant to the sort of real world problems like terrorism and people smuggling that would be at the heart of the security relationship just a few years later.

The final agreement, announced on 14 December 1995, was just over a page long. The preambular paragraphs placed its provisions in the context of the United Nations and noted that nothing in it affected the existing international commitments of either party. The three key operative paragraphs provided for Australia and Indonesia to:

- consult at ministerial level on a regular basis about matters affecting their common security and to develop such cooperation as would benefit their own security and that of the region;
- consult each other in the case of adverse challenges to either party or to their common security interests, and, if appropriate, to consider measures which might be taken either individually or jointly and in accordance with the processes of each party; and

- promote—in accordance with the policies and priorities of each—cooperative activities in the security field.[15]

The agreement was therefore simple, direct and provided a foundation for closer defence cooperation; yet it also had an active element—the agreement to consult in the event of adverse challenges and to consider individual or joint measures to respond.

The agreement was generally well received. The press was largely positive and the Opposition immediately expressed its support. What criticism there was took the form of complaints that the agreement was a 'secret treaty'. It had not been announced to the public in advance and, highly unusually in Canberra, nothing about it leaked. But its purpose, direction and form were consistent with the published and spoken comments that the government had made about its wish to strengthen defence cooperation with Indonesia.

The agreement was certainly a product of the personal relationship between Keating and Suharto. In both countries it was driven from the top. The decision-making process on the Indonesian side was difficult to read but all the evidence pointed to Suharto, who consistently showed himself to have a broader view of the relationship with Australia than many of his senior officials, having personally overcome opposition within the Indonesian military and government to secure agreement.

After ratification, the agreement largely disappeared from the public debate, but it provided the foundation for a very intense period of activity between the two armed forces. A new bilateral defence structure was put in place with annual ministerial meetings—an Australia–Indonesia Defence Policy Committee (chaired by the two chiefs of the defence forces) and an Australia–Indonesia Defence Coordinating Committee (with five working groups, including on operations and exercises, electronic warfare technology and logistics).

Indonesia transformed

The first major statement of strategic policy from the new Howard government came with the 1997 Defence White Paper which concluded: 'In recent years the sense of shared strategic interests between Australia and Indonesia has grown. This has been reflected in the Agreement on Maintaining Security signed by our governments in 1995.'[16]

Yet soon after the publication of the White Paper, two equally unanticipated events transformed the nature of the Australia–Indonesia security relationship: the 1997 financial crisis (which devastated Indonesia's economy and brought about the end of the New Order government) and the Bali bombings of 12 October 2002 (which contributed to a dramatic change in the content of the security relationship between the two countries).

The financial crisis began in Indonesia in mid-August 1997 when the government was unable to sustain its informal currency peg with the US dollar. Indonesia's large private foreign debt, around US$30 to $40 billion in loans and hot money on the stock exchange, was mostly unhedged.[17] With businesses unable to repay their debts, systemic weaknesses in the local banking system and poor prudential control were exposed. The International Monetary Fund (IMF) was called in to help, but made matters worse. Under pressure from the United States, which with the end of the Cold War no longer viewed Indonesia as an important strategic partner and wanted to put pressure on Suharto for human rights reforms, the IMF imposed onerous and unrealistic conditionality on its assistance. Paul Blustein, an historian of the crisis, described Indonesia's experience during this period as 'a tale of error piled atop error, with each side's bad moves—both the Fund's and the Indonesians'—compounding the other's and dragging the country to depths nobody had previously imagined possible'.[18] The result was that the Indonesian economy shrank by 20 per cent as money, including local money, fled the country. Unemployment doubled and inflation grew by 80 per cent. Few countries in the world of Indonesia's size and level of development have faced such sharp decline.

There was an immediate political impact. In the words of Suharto's biographer Robert Elson: 'The crisis was ... the catalyst which allowed a broad constellation of factors, many of them the products of long gestation, to come together and build so much pressure that Suharto found himself with no option but to stand down.'[19] The President resigned in a public speech in May 1998, handing over power to his vice-president, B. J. Habibie, an eccentric aeronautical engineer who had no independent power base.

Habibie was ready to test a number of the policy assumptions of the New Order government of Suharto, including those relating to the province of East Timor, where 20 years of indifferent and sometimes brutal Indonesian control had done little to reconcile its inhabitants to Indonesian sovereignty. Habibie expressed his willingness to consider prisoner releases and a 'special status' for East Timor, provided it was 'recognized as an integrated part of the Republic of Indonesia.'[20] This led to a revived effort within the UN-sponsored talks on the East Timor problem.

The Australian government wanted to play a part in the new discussions. Public opinion in Australia was clearly opposed to Indonesia's control and the Labor Opposition was now taking a stronger position. At the recommendation of the Foreign Minister Alexander Downer, the prime minister decided to send a letter to Habibie setting out Australia's views on the issue and offering some suggestions. Howard's letter of 19 December 2005 stated that Australia's view of Indonesia's sovereignty over East Timor was unchanged, as was Australia's view that the interests of Australia, Indonesia and East Timor were best served by East Timor remaining part of Indonesia. He argued, however, that Habibie should enter direct negotiations with East Timorese leaders and consider ways of addressing public opinion such as the Matignon Accords in New Caledonia, which had enabled France to postpone a referendum on independence for many years. Successful implementation 'of an autonomy package with a built-in review mechanism would allow time to convince the East Timorese of the benefits of autonomy within the Indonesian Republic',[21] Howard wrote.

Although Habibie rejected the Matignon concept immediately, he used the letter, with its implicit suggestion of possible movement in Australia's support for Indonesian sovereignty, to push ahead with rapid change. After a Cabinet meeting on 27 January 1999 Foreign Minister Ali Alatas announced that Indonesia would hold a referendum within a year in which the East Timorese could choose between independence and special autonomy. In May, Portugal and Indonesia asked the United Nations to conduct a 'popular consultation'. The UN Mission in East Timor (UNAMET) was established on 11 June 1999 to supervise the referendum. However, the situation in East Timor began to deteriorate with violence against supporters of independence and the arming by Indonesian forces of pro-Jakarta militias. Australia began surreptitiously building up its forces in Darwin in response, while denying that this was directed against Indonesia. The relationship was becoming more fragile.

On 30 August 1999, East Timorese voted by a margin of four to one in favour of independence, with a near universal turnout of voters. When the result was announced on 4 September 1999, pro-Indonesian militias reacted violently, their actions facilitated by elements of the Indonesian armed forces. With the agreement of the Indonesians, Australian forces entered Timor to evacuate Australian and UNAMET personnel as well as East Timorese. A fortuitously timed APEC meeting in Auckland enabled Howard, Habibie, US President Bill Clinton and other leaders to discuss the response. Under intense international pressure, Habibie agreed on 12 September to accept international assistance.

When Howard was asked a question in a radio interview about the relevance of the Agreement on Maintaining Security, he made a disparaging response which Habibie seems to have interpreted as a threat that Howard might move to abrogate the agreement. Indeed, on 16 September 1999, Habibie announced that the agreement had been abrogated, and cited Howard's remarks as the reason.

Just three years old, the agreement had not been in existence long enough to become institutionalized in the relationship between the two countries. It had not become part of the common fabric of thinking and, most importantly, because in both countries the leadership had changed, neither of the principals had a political interest tied to its success. In a crunch—and the period of East Timor's independence was certainly that—it was dispensable.

Under the terms of a unanimous UN Security Council resolution which authorized International Force East Timor (INTERFET), a multinational force under Australian control, the first Australian forces were deployed on 20 September 1999. INTERFET's mandate was to restore peace and security in East Timor, to protect and support UNAMET and to facilitate, within force capabilities, humanitarian assistance missions in East Timor.

The force was lead by General Peter Cosgrove, with a Thai as deputy commander. Force participants included—with Indonesia's agreement—a number of its ASEAN partners (Malaysia, the Philippines, Singapore and Thailand), contributions from New Zealand, Britain and Canada and logistical help from the United States. In addition, Japan made a substantial financial contribution. With 5,500 troops at its height, it was the largest commitment of Australian forces overseas in three decades. By year's end, INTERFET had the territory under control and the UN Transitional Administration for East Timor (UNTAET) took over to supervise Indonesia's transition to independence.

The military operation was very successful, not least because of the cooperation of the Indonesian authorities. The value of the people-to-people links the military cooperation program had been emphasizing for many years became clear.

However, the political implications for Australia–Indonesia relations were serious. Merle Ricklefs described the public relations of INTERFET as a 'disaster': 'It was as if Australia, rather than partnering others in a regional police action was again sending off the troops to Gallipoli as the band played 'Waltzing Matilda'. ... Military triumphalism was the prime ministerial style of the day.'[22] Indonesian nationalists responded to the perceived humiliation of the affair. The Australian Embassy in Jakarta was attacked, including with Molotov cocktails, and shots were fired. The experience in East Timor seriously undermined Indonesian military confidence in itself. The perception grew that friends had turned against them while they were weak, and that Australia was a cause of Indonesia's disgrace.

Yet the independence of East Timor was just one of a number of fundamental political changes with which Indonesia was struggling. After the stability of the New Order period—a stability which had, in the end, stagnated—political change in Indonesia appeared on the horizon. In June 1999, as a result of a new constitution introduced by Habibie, more than 100 million Indonesians took part in free elections. The Indonesian Democratic Party-Struggle (PDI-P)—a secular nationalist party headed by Sukarno's daughter Megawati Sukarnoputri—emerged as the dominant party in parliament, but it lacked the numbers to overcome a hostile coalition aimed at preventing Megawati becoming president. That impasse was resolved with the election by the parliament of Abdurrahman Wahid (Gus Dur), an Islamic scholar and leader of the moderate Islamic group Nahdlatul Ulama. Megawati became his vice-president. But scandals over money (not helped by a chaotic administrative style) eventually undermined Wahid's position and led in July 2002 to a constitutional stand-off between president and parliament. Parliament eventually voted by a unanimous 591 votes to impeach and dismiss Wahid, and Megawati finally moved into her father's old office.

In August 2002 further important constitutional changes were passed, including a provision for the direct election of the president. In September

2004 a former general (and Megawati's security minister) Susilo Bambang Yudhoyono, building a political base outside the established parties of the New Order, became Indonesia's first democratically elected president. The role of the military in Indonesia was also transformed as its structural role in the political system was diminished.[23]

A broadening security agenda

At the same time that Indonesia was struggling with these deep political changes, a very different security agenda was imposing itself on the Australia–Indonesia relationship—broadening it well beyond the familiar military-to-military links.

In 1998–9, immediately before the East Timor intervention, expenditure on Australian–Indonesian defence cooperation totalled A$6 million. This included support for the longstanding *Nomad* aircraft program, and training courses for more than 128 Indonesian military personnel. Engagement between the ADF and the Indonesian armed forces occurred at many different levels and included combined ground exercises in Bandung in March 1999.

Following the Timor operation, most of this program went into a deep freeze. Actual expenditure on defence cooperation in 2000–1 was just A$3.3 million, compared with the budgeted A$7.2 million. Exercises and high-level visits were all put on hold but, despite the tension in the relationship, the program was never abandoned completely. Implicitly at least, both sides wanted it to continue. Personnel and logistics support for the *Nomad* program continued and Australian students attended Indonesian staff colleges. Therefore, even during the most difficult period, Australian observers believed that TNI's leadership recognized that the relationship would go through a period of damage control followed by repair and rebuilding.

The relationship was built up again slowly through 2004 with reciprocal senior visits and the resumption of high-level strategic dialogue and service-to-service talks. Capacity-building cooperation shifted from TNI headquarters to the defence ministry and included strategic analytical capabilities. Around 100 Indonesian defence personnel were once more training annually in Australia. By 2004–5, the expenditure on defence cooperation was again around A$6 million.

More importantly, the security relationship was developing in new areas. From 2001, Australia had been developing a greater interest in cooperating with Indonesia over rising levels of people smuggling and illegal fishing. Then the 11 September 2001 attacks in New York, and Washington added terrorism to the agenda. This issue picked up urgency after the October 2002 Bali bombings (in which 88 Australians died),[24] the August 2003 Marriott Hotel and September 2004 Australian Embassy bombings in Jakarta, and the October 2005 Bali bombings (which killed 20 people, including four Australians). These events greatly deepened the urgency and broadened the extent of the cooperation between the law enforcement and intelligence agencies of the two countries, especially the Australian Federal Police (AFP) and the Indonesian National Police, which had been formally separated from the military in the reform process that followed the end of the Suharto government. As the significance of the threat posed by the *Jemaah Islamiyah* group became clearer, Australia recognized, in the words of the 2005 Defence Update, that Indonesia had a 'pivotal role to play in counter-terrorism in the region'.[25]

After the Bali bombings in 2002, counterterrorist planning became a greater feature of the relationship, including, sensitively, with *Kopassus*—the Indonesian special forces which would probably form the main Indonesian strike body in any counterterrorism operation.

This broader security agenda was reflected in a Memorandum of Understanding on counterterrorism signed in February 2002. In October that year Prime Minister Howard announced a A$10 million four-year counterterrorism assistance package, which was increased to $20 million in October 2004. One concrete result of this cooperation was the establishment in 2004 of the Jakarta Centre for Law Enforcement Cooperation (JLEC) which has provided counterterrorism training to law enforcement officers from Indonesia and across Southeast Asia. A Transnational Crime Centre in Jakarta, officially opened in February 2006 (and also jointly funded by Australia), was established to enhance the Indonesian National Police's capacity to address terrorism, drug trafficking, cyber crime and money laundering.

The Australian government has claimed that close cooperation between the AFP and the Indonesian police was instrumental in bringing more than 160 terrorists and their collaborators to justice.[26] Other bilateral agreements were reached covering transnational crime and police cooperation (June 2002) and the exchange of financial intelligence (February 2004). The two countries also cooperated regionally by co-hosting meetings on the counterterrorism agenda.

This broadening security cooperation was reflected in the rather different sort of language which Australian policymakers used to describe Indonesia in the 2005 Defence Update as compared with earlier defence analyses:

> As a country of 230 million people, Indonesia's importance to the Asia–Pacific region and to Australia should not be underestimated. Its size, historical legacy and economic potential give it a strategic importance undiminished by the significant domestic economic and political challenges of recent years. Indonesia has a pivotal role to play in counter-terrorism in the region.
>
> Australia attaches high priority to working with Indonesia on common security issues, particularly terrorism and border security. We have rebuilt the defence relationship after the stresses of East Timor. Our focus is on developing activities, at a pace comfortable to both countries, that will confer practical benefits. Developing mutual confidence and awareness between our forces will be an asset for both countries.[27]

This new agenda again generated political interest in the idea of an overarching security arrangement between the two countries.

President Yudhoyono had dealt effectively with Australia in his earlier positions, including as an army general and as coordinating minister for security under President Megawati Sukarnoputri. His election as president gave a strong new impetus to Australia–Indonesia cooperation. This began, tragically, with the disaster of the Indian Ocean tsunami on 26 December 2004 which killed more than 130,000 Indonesians and displaced half a million people in Aceh and North Sumatra. The Australian government and community responded quickly and generously to the crisis. Under Operation Sumatra Assist, the ADF provided humanitarian support including emergency relief, engineering and aeromedical evacuation. In January 2005, Prime Minister Howard announced a A$1 billion aid program over five years under a new Australia–Indonesia Partnership for Reconstruction and Development. An earthquake in Nias and neighbouring islands in March 2005 resulted in another humanitarian operation by the ADF, in which nine Australians lost their lives in the *Sea King* helicopter disaster.

In April 2005, President Yudhoyono visited Australia. Speaking to a parliamentary lunch in Canberra, he said: 'We now live in geopolitical and geo-economic environments that are different from the ones of the previous decades. ... It is not enough for us to be just neighbors. We have to be strong partners.'[28] He referred again to a subject he had first raised in an earlier visit as security minister in 2003—the idea of a new security treaty. Following discussions between the two governments, a new Agreement between the Republic of Indonesia and Australia on the Framework for Security Cooperation was signed by the Australian and Indonesian foreign ministers in Lombok on 13 November 2006.[29] Foreign Minister Downer described the agreement as providing 'a strong legal framework for encouraging intensive dialogue, exchanges and implementation of cooperative activities and ... a firm basis for the conclusion of separate arrangements in specific areas'.[30] The stated purpose of the agreement is to

> provide a framework for deepening and expanding bilateral cooperation and exchanges as well as to intensify cooperation and consultation between the Parties in areas of mutual interest and concern on matters affecting their common security as well as their respective national security.[31]

The Lombok Treaty is different in form from the 1995 Agreement on Maintaining Security. At its heart lies a non-aggression pact. Under Article 2, the parties to the treaty agree to 'refrain from the threat or use of force against the territorial integrity or political independence of the other'.[32] The familiar 'mutual respect for the sovereignty, territorial integrity, national unity and political independence of each other' are emphasized and the parties agree that, 'consistent with their respective domestic laws and international obligations', they shall not in any manner support or participate in activities by any person or entity which constitutes a threat to the stability, sovereignty or territorial integrity of the other Party, including those who seek to use its territory for encouraging or committing such activities, including separatism, in the territory of the other Party.[33]

This article in particular bears the marks of a bruising period in Australia's relations with Indonesia. It shows the effect of the East Timor intervention, the tension over Papuan asylum seekers in 2006 (further discussed below) and a residual Indonesian concern over Howard's December 2002 comments that Australia had the right to preempt terrorist attacks in the region. It is a reversion to familiar forms and language in Indonesian security policy.

The commitment that the two sides will 'not in any manner support or participate in the activities by any person or entity which constitutes a threat to the stability, sovereignty or territorial integrity of the other party' goes beyond the longstanding position of both major political parties in Australia to support Indonesia's established borders. Yet this clause would seem to offer Australia as much scope to press Indonesia on *Jemaah Islamiyah* and other terrorist groups as for Indonesia to pressure Australia on Papua. Either way, though, it seems to store up rich political problems for the future.

There follows in Article 3 of the Lombok Treaty a list of the general areas in which cooperation might take place, together with a commitment to cooperate (although this is hedged in most places by caveats). The clause on intelligence cooperation, for example, reads 'cooperation and exchange of intelligence on security issues between relevant institutions and agencies, in compliance with their respective national legislation and within the limits of their responsibility'. Other areas identified for cooperation include the defence forces; law enforcement in areas such as drugs, illegal fishing, people smuggling, corruption, cyber crimes and money laundering; counterterrorism cooperation; intelligence cooperation; maritime security; aviation safety; and the proliferation of weapons of mass destruction (WMD).

The implementation mechanism for the Lombok Treaty is the annual Indonesia–Australia Ministerial Forum.

Compared with the 1995 agreement, the Lombok Treaty is more traditional in form and more bilaterally focused. The main difference lies in its ambition. In the 1995 agreement, the two sides agreed to 'consult each other in the case of adverse challenges to either party or to their common security interests, and, if appropriate, consider measures which might be taken either individually or jointly and in accordance with the processes of each party'; in other words, to act together to address challenges that might threaten both. The new treaty is much more concerned with the bilateral relationship. The idea of the two countries identifying common external interests and then acting together to pursue them is much less prominent. Still, it underlines the commitment of both governments to work together to build closer ties. It was negotiated quickly and it reflects a dialogue on these subjects that is broadening out well beyond the two defence forces.

The future of the relationship

For nearly 50 years, Australia had to deal with just two Indonesian presidents; yet there were four in less than a decade after the fall of the New Order regime, together with a more active and involved parliament. For the Australia–Indonesia relationship as a whole, and for its security dimensions in particular, Indonesian democracy will yield more surprises and unexpected turns than did Indonesian authoritarianism.

This will give public opinion an increasing role in the relationship. In this regard, the findings of a Lowy Institute public opinion survey in 2006 were revealing.[34] The first poll to be conducted in both countries, it showed quite high levels of suspicion and ignorance. Just 50 per cent of Australians expressed positive feelings about Indonesia, markedly less than the results for most other Asian countries. For Indonesians, the attitude to Australia was not dissimilar, with only around 51 per cent expressing positive feelings.

Respondents in Australia agreed strongly with statements that Indonesia was essentially controlled by the military and that it was a dangerous source of Islamic terrorism. A clear majority supported the view that 'Australia is right to worry about Indonesia as a military threat'. Australians were ambivalent about whether 'Indonesia is an emerging democracy'.

On the Indonesian side, respondents felt strongly that 'Indonesia is right to worry that Australia is seeking to separate the province of West Papua from Indonesia', that 'Australia has a tendency to try to interfere too much in Indonesia's affairs' and also that 'Australian policy towards Indonesia and the region is shaped too heavily by its alliance with the United States'. Neither set of respondents displayed much political knowledge of the other country. When asked to name the other country's leader, only a quarter of Indonesians and one fifth of Australians could do so correctly. On a more positive note, however, the survey also found that clear majorities in both countries felt that 'it is very important that Australia and Indonesia work to develop a close relationship', although more Australians (77 per cent) expressed support for this view than Indonesians (64 per cent).

Yet, short of the emergence in Jakarta of an Islamist government committed to Salafi-Jihadist aims (of which there is no evidence at all, either from the past history of Indonesian Islam or from the patterns of Indonesian voting preferences in elections since the end of the New Order government), Indonesian democratization should not deliver any fundamental conflicts of strategic interest with Australia.

Within the reasonable time horizons of strategic planning, it is far easier to see similar approaches to Australian and Indonesian strategic objectives in East and Southeast Asia than to imagine differences. Indonesia will want ASEAN to remain a strong and resilient element in regional security and economic affairs, if only to ensure a hedge against China's growing power. That will suit Australia. Neither, on any realistic estimate, is Indonesia likely to develop the economic foundation to enable it to establish an extensive military projection capability in its own right, still less the interest in turning such a capability against Australia. It is equally hard to see why it would facilitate the projection of power by any adversary (presumably China under some scenarios) which might threaten Australia.

So Australian and Indonesian strategic objectives in Asia are likely to remain fundamentally congruent.

Any security problems are more likely to appear in border areas. Richard Chauvel has pointed to the 'centrality of the periphery' in the Australia–Indonesia relationship.[35] East Timor remains a concern for Australian security and foreign policy, but it is now less of a problem in the context of our relationship with Indonesia. This is not to say that mismanagement in East Timor, Indonesia or Australia could not make it so again, but it would be a problem of a different sort and, most likely, of a lesser order.

However, Papua remains a key challenge for both countries. If both sides fail to handle this effectively, it has the potential to disrupt and derail the Indonesia–Australia relationship in the early twenty-first century, just as East Timor did in the late twentieth century. As noted earlier, Papua occupies a sensitive place in the history of Australia–Indonesian relations. Contrary to some expectations, however, it has not been a central issue in the years since the 'Act of Free Choice'. PNG and Indonesia have generally managed their border relationship smoothly and, for Australia, East Timor loomed much larger in the bilateral relationship. Nevertheless, memories of the earlier suspicions continue to resonate in the minds of both Australians and Indonesians.

With East Timor's independence in 1999 and the democratization of Indonesia, the public focus on Papua in Australia resumed when a number of the Christian church, human rights and other Australian NGOs (which had focused on East Timor) shifted their attention to Papua. The issue came to a head again at the governmental level in early 2006 when a group of 43 Papuan asylum seekers reached the Australian mainland by boat and sought asylum as political refugees. Forty-two were granted refugee status after their cases were considered by an Australian official acting as an independent decisionmaker under the terms of the 1951 Refugee Convention. This result came despite a personal assurance by President Yudhoyono to Prime Minister Howard that the Papuans would not be harmed if they returned home. Despite firm reassurances by the Australian government of its commitment to Indonesia's territorial integrity, the reaction from Indonesia was sharp. It included the recall of the Indonesian Ambassador to Australia—a step which was never taken during the fraught relationship over East Timor.

Papua brings together a range of so-called 'new' security issues encountered in other parts of Melanesia (such as illegal people movement, refugees, health and environmental problems) with the most traditional questions of nationalism and state sovereignty. For Indonesia, it involves deep questions regarding the scope and nature of the Indonesian state and engages immediate suspicions of Australian intentions. Moreover, because any large-scale unrest in Papua could spill over into PNG, with which Australia has security links (including a treaty commitment to consult in the event of external armed attack), it also potentially involves a third state. It is where the 'old' security issues and the new ones intersect most immediately for Australia.

The capacity and willingness of the two countries to engage with each other in these circumstances is limited, but will be vital. Rodd McGibbon has pointed to a number of ways in which this might be done such as by boosting bilateral cooperation (including aid), supporting democratic insti-tution building in Indonesia (including special autonomy for Papua) and winning the 'battle for ideas' in Australia. Australian officials, he correctly points out, 'need to fashion an approach over Papua that can navigate between the contending pitfalls of policy inaction and policy overreach'.[36]

Hugh White has argued that Australia's defence relationship with Indonesia

> will always be based on a deep ambivalence, in the literal sense of that word. Indonesia impinges on Australia's deepest strategic preoccupa-tions in two ways. It is the only large country within easy range of Australia; because of its proximity and sheer size, it has the strategic potential to pose a serious military challenge to Australia directly. And it is the only one strong enough to help defend our neighbourhood against an intruder. Whether it is strong or weak, Indonesia offers both potential protection and potential threats to Australia. ... When Aus-tralian strategists have looked at our neighbourhood in isolation, as a self-contained strategic system, a strong Indonesia looks like a liability. But when we look at our neighbourhood as an element of the wider Asia–Pacific strategic system, it looks like an asset. Australia has this kind of strategic ambivalence with no other country.[37]

Other analysts have gone beyond the idea of ambivalence to underline bar-riers. According to Bilveer Singh,

> the asymmetries between the two countries are so deep and intense, and the cultural divide so immense, it is unlikely that the strangeness between Australia and Indonesia will be reduced in the short term and to that extent, the great barrier between the two will last longer than expected.[38]

For Indonesia, Australia is less important to its strategic outlook. Throughout the New Order period and since, Indonesia's security policy, as well as its wider approach to international relations, has been based on 'an implicit adherence to a "concentric circles" approach'.[39] This was refined in Indonesia's 1995 Defence White Paper:

In a geostrategic context Indonesia's basic defence and security strategy is one providing for layered security. The deepest layer is domestic security, followed by sub-regional (ASEAN) security, regional (Southeast Asia) security and security of neighbouring regions, in that order. This strategy is called defence-in-depth.[40]

It is not just that we begin with a naturally different perspective on the relationship; it is also that we think about the world in different ways. The negotiations over the 1995 and 2006 security agreements each underlined how readily Australians think of their security from the outside in, in terms of alliances and bilateral agreements, and how naturally Indonesians think about security from the inside out and in alliance terms how Indonesians think multilaterally.

White concludes that

> it is only sensible to recognize that nothing can be done to help reduce Indonesian suspicion of Australia, and to start rebuilding trust, without both sides being willing to make a substantial effort, to take some real political risks and to pay some real political costs. Today this is as true in Jakarta as it is in Canberra.[41]

He urges that we avoid 'unrealistic expectation' and work on the 'humble but vital business of helping each side to understand the other's policies, and our respective views of how our long-term regional goals and policies intersect'.[42]

This is a sober and persuasive analysis of—and policy prescription for—the relationship. Yet I would go further. In fact, the only effective way in which Australia can look at Indonesia is not in terms of a self-contained neighbourhood strategic system, or even as an 'element of the wider Asia Pacific strategic system', but as part of a wider strategic system than that—one that encompasses the security threats from non-state actors like Salafi-Jihadist terrorism and the increasingly important links between an East Asia hungry for energy and a Middle East that is the only place from which such resources can come.[43]

In those circumstances, Indonesia's strategic ambivalence toward Australia is diminishing, while its strengths as a potential partner for Australia (and the countries of most importance to Australia's continuing prosperity and security) are increasing.

Notes

1 P. Dibb, *Review of Australia's Defence Capabilities: Report to the Minister for Defence by Mr Paul Dibb*, Canberra: Australian Government Publishing Service, 1986, p. 4.
2 Quoted in L. Metzemaekers, 'The Western New Guinea problem', *Pacific Affairs*, vol. 24, no. 2, June 1951, p. 140.

3 D. Lee and M. Dee, 'Southeast Asian conflicts', in D. Goldsworthy (ed.) *Facing North; A Century of Australian Engagement with Asia, Vol. 1*, Melbourne: Melbourne University Press, 2001, p. 277.
4 D. Goldsworthy, D. Dutton, P. Gifford and R. Pitty, 'Reorientation', in ibid., pp. 352–76.
5 R. Woolcott, *The Hot Seat: Reflections on Diplomacy from Stalin's Death to the Bali Bombings*, Sydney: HarperCollins, 2003, p. 145.
6 The official documents for this period can be found in 'Australia and the Indonesian incorporation of Portuguese Timor 1974–76', *Documents on Australian Foreign Policy*, Melbourne: Department of Foreign Affairs and Trade, 2000.
7 Goldsworthy *et al.*, 'Reorientation', p. 361.
8 Dibb, *Review of Australia's Defence Capabilities*, p. 33.
9 *Strategic Review 1993*, Canberra: Department of Defence, 1993, p. 25.
10 B. Hawke, *The Hawke Memoirs*, Melbourne: Mandarin, 1996.
11 P. Keating, *Engagement: Australia Faces the Asia Pacific*, Sydney: Pan Macmillan, 2000, p. 126.
12 *Strategic Review 1993*, p. 24.
13 Reproduced in M. Ryan (ed.) *Advancing Australia: The Speeches of Paul Keating, Prime Minister*, Sydney: Big Picture Publications, 1995, p. 203.
14 Ibid., p. 142.
15 For full text, see B. Singh, *Defence Relations between Australia and Indonesia in the Post-Cold War Era*, Westport, CT: Greenwood Press, 2002, Appendix 3.
16 Commonwealth of Australia, *Australia's Strategic Policy*, Canberra: Department of Defence, 1997, p. 11.
17 H. Hill, 'The Indonesian economy', in G. Forrester and R.J. May (eds) *The Fall of Soeharto*, Singapore: Select Books, 1999, p. 95.
18 P. Blustein, *The Chastening: Inside the Crisis that Rocked the Global Financial System and Humbled the IMF*, New York: Public Affairs, 2001, p. 88.
19 R.E. Elson, *Suharto: A Political Biography*, Cambridge: Cambridge University Press, 2001, p. 293.
20 Cited in D. Goldsworthy, 'East Timor', in P. Edwards and D. Goldsworthy, *Facing North: A Century of Australian Engagement with Asia, Vol.2*, Melbourne: Melbourne University Press, 2003, p. 223.
21 Ibid., p. 228.
22 M.C. Rickefs, 'Australia and Indonesia', in R. Manne (ed.) *The Howard Years*, Melbourne: Black Inc, 2004.
23 See M. Mietzner, *The Politics of Military Reform in Post-Suharto Indonesia: Elite Conflict, Nationalism and Institutional Resistance*, Washington, DC: East West Center, 2006.
24 An account is given in A. Gyngell and M. Wesley, *Making Australian Foreign Policy*, Port Melbourne: Cambridge University Press, 2003, p. 161.
25 *Australia's National Security: A Defence Update 2005*, Canberra: Commonwealth of Australia, 2005, p. 8.
26 Australian Government, 'Indonesia country brief', Department of Foreign Affairs and Trade, December 2006.
27 *Australia's National Security: A Defence Update 2005*, pp. 8, 14.
28 Speech by His Excellency Dr. Susilo Bambang Yudhoyono, President of the Republic of Indonesia, at the Great Hall, Parliament House, Canberra, 4 April 2005.
29 *Agreement between the Republic of Indonesia and Australia on the Framework for Security Cooperation*, 13 November 2006.
30 The Hon. Alexander Downer MP, Minister for Foreign Affairs, Australia, 'Signature of the Australia Indonesia Agreement for Security Cooperation', media release FA124, 13 November 2006.

31 *Agreement between the Republic of Indonesia and Australia on the Framework for Security Cooperation*, Article 1.
32 Ibid., Article 2.
33 Ibid.
34 I. Cook, *Australia, Indonesia and the World: Public Opinion and Foreign Policy*, Sydney: Lowy Institute for International Policy, 2006.
35 R. Chauvel, 'The centrality of the periphery: Australia, Indonesia and Papua', J. Monfries (ed.) *Different Societies, Shared Futures: Australia, Indonesia and the Region*, Singapore: Institute of Southeast Asian Studies, 2006.
36 R. McGibbon, *Pitfalls of Papua*, Lowy Institute paper 13, Sydney: Lowy Institute for International Policy, 2006, p. xii.
37 H. White, 'The new Australia–Indonesia strategic relationship: a note of caution', in Monfries, *Different Societies, Shared Futures*, p. 45.
38 Singh, *Defence Relations between Australia and Indonesia in the Post-Cold War Era*.
39 L.C. Sebastian, 'Indonesia's management of regional order', in J.C.C. Liow and R. Emmers (eds) *Order and Security in Southeast Asia: Essays in Memory of Michael Leifer*, London: Routledge, 2006.
40 The Policy of the State Defence and Security of the Republic of Indonesia, Jakarta: Ministry of Defence and Security, 1995, pp. 16–17.
41 White, 'The new Australia–Indonesia strategic relationship', p. 52.
42 Ibid., p. 53.
43 M. Thirlwell and A. Bubalo, 'New rules for a new "great game": Northeast Asian Energy Insecurity and the G-20', Lowy Institute for International Policy Brief, November 2006.

8   Australia–South Pacific

Hugh White

The Howard Doctrine

No element of Australia's regional policy has changed as sharply in recent years as its approach to the small island nations of its immediate neighbourhood in the Southwest Pacific, and arguably nowhere does Australian regional policy face a tougher challenge and a lonelier test. One might also say that no policy bears so strongly the mark of the present government and of Prime Minister John Howard himself. If any of the foreign or strategic policies of the Howard government deserve to be called the 'Howard Doctrine', it is the engaged and muscular approach to Australia's interests in, and responsibilities toward, its smaller neighbours that has emerged over recent years. This new approach was most clearly inaugurated with the launch of the Regional Assistance Mission to Solomon Islands (RAMSI) in July 2003, but it started to emerge somewhat earlier in the Howard years. It was already evident, for example, in 1999 when during an interview John Howard acquiesced to the idea that Australia might be America's 'regional deputy' in looking after problems in its backyard.[1] This became Howard's most famous foreign policy pronouncement, and was called at the time and since the 'Howard Doctrine'. Yet its significance has often been misunderstood. Most commentators have interpreted Howard as accepting for Australia a subordinate role to that of the United States in regional affairs. However the context of the interview, and the wider circumstances of the time, suggest a very different reading. It was conducted at the height of the East Timor crisis in September 1999, when Australia was taking an unprecedented leadership role in the affairs of its immediate neighbourhood. Moreover, it seemed to many at the time—including, apparently, Howard himself—that Australia was receiving relatively little support from the United States. It seems much more plausible to read Howard's position at this time to be an assertion that Australia had unique interests, responsibilities and capacities to manage problems in Australia's 'arc of instability', and intended to continue to do so. This is the Howard Doctrine.

No one could accuse Howard of playing it safe. The emergence of the Howard Doctrine in its current form—involving simultaneous, prolonged, high-profile security-oriented intervention missions in several regional neighbours—constituted a very distinct new policy direction for Australia. When he announced RAMSI in June 2003, John Howard himself acknowledged that the initiative marked a reversal of previous approaches[2]—perhaps the only time that Howard has acknowledged a significant change of direction on any foreign and strategic policy. Moreover, there is no major issue on Canberra's international agenda in which Australia is so clearly going it alone, forced to take the major responsibility for framing, promoting and delivering policy outcomes in very complex circumstances. Success will be highly visible, and so will failure. So far the signs are not promising, and there seems a significant likelihood that Howard will not succeed in achieving the goals he has set. If not, the implications for Australia could be very serious. And yet the motives and purposes which underlie the Howard Doctrine are themselves rather unclear.

This chapter will explore, and aim to illuminate, the interests behind the Howard Doctrine, the circumstances of its evolution, the problems encountered so far, the prospects for the future and the conditions of success. In brief, it will argue that the policy reflects deep and enduring Australian strategic interests, and may be the only effective approach to protecting those interests in present circumstances, but that it is failing at present and is in danger of continuing to do so.

Permanent interests

While much about the Howard Doctrine is new, its basic motives are not. The mainspring of Canberra's new engagement in its neighbourhood is a conception of Australia's interests and regional responsibilities that is as old as Australian strategic thinking. Australia has long identified developments in the islands to its north as key factors in its own security. Australia's earliest strategic concerns focused on the intrusion of potentially hostile European powers into these islands in the later nineteenth century, and worries that they could provide bases to support attacks on Australia itself by these powers. In response, Australian statesmen proposed a Monroe Doctrine for the South Pacific, aimed at excluding non-British intrusion into the immediate neighbourhood. As early as 1870, the Australian colonies took united action to urge London to colonize Fiji to preempt US or German interest.[3] In 1884, when London rebuffed Queensland's attempt to forestall German intrusion by annexing Papua, the colonies launched themselves on the path to federation to strengthen their hand.[4] During and after the First World War, promoting Australia's version of the Monroe Doctrine became the key strategic objective of Australian diplomacy, especially under Prime Minister Billy Hughes.[5] Nor were these strategic issues the only Australian concerns in the neighbouring islands: the problems of indentured labour, for example, provided a precedent for today's concerns about transnational criminals operating outside the scope of effective laws in these territories.

The solution of course was colonialism: Australia directly took responsibility for what is now Papua New Guinea, and urged Britain to take on colonial responsibilities in the Solomon Islands, Vanuatu, Fiji and elsewhere.

Colonial rule was an effective, if costly, way to protect Australia's interests in its island neighbourhood, but it was not one that could long survive the winds of change that swept colonialism away in the decades after the Second World War. By the late 1960s it was clear that a number of small independent nations would emerge on Australia's doorstep as colonial rule was withdrawn. Most attention was paid to PNG, of course, which was the biggest of the emerging new neighbours, was Australia's own colony, and in some ways posed the biggest strategic concerns because of its border with Indonesia. But, as it happened, the transition to independence coincided with a relatively benign period in Australia's regional affairs. Japan was embedded in the Western alliance, relations with China had been opened, and Indonesia (East Timor notwithstanding) had settled into the more congenial policies of Suharto's New Order. It was possible to argue that PNG and other island neighbours were no longer as important to Australian security as they had once been.[6] Nonetheless, there were real doubts about whether these new, small island states could survive and function in ways which would meet Australia's aims and protect its interests. Many of the problems we now recognize in PNG and elsewhere in Australia's close neighbourhood were accurately diagnosed by observers like Peter Hastings before independence.[7]

Australian policy towards its new neighbours in their first years of independence thus reflected a certain ambivalence. On the one hand, Australia provided generous if not always well-directed aid, including defence assistance under the Defence Cooperation Program (DCP). In the smaller states, to the extent that these programs had an explicit strategic rationale at all, they were intended to establish and maintain a benign Australian military presence in the islands, and to foster an image of Australia as their natural strategic partner, as well as contributing in broader and often unspecified ways to national development. In PNG the aim was more specific and ambitious: Australian defence assistance was intended to build up the PNG Defence Force (PNGDF) so that, in the event of low-level problems, most probably with Indonesia, PNG would have a reasonable chance of looking after itself without calling on Australia for assistance. This thinking recognized that Australia would, almost instinctively, be drawn into supporting PNG if there was a clash with Indonesia which PNG could not manage on its own. The risks of such a clash, arising out of the presence of Papuan separatist activists and sympathizers in PNG, was probably the scenario for regional conflict which was most closely studied by Australian defence planners in the 1980s, and which was seen to pose the most credible risk of drawing Australia and Indonesia into conflict.

On the other hand, there was no formal security agreement or undertaking between Australia and PNG, or any of the other Pacific Island countries (PICs), until late 1987 when the Joint Declaration of Principles (JDP) between Australia and PNG was signed.[8] The JDP includes a clause committing the two countries to consult about their response to an armed attack on either. This reflected a broader policy disposition to limit Australia's liabilities and commitments in the PICs. There was a general view that although Australia should be generous with aid, it should avoid becoming closely involved in its small neighbours' internal affairs. Underpinning this view was a basic optimism that the PICs would succeed in building themselves into stable states with effective and responsible governments which would be able, with financial and technical help, to look after the basic needs of their peoples. The obvious problems among them were seen as those arising from the transition from colony to independent state, rather than deep-seated systemic problems reflecting more fundamental weaknesses.

These optimistic assumptions were not to last, however. In retrospect one can argue that they started to wane after the first Fiji coup in 1987 and were further eroded by other developments and incidents around the same time, especially political instability in Vanuatu, including the establishment of links with Libya, which was at that time a notorious rogue state. However, the biggest blow was the Bougainville crisis which erupted in 1989 in PNG. The long-running crisis that followed revealed deep flaws in the PNG state, and profound weaknesses in some of its key institutions. In particular it revealed deficiencies in the PNGDF, which was shown, albeit under very testing circumstances, to be both ineffective and brutal. From around that time onwards, it became more commonplace for Australian policymakers to stress the depth of problems facing the PICs, and to acknowledge the likelihood that Australia would be drawn more deeply into efforts to address those problems and resolve any resulting crises. As early as November 1989, Australian defence planning documents were acknowledging the likelihood that in future Australia would need to take a more active and engaged role in the South Pacific, including the use of its armed forces to help support internal security.[9] In 1991 Australia adopted a much tougher approach to defence aid to PNG, arguing forcefully that further DCP assistance would be conditional on major reform of the PNGDF. Over the early 1990s, as the Bougainville crisis dragged on, it became widely accepted that the problems of its Pacific Island neighbours were among Australia's gravest foreign and defence policy challenges.

The man behind the white picket fence

When the Coalition won the election in 1996, it came to government with no clear foreign policy agenda. Apart from an unfocused instinct to promote and preserve the US alliance, the new Australian government's main aim seemed to be to avoid what it saw as the rhetorical excesses and immodest pretensions of its immediate predecessors. Yet John Howard quickly showed that in one area, at least, he had ambitions to play a larger role. Perhaps appropriately for a leader who had identified himself with the modest aspirations of Australia's suburbs, Howard's first and most enduring foreign policy priority has been Australia's own backyard. Characteristically, he has chosen a small pond but has shown determination to act the big fish in it. This pattern was first evident in the first weeks of the new government, in a clear impatience with Australia's attitude of reluctant resignation to the horrors of the Bougainville situation and its inability to do much to help. In early policy reviews, Howard and his colleagues made it clear that they were willing to examine more broadly options to engage in Bougainville than had their predecessors. They were put to the test early the following year, when the Sandline crisis erupted over attempts by the PNG government to hire mercenaries to suppress the separatist forces on Bougainville. Howard responded very strongly, making it clear that he was willing, if necessary, to use the Australian Defence Force (ADF) both to interdict the mercenaries and to suppress the military coup, which seemed to loom in Port Moresby once the presence of the mercenaries become known.[10] In the end this did not prove necessary, but the Australian government's concerns about threats to regional stability, and its commitment to take big risks and bear heavy costs to address them, had been clearly demonstrated.

The real test came, of course, two years later in East Timor. The Howard government did not set out to play the leading role in East Timor's transition to independence that events conspired to thrust upon it, but when the time came it accepted the challenge relatively willingly. Moreover, as Howard's acceptance of the 'regional deputy' label suggests, he was happy enough, even before success was assured, to see East Timor as something of a template for Australia's future role in its close neighbourhood. This new activism was strongly reflected in the government's 2000 Defence White Paper, which was of course produced in the months after the East Timor deployment and was in these respects strongly influenced by it. The White Paper explicitly identified the preservation of stability in Australia's immediate neighbourhood as one of Australia's core strategic challenges, and one of the ADF's key tasks. Its account of the PICs' prospects was notably pessimistic,[11] and the implications of their instability for Australia's strategic interests were clearly spelled out.[12] The White Paper not only reaffirmed the security commitments to PNG under the JDP in very clear terms:[13] it also broke new ground by articulating what was, in effect, a unilateral security guarantee by Australia to the islands of the South Pacific, when it said: 'We would be very likely to provide substantial support in the unlikely event that any country in the Southwest Pacific faced substantial external aggression.'[14] The importance of these tasks in shaping the ADF's capability needs was clearly increased, with the army in particular shaped and sized specifically for stabilization operations in the immediate neighbourhood.[15] Howard, in particular, viewed the enhancement of the ADF's capacity for stabilization operations in the immediate neighbourhood as the key strategic imperative driving the White Paper process.

Even so, it was not until 2003 that the Howard Doctrine was finally implemented in its current form. Until that time, the muscular interventionism that had evolved over the 1990s remained counterbalanced by a deep caution about becoming bogged down in protracted and unwinnable deployments involving complex and ambiguous domestic political situations, and tainted by suspicions of neocolonialism. Throughout the crisis in the Solomon Islands from 2000 until mid-2003, during which time Canberra was urged to intervene by the Solomon Islands government, it consistently refused on the grounds that these were problems to be solved by the people of the Solomon Islands themselves. As Foreign Minister Alexander Downer wrote in January 2003:

> Sending in Australian troops to occupy Solomon Islands would be folly in the extreme. It would be widely resented in the Pacific Region. It would be very difficult to justify to Australian taxpayers. And for how many years would such an occupation have to continue? And what would be the exit strategy? The real show-stopper, however, is that it would not work—no matter how it was dressed up, whether as an Australian or a Commonwealth or a Pacific Islands Forum initiative. The fundamental problem is that foreigners do not have the answers for the deep-seated problems afflicting Solomon Islands.[16]

He returned to the same themes when launching the government's Foreign Policy White Paper in February 2003:

> In the South Pacific, Australia has a particular responsibility to help the small, fragile island countries deal with deep-seated problems. But we can help effectively only if the Pacific Island countries are prepared to help themselves. We are not a neocolonial power. We can't impose solutions.[17]

Catalysts for intervention

What then brought about the change in policy that led to the deployment of RAMSI only a few months later, and a few months after that the initiation of a highly ambitious program of security assistance to PNG under the Enhanced Cooperation Program (ECP), and which has since seen Australian forces return to East Timor in what looks to be a protracted and very complex engagement in the political reconstruction of that country? Five sets of factors can be identified—some of which had built up over many years, others emerging more recently.

First, by 2003 governments and publics around the world, including in Australia, had become highly aware of the ways in which chaos and disorder in weak states can pose security problems for other countries, both near and far. The most obvious catalyst for this anxiety was of course the

11 September 2001 terrorist attacks, yet even without those attacks, concerns about transnational security problems from weak states had been growing for some years.[18] In Australia's case, this was amplified by a growing sense that in the less certain and potentially quite unstable strategic milieu of post-Cold War, twenty-first century Asia—where rising powers like China were challenging the strategic status quo—Australia's traditional concerns about the vulnerability of its island neighbours to hostile intrusion seemed to regain something of its earlier importance. This was quite explicit in the 2000 White Paper, which clearly identified Australia's primary strategic interest in its immediate neighbourhood as preventing the intrusion of potentially hostile forces,[19] but it had been a growing concern throughout the 1990s.[20] Overall, Australians had an increased sense that what happened in their immediate neighbourhood mattered for their security.

Second, in the years leading up to 2003 many Australians may have developed a clearer sense of how grave the situation had become in some South Pacific countries, especially PNG and the Solomon Islands—the result not so much of any single development but of a long steady pattern of grim news and negative images.

Third, the acceptability of a policy of active engagement or intervention had been markedly transformed over the preceding decade or more. In the years after a number of South Pacific countries had gained independence, Australia was very cautious to avoid accusations of neocolonialism. During the 1990s, however, norms of humanitarian intervention had evolved around the world in response to crises in many places including the Balkans, Rwanda, Somalia, Cambodia and East Timor. These interventions legitimized highly intrusive engagement by the international community in the affairs of sovereign states in ways that, until the end of the Cold War, would have been regarded as an unacceptable violation of national sovereignty, and as unacceptably neocolonialist. By the decade's end, the principle had been firmly established that the international community had not just a right but a positive responsibility to intervene (under certain circumstances) in sovereign states, with or without the consent of the government, in order to prevent brutality, injustice and hardship. This global development obviously made it much easier for Australia to develop and to justify, both at home and internationally, a policy of closer engagement and intervention in Australia's nearer neighbourhood.

Fourth, by 2003 Australians (like many others around the world) had become more confident of their ability to make interventions—especially military action—work. After Vietnam there had been an understandable reaction against the idea that Western countries, and especially Western military forces, could do much if anything to help stabilize other lands and societies. In Australia's case, there was significant scepticism that the ADF had the resources or the skills to successfully intervene in major regional crises. At the time of the first Fiji coup in 1987, government ministers briefly considered and quickly dismissed the idea that Australian forces might intervene to restore the Bavadra government, and in 1989 they firmly decided against Australian military intervention in Bougainville to keep the Panguna mine open. During the 1990s, confidence in Australia's military capacities gradually grew; yet even in early 1999 there was little confidence in official circles that Australian forces could do much independently, or even with partners, to impose peace in East Timor if law and order broke down. It took the crisis of September 1999, when Canberra had no choice but to throw caution to the wind and lead the International Force for East Timor (INTERFET) operation in East Timor, that Australians—government and people—regained a measure of confidence that Australia, and especially the ADF, could contribute substantially to stabilizing Australia's nearer neighbours. In the 2000 White Paper—prepared immediately after the East Timor intervention—the government specifically reoriented the roles and structures of the army to give capacity for future interventions along similar lines in Australia's immediate neighbourhood.[21]

Finally, there is the complex influence of the terrorist attacks of 11 September 2001 and the global 'war on terror' that followed. It has been easy to assume that Canberra's more interventionist policy in its own neighbourhood is simply a local manifestation of the Bush administration's post-11 September strategic policy of using military force to preempt threats from failed and rogue states. My hunch is to the contrary: even without 11 September and the subsequent 'war on terror', the four factors listed above would have pushed Australia towards a more active policy in its backyard. However, the 'war on terror' provided a context in which it was easier for the government to overcome public reservations about overseas commitments, and the invasion of Iraq made it harder to deflect the arguments of those who urged more active engagement by citing, as Downer had done, the need to respect the sovereignty of others. Indeed, the timing of the government's decision to mount the RAMSI operation may have been influenced by the withdrawal of Australia's main combat forces from Iraq only a few weeks earlier.

The Howard Doctrine in action

Since Australia's new policy direction in its immediate neighbourhood was inaugurated with the launching of RAMSI in 2003, there have been significant opportunities to test its nature, scope and limits. RAMSI itself has remained in place for three years, and has scored some important successes as well as encountering some significant problems. The ECP in PNG, announced in 2003, initiated in 2004 and largely abandoned in 2005, offered important lessons in what not to do. And Australia's more recent regional commitment, the reinsertion of Australian forces along with others in East Timor in May 2006 raises further questions about what the Howard Doctrine can actually achieve. This chapter does not provide the opportunity to explore these three ventures in any detail, but we can usefully draw some broad lessons from the ways they have unfolded so far, and point to a number of important conclusions about the conditions for the success of Australia's new policy of regional engagement.

The first point to make is that none of these operations can be considered a success—at least not yet. In the Solomon Islands the initial military and police operations to restore law and order in Honiara and on the Weather Coast of Guadalcanal were highly successful, and the placement of Australian and other RAMSI officials in key government departments has restored a measure of fiscal and administrative discipline. Yet the longer-term efforts to rebuild the Solomon Islands government institutions, and to restore the faith of Solomon Islanders in their government system, have been much less successful. The riots in Honiara in April 2006, and the political instability since, have shown how little has been achieved in addressing the deeper sources of state weakness in the Solomon Islands over the past three years. As regards PNG the report is even gloomier. The ECP, which aimed to place Australian policeman in relatively large numbers into line positions in the PNG police force, and to place officials in line positions in key ministries, was dogged from the outset by deep reservations among many in the PNG government, and among wider elites, about the nature of the program and its suitability to PNG. These doubts, mobilized by characteristic displays of political opportunism, resulted in the ECP being thrown out on legal grounds within 12 months of the initial deployments. Even without these difficulties, there are real reasons to doubt that the program, though well funded, would have achieved its objectives, conceived as it was in haste, with little understanding of the deeper sources of PNG's law and order issues, and their place in the country's wider problems. In East Timor, Australia's deployment of troops and police in May 2003 may have helped prevent a major constitutional crisis and perhaps more widespread violence, but it has not helped to resolve the major political rift that was the key cause of the unrest in Dili; nor has it provided a framework for addressing the deeper-seated constitutional and social issues that underlie East Timor's fractious politics. Law and order remains fragile, politics remains fractious, and there is no clear end in sight to the role that Australia, with some others, has taken on to maintain stability.

These problems that Australia has encountered in implementing the new policy of active engagement in its neighbourhood follow a characteristic pattern. First, in each case Australian interventions have been prompted by, and focused on, overt security problems in Honiara, Port Moresby and Dili. These problems have been real enough, and serious in their impacts on the well-being of citizens, economic development and the emergence of effective government. Yet in all cases the security problems themselves are only the manifestations of much deeper institutional, political and social issues. Stopping the violence in Honiara or Dili is a necessary first step—but only a first step—towards addressing these deeper problems. Without a strategy to tackle the deeper problems, Australian intervention is merely a band-aid on a running sore. It is easy to suspect that Canberra has been tempted to focus on the immediate law and order problems not only because they are serious (and newsworthy) in themselves, but also because it has believed that in the ADF and the Australian Federal Police (AFP) it has, or is developing, policy instruments that can address them. We have discovered, however, that our policy instruments are not well suited to attending to these problems and, even if they were, they would be of little value as long as the deeper sources of lawlessness and disorder were also not effectively addressed. As we have seen in Dili, Australian soldiers are not really trained, equipped and organized for low-level law and order tasks, and when confronted with violent street gangs they have few effective responses short of lethal force. Civil policing is a highly complex and specialized business, best left to police. But even Australian police find it difficult to operate effectively in such alien and complex environments as PNG, East Timor and the Solomon Islands. Barriers of legal systems, cultures and most of all language make it extremely difficult to work effectively, and the problem of deploying and sustaining police in sufficient numbers to make a real difference remains insuperable, even with generous additional funding for extra police numbers.

The clear conclusion is that if Australia is to make any lasting difference to the security and stability of our closer neighbours, we need to develop patterns of intervention which do not rely solely or primarily on the insertion of Australian uniformed forces. Instead, Australia needs to develop programs to help its neighbours address the deep-seated weaknesses in state institutions, political systems and social structures that underlie and cause the law and order problems that flare on Australian TV screens. This is an immensely challenging task. It is not one faced by Australia alone: since the 11 September 2001 terrorist attacks, Western governments have become more aware of these challenges. For Australia the problem is more immediate, because alone among OECD countries Australia faces the risk of state failure among its closest neighbours.

The questions raised by the need to help nations build better and more effective government institutions and systems has received a lot of attention, but little in the way of clear answers have emerged.[22] What has become clear is that traditional 'aid' approaches are unlikely to succeed. A number of donor countries, including Australia, have sought to reorient their official aid programs to support 'governance', and Australia's recent White Paper on aid contains some important policy initiatives.[23] Yet aid, as traditionally conceived, only works for countries whose systems of government have reached a reasonable level of functionality: among the dysfunctional states of Australia's nearer neighbourhood there is still much further to go.

Effective intervention will require Australia to develop new forms of closer interaction with its near neighbours to help them overcome their deep-seated problems. We have no ready model of what that will look like:

clearly it cannot be a return to colonialism, but equally we can now judge that little will be gained by persevering with the kind of detachment that characterized our earlier policy approaches. It will need to involve much closer connections between Australia's economy and society with those of our smaller neighbours, including through measures like labour-market mobility that Canberra has so far shunned. It will need to be based on much closer consultation and the forging of a real consensus between Australian leaders and their neighbouring counterparts on the goals that are set and the nature and scope of Australia's role in helping to achieve them. And that will require a sustained effort to build closer, more trusting bilateral relationships, which avoid the petty squabbling that so often mars the conduct of these relationships from both sides.[24]

All this suggests that although the Howard Doctrine correctly identifies Australia's key interests and responsibilities in the stability of its small near neighbours, the government is still a long way from developing a comprehensive, effective policy approach to meeting the goals it has identified. This is a long-term issue and one that is probably generational in scope. But starting to work more effectively than we have done so far is quite urgent, as the problems to be addressed become harder with the passage of time. For that reason, finding new ways for Australia to help build effective governments among its near neighbours is among the more pressing and important of Australia's foreign policy challenges.

Notes

1 F. Brenchly, 'The Howard Defence Doctrine', *The Bulletin*, 28 September 1999, pp. 22–4.
2 Commonwealth of Australia, Parliamentary Debates, House of Representatives, Official Hansard, no. 10, 25 June 2003, pp. 17483–4.
3 N. Meaney, *The Search for Security in the Pacific 1901–14*, Sydney: Sydney University Press, 1976, p. 14.
4 Ibid., p. 18.
5 P. Spartalis, *The Diplomatic Battles of Billy Hughes*, Sydney: Hale & Iremonger, 1983.
6 O. Harries, 'Australia's New Guinea question', in W.J. Hudson (ed.) *Australia's New Guinea Question*, Melbourne: Nelson/Australian Institute of International Affairs, 1975, pp. 143–60.
7 P. Hastings, *New Guinea: Problems and Prospects*, Melbourne: Cheshire/Australian Institute of International Affairs, 1969.
8 Commonwealth of Australia, *Defence 2000: Our Future Defence Force*, Canberra: Department of Defence, 2000, p. 43.
9 See, for example, Commonwealth of Australia, *Australia's Strategic Planning in the 1990's*, Canberra: Department of Defence, September 1992, p. 26.
10 M. O'Callaghan, *Enemies Within: Papua New Guinea, Australia and the Sandline Crisis: The Inside Story*, Sydney and New York: Doubleday, 1999.
11 Commonwealth of Australia, *Defence 2000*, pp. 22–3.
12 Ibid., pp. 30–1.
13 Ibid., p. 43.
14 Ibid., p. 44.

15 Ibid., pp. 79–80.
16 A. Downer, 'Neighbours cannot be recolonised', *The Australian,* 8 January 2003, p. 11.
17 The Hon. Alexander Downer MP, Minister for Foreign Affairs, Australia, 'White paper on foreign affairs & trade: advancing the national interest', speech to the National Press Club, Canberra, 12 February 2003.
18 Commonwealth of Australia, *Australia's Strategic Planning in the 1990's,* p. 8.
19 Commonwealth of Australia, *Defence 2000,* pp. 30–1.
20 Commonwealth of Australia *Defending Australia: Defence White Paper 1994,* Canberra: Department of Defence, 1994, p. 92; and Commonwealth of Australia, *Australia's Strategic Policy,* Canberra: Department of Defence, 1997, p. 13.
21 Commonwealth of Australia, *Defence 2000.*
22 F. Fukuyama, *State-Building: Governance and World Order in the 21st Century,* Ithaca, NY: Cornell University Press, 2004.
23 Commonwealth of Australia, *Australian Aid: Promoting Growth and Stability. A White Paper on the Australian Government's Overseas Aid Program,* Canberra: AusAID, 2006.
24 H. White and E. Wainwright, *Strengthening our Neighbour: Australia and the Future of Papua New Guinea,* Canberra: Australian Strategic Policy Institute, 2004.

9   Australia–New Zealand

Robert Ayson

As a pair of countries, and natural alliance partners, Australia and New Zealand form a rather unique combination in international politics. Yet they are by no means identical twins. They are more akin to being very close, but sometimes competitive, brothers. Australia is the much larger sibling and is older too—in geological, pre-European and European settlement terms. It has historically experienced the advantages and risks of its much closer proximity to Asia. Half a world away from traditional protectors, this distance has helped generate a steely Australian determination towards self-help and self-reliance. At the same time commonly regarded (including by some other countries) as a medium regional power with a major stake in the regional balance, Australia has had a natural inclination to look first to those larger and stronger powers with similar traditions and/ or interests. For the past 60 years this has meant, more often than not, the United States. What it will be in another 60 years is interesting to speculate, but the enmeshing of Australia with East Asia is leading to some very interesting relationships.

New Zealand is the far smaller and younger of the two. While it has no pretensions of medium power status, New Zealand has a strong independent streak and a well-developed capacity to promote its own national interests. Less exposed by geography than Australia, New Zealand has sometimes given the impression of pursuing internationalist causes as luxuries only the unthreatened can afford. But its small size (geographically and economically) and isolation also generate a particular sense of vulnerability and have encouraged it to look west for the natural protection which the island continent of Australia provides. These features have also given New Zealand an experience of small state politics which has come in handy when engaging with some of the micro-polities of the South Pacific (with whom it has strong cultural connections).

As the smaller sibling, Wellington's first instinct has often been to wonder what Canberra is thinking or doing about a particular issue—although this has sometimes arisen from competitive as well as cooperative impulses. The reverse applies much less frequently. Australia has fewer natural reasons to consider developments across the Tasman Sea, and the interest in trans-Tasman defence cooperation is generally stronger in New Zealand than it is in Australia. This sets up a fascinating asymmetry between these two Australasian countries—one which has not always helped them to build the strongest of alliance relationships. The main concern of this chapter is to determine what factors have encouraged direct alliance cooperation between them, as well as the factors which have tended to be less helpful in this regard.

ANZUS and great and powerful friends

There is more than one way to approach the bilateral alliance relationship between Australia and New Zealand. Given the importance of Australia's own ANZUS relationship with the United States in Canberra's strategic planning, however, it is appropriate for the purposes of this volume to begin by considering the Australia–New Zealand relationship as the least talked about and third leg of that trilateral treaty. Of course, New Zealand is rather more famous (or infamous) for having taken on the mantle of a suspended alliance partner after its mid-1980s rift with the United States over port visits by nuclear capable American vessels.

Under ANZUS the two Australasian neighbours remain committed to 'act to meet the common danger' in the event that either country is attacked directly or if their armed forces are attacked in the 'Pacific area'. Perhaps because security cooperation between Australia and New Zealand has sometimes been assumed as a natural given, and also because they were the two junior parties to the 1951 ANZUS Treaty, very little public attention has been devoted to the trans-Tasman application of this provision. Instead, the major focus of ANZUS from its establishment was in terms of the security relationships that Canberra and Wellington each were able to enjoy with the United States. At the time the treaty was signed, both were still concerned about Japan's possible rearmament: the alliance helped cement the US regional presence as insurance against inimical changes in the Asian balance. This was especially important for security-conscious Australia lying far closer than New Zealand to the East Asian zones of conflict.[1] A key imperative for Canberra was what the alliance might mean should Australia get into a difficult situation with one of its large northern neighbours in Southeast Asia, such as Indonesia. For Washington, the treaty recognized the support it was receiving in Korea in the early 1950s from Canberra and Wellington.

Indeed, ANZUS linked the two Antipodean democracies into Washington's San Francisco system of alliances which was designed to contain the communist challenge in Asia. The sense of their own bilateral alliance relationship in this period rested considerably on a series of parallel commitments to regional conflicts under either US or British leadership.[2] In addition to the Korean War commitment, the two Australasian states also contributed forces to the US-led war in Vietnam. Alongside Britain, they committed forces to the Emergency in Malaya and then in the mid-1960s to

Malaysia in its struggle against the *Konfrontasi* policy of Indonesia's then President Sukarno. Moreover, alongside Britain and the United States (and also France, Pakistan, Thailand and the Philippines), they were parties to the Southeast Asia Treaty Organisation (SEATO) until that 1954 agreement terminated in the mid-1970s, and with Britain to the Australia, New Zealand and Malaya arrangement from 1949–71. New Zealand and Australian forces were stationed forward alongside each other in Southeast Asia as major co-contributors to the Commonwealth Strategic Reserve. And then, upon Britain's withdrawal from East of Suez, they became parties in 1971 with London to the Five Power Defence Arrangements (FPDA) for the external defence of Singapore and Malaysia.

Hence the idea of an alliance relationship between Australia and New Zealand was shaped more by their common involvement in multilateral alliance relationships involving other powers than it was by direct trans-Tasman defence cooperation.[3] This showed up as well in the series of intelligence relationships which they shared with Britain and the United States[4] and in the way both countries came to signify ANZUS as the cornerstone of their respective defence policies. Their mutual commitment to forward defence in Asia in the 1950s and 1960s was more a coincidence of focus than a grand bargain directly between them.

Something similar might be said of their respective commitments in an earlier age—as loyal members of the British Empire—to the Boer War and the First World War. The latter did of course produce the Australia and New Zealand Army Corps (ANZAC) in 1914—a name immortalized on the unforgiving hillsides of Gallipoli in the following year. But this tradition did not develop an especially strong pattern of direct cooperation which would outlast the First World War. Neither had the dispatch some half a century earlier of Australian colonial soldiers to help fight the New Zealand wars.

Around the middle of the twentieth century one can locate a moment when the two countries sought formally to establish a direct alliance relationship with each other without anyone else in the room. This was the Canberra Pact signed in 1944 as both countries looked to their mutual interests in cooperation on security in the immediate regional neighbourhood once the Second World War had ended, in part out of concerns that their mutual interests would not be recognized by major allies in the forthcoming postwar period.[5] And unlike ANZUS, the Canberra Pact was not built on an effective promise to render assistance in the event of external attack. Instead, it was more a promise to share the security burden in the South Pacific, envisioning 'a regional zone of defence comprising the South West and South Pacific areas ... based on Australia and New Zealand, stretching through the arc of islands north and northeast of Australia to Western Samoa and the Cook Islands'.[6]

This zone was never established in any formal sense. Instead there was an ongoing and largely tacit regional division of labour between the two countries, with Australia having greater responsibility for security in Melanesia (including its then territory Papua New Guinea (PNG)) and New Zealand a greater focus upon security in the Polynesian subregion (including for its own territories of the Cook Islands, Niue and Tokelau, as well as Western Samoa). During the first four decades of the postwar period the main task was to help steer a number of these entities to independent statehood: Samoa achieved this status, for example, in 1962 and PNG did so some 13 years later. However, there were few developments on their local security front, and little enthusiasm in either capital to respond to them, to bring the Australia–New Zealand strategic relationship into prominence. Instead it was as team members of the larger British and US-led enterprises in East Asia that precipitated their major combat commitments, force structure purchases and strategic guidance. And even this did not see extensive attention focused on the bilateral alliance relationship between the two Australasian countries as a priority in and of itself.

Self-reliance, the ANZUS crisis and Closer Defence Relations

When that forward defence team effort ended with the withdrawal of British forces from the region and the Nixon administration's Guam Doctrine, Australia and New Zealand had more reason to consider their own immediate security environments. They were to some extent now unified by a mutual sense of strategic loneliness. This helped generate momentum for greater practical cooperation. Having signed a Memorandum of Understanding (MOU) in 1969 on Cooperation in Defence Supply,[7] the two countries established the Australia–New Zealand Consultative Committee on Defence Consultation three years later which reported to annual meetings between the respective defence ministers and which encouraged subsequent movement towards greater collaboration in equipment supply, defence activities, exercises and training.[8] By 1977 officials from the two countries were meeting annually in the Australian–New Zealand Defence Policy Group.[9]

At a broader strategic level, the two countries' experiences during this period were similar but by no means identical. For Canberra, the transition from forward defence was especially significant and decisive. By the early 1970s, strategic visionaries such as Arthur Tange were ready with ideas of Australian defence self-reliance[10] which came into full view in the 1976 Defence White Paper and later underpinned the defence of Australia logic in the momentous review by Paul Dibb of Australia's defence capabilities.[11] In alliance terms this actually encouraged a continuing Australian focus on its ANZUS relationship with the United States: cooperation in defence training, equipment and in intelligence with the leader of the Western world was a prerequisite for effective Australian self-reliance, especially if this included the capacity to mount independent missions in the local area.

Looking back on that era, one is tempted to argue that New Zealand found it rather more difficult to identify a clear and lasting focus for its defence efforts with the ending of forward defence. This difference was symbolized in the fact that its forces took many years longer than their Australian counterparts to return home from Singapore, although this had as much to do with the need for additional base infrastructure in New Zealand as any other factor. In part because of the country's benign strategic isolation, the defence of New Zealand did not translate especially well as an organizing concept. If there was a closer to home focus it was in terms of New Zealand's interests in Pacific security, which received increasing emphasis in the 1978 and 1983 Defence White Papers,[12] and which also helped energize Australia–New Zealand cooperation.

That same isolation (as distinct from isolationism) made New Zealand more ready to question the priority of its own alliance relationship with the United States. When David Lange's Labour government was elected in 1984 with a strong anti-nuclear policy platform, most New Zealanders still supported ANZUS. Yet events transpired to allow them to have only one of the two: once the ban on visits by nuclear capable vessels (armed and powered) became legislation as the 1987 New Zealand Nuclear Free Zone, Disarmament and Arms Control Act, the Reagan administration's approach became unyielding, suspending its ANZUS obligations to New Zealand.[13] ANZUS had clearly lost the use of one of its three legs.

This diplomatic crisis stimulated both tensions and cooperation in Australia–New Zealand alliance relations which at long last were also in the spotlight. On the debit side of the ledger, Canberra was disappointed that its neighbour had allowed the anti-nuclear cause to wreak havoc on the New Zealand–US security relationship (although it must be said that Canberra benefited from the flattering contrasts which highlighted its own alliance loyalty in American eyes). An ongoing Australian bilateral defence relationship with New Zealand meant the establishment of a separate set of exercises now that Wellington had been excluded from such activities involving US forces. Limits also applied to the sharing of US-sourced intelligence with New Zealand.[14] Moreover, without close US–New Zealand security links, there were prospects of significant gaps between the experiences (and proficiency) of the two Australasian defence forces, potentially affecting their ability to operate with one another.[15]

Despite this, the net result from Wellington's dispute with Washington was greater encouragement for trans-Tasman defence cooperation.[16] In a sense, Australia was now New Zealand's (last) great and powerful friend. As part of the down payment for further bilateral cooperation, the Labour government entered into the ANZAC frigate project, ordering two vessels with the potential (and expectation) to acquire two more. Wellington and Canberra were both becoming increasingly concerned about Pacific security—what had hitherto seemed a rather peaceful lake had been ruptured by instability in Vanuatu and most especially by the 1987 coups in Fiji. New Zealand's 1987 Defence White Paper was remarkable most of all for its emphasis on Pacific security and on cooperation with Australia. The two countries also cooperated extensively in the establishment of a South Pacific nuclear-free zone, confirmation that the Hawke Labor government in Canberra also had strong anti-nuclear convictions.

Australia's emphasis on the defence of its northern maritime approaches also connected with trans-Tasman policy. New Zealand's frigates and its combat and maritime patrol aircraft potentially (or perhaps apocryphally) added 20 per cent or more to the effective Australian order of battle should any crisis arise. In this way, the defence of Australia was effectively becoming a priority mission for New Zealand as well. The institutionalization of Australia–New Zealand policy coordination was also moving forward. On the economic front there had already been significant progress in policy harmonization and collaboration, symbolized and encouraged by the arrival in 1983 of Closer Economic Relations (CER)—a replacement for the less effective New Zealand–Australia Free Trade Agreement of mid-1960s vintage,[17] a pathway to a single economic market between the two countries and a stimulus to the free-trade agreements which Australia and New Zealand were to seek with other regional countries in coming years.

Formal measures for defence cooperation had also been developing. In that same year the two countries signed a new MOU on Defence Logistic Cooperation[18] and in 1991 they launched Closer Defence Relations (CDR). This more comprehensive process was established to encourage further consultation and cooperation on detailed defence matters (including force structure development, equipment procurement, interoperability and training[19]) and raised in some minds (including then Australian Defence Minister Robert Ray) the rather distant prospect of an eventually combined defence force. By this time New Zealand also had a National Party government back in office which had committed itself to strengthening and restoring traditional security partnerships and which returned to speaking of Australia and New Zealand as a 'single strategic entity'. This phrase had been used by the prime ministers of both countries in a 1976 meeting in New Zealand[20] and had featured in the 1983 White Paper: Ball is correct to note the degree of hyperbole in such a notion.[21]

That unity, and the collaboration which was occurring under CDR, still did not apply in any event to the sort of alliance relationships which the two countries could enjoy (or in Wellington's case, not enjoy) with the United States. The logic of domestic politics meant that New Zealand's non-nuclear legislation remained in place under the Bolger National governments and, with it, the suspension of formal US–New Zealand defence relations. Moreover, many officials and observers in Canberra became increasingly disappointed at Wellington's limited commitment to defence expenditure—which had been capped after an early 1990s recession, putting at risk future ANZAC frigate purchases and other forms of substantial defence collaboration.

That said, common concerns about Pacific security continued to develop as a thread keeping the two countries in effective cooperation—in 1997, for example, New Zealand led an unarmed Truce Monitoring Group to Bougainville after the signing of the Burnham Agreement outside Christchurch.[22] Australia contributed heavily to this mission. While it was not possible for Canberra to take the lead initially because of its close historical relationship with PNG, it headed the subsequent Peace Monitoring Group in which New Zealand remained substantially involved. Further afield, Australian and New Zealand forces also continued to work together in multilateral exercises under the FPDA, although Canberra's extensive investment in force structure suitable for possible combat operations in East Asia made it a much more attractive partner for Singapore in particular.

Divergence, convergence and the Pacific factor

By the close of the twentieth century the bilateral alliance relationship between Australia and New Zealand was demonstrating contending patterns of collusion and collision. The latter theme appeared to have taken over completely in the aftermath of New Zealand's 1999 general election which brought to power the first of a series of left-of-centre coalition governments led by Helen Clark's Labour Party. The new government's first major decision on defence was to cancel its predecessor's option to purchase F-16 combat aircraft to replace the Royal New Zealand Air Force's ageing A-4 *Skyhawks* (which were eventually removed from service, including from Nowra in New South Wales where about half of them had come to be based since 1991). In addition, the new government confirmed Australian suspicions that there would be no additional ANZAC frigates and also toyed at one stage with the idea of removing from service the valuable P-3 *Orion* maritime patrol aircraft.

In place of a small, balanced New Zealand Defence Force (NZDF), the Clark government opted for a strengthened army and emphasized the supporting functions of the reconfigured air force and navy. For an Australia committed to strengthening its own maritime combat capabilities, with one eye on the wider Asian region and the other on its own maritime approaches, this might well have been the final straw in the bilateral relationship. Some observers on both sides of the Tasman Sea saw this as evidence of a significant and potentially mortal divergence in strategic policy.[23]

Fortunately, external events of the time conspired to strengthen rather than demolish this strategic partnership. In the second half of 1999, New Zealand had joined the Australian-led INTERFET force in East Timor in the aftermath of the severe post-referendum violence in that soon-to-be independent country. New Zealand's largest military deployment since the Korean War helped underscore the value of trans-Tasman defence cooperation in the nearer neighbourhood—not on the basis of a formal agreement but, rather, in terms of real-time cooperation in regional crisis management. Given Australian concerns about what some of its leading analysts have called 'the arc of instability,'[24] an NZDF restructured with these sorts of mission in mind could be especially useful.[25] Indeed, four years later New Zealand also contributed forces to another Australian-led multilateral mission—the Regional Assistance Mission to Solomon Islands (RAMSI). In 2006, as street violence erupted in the Solomon Islands capital of Honiara and then in East Timor's Dili, Australia and New Zealand were quick to send additional forces back to these two fragile small states.

This is not to imply a complete harmony of approach: Australia tended to prefer a stronger military component to missions, whilst New Zealand gave more emphasis to the police and civilian-led components of these endeavours. But the difficult challenges of encouraging stability in a number of Melanesian states have concentrated minds in both Canberra and Wellington and helped energize the bilateral security relationship between them. To this extent at least, bad news in the immediate neighbourhood has been good news for Australia–New Zealand security relations—a broader trend which might be traced back as early as 1883 when the convention held by the Australian colonies and New Zealand attempted to draw London's attention to their concerns about non-British penetration in the Pacific.[26]

The alliance impact of the 'war on terror'

A similar unifying effect might also be said of the 'war on terror' period which began in the wake of the 11 September 2001 attacks on the United States. Given the closeness of US–Australian strategic relations (and the fact that Prime Minister John Howard was in Washington on that fateful day), Canberra's response was always going to be more prominent. As discussed elsewhere in this volume, Australia invoked ANZUS for the first time (and if one had polled the signatories in 1951 about the likely catalysts for that first invocation, it is unlikely an attack on the American eastern seaboard would have rated much mention). The Howard government then dispatched significant elements of the Australian Defence Force to Afghanistan to help remove the Taliban and seek out al Qaeda. And when the call came from Washington to join the 2003 invasion against Saddam Hussein's Iraq, Canberra joined the small 'coalition of the willing' who contributed to the initial combat phase. Australian forces remain stationed in both Afghanistan and Iraq and have been expanded in their size and scope in response to the deteriorating internal security circumstances in both countries.

The Iraq case might well be used as evidence for the case for divergence in Australian and New Zealand strategic policies, and as possible signs of strains in their relationship in the US-led 'war on terror'. It is certainly true that the Clark Labour government did not join the war against Iraq, and unlike the Howard, Bush and Blair administrations, it argued that diplomacy through the United Nations needed to be given more time. New Zealand did, however, make a modest subsequent contribution to the nation-building project in Iraq: army engineers were deployed for approximately 12 months from September 2003. Moreover, while Wellington did not invoke ANZUS after 11 September 2001, its contribution to Afghanistan, including special forces and later a Provincial Reconstruction Team, represented something of a parallel commitment with Australia to an overseas conflict situation. The work of Australian and New Zealand forces in Afghanistan alongside their NATO colleagues has also raised the possibility of increased NATO collaboration with the two Antipodean defence forces.[27]

It is certainly true that Washington has given especially significant recognition to the Australian commitments to Iraq and Afghanistan. According to the Pentagon's 2006 Quadrennial Defense Review, the 'unique' relations the United States enjoyed with Australia and the United Kingdom were 'models for the breadth and depth of cooperation that the United States seeks to foster with other allies and partners around the world'.[28] But the George W. Bush administration has also warmed to New Zealand's contribution to the campaign against international terrorism, symbolized by the award in 2004 of a US Navy Presidential Unit Citation to New Zealand's special forces. While a return to a fully functioning trilateral ANZUS is not necessarily on the cards, there are elements of a slightly thawed US–New Zealand defence relationship, including Washington's recognition of the joint effort Australia and New Zealand have been making in their own region.[29] On the whole, Washington has regarded the 'arc of instability' as an arena for Canberra's leadership, but there is also awareness of New Zealand's contribution.

Here the logic of the 'war on terror' has worked to both Canberra and Wellington's advantage. Since 11 September 2001 Washington has been especially wary of the dangers which may develop in and from weak and failing states and, with a good part of the arc seeming to be at risk of such status, trans-Tasman cooperation in regional stabilization has been welcomed by the senior ANZUS member. Yet there are reasons aside from the 'war on terror' *per se* which have motivated the two Pacific hegemons and which have also invigorated their own bilateral relationship. Both have been keen, for example, to boost cooperation among Pacific police and customs agencies in the fight against transnational crime, and both also have broader concerns about the future stability of a number of Pacific polities. Indeed Pacific security issues tend to dominate the regular meetings between the defence ministers of the two countries, which serve to testify to the strength of the bilateral relationship and which reflect the pragmatic understanding in both capitals of their different but by no means incompatible defence outlooks.

Australia, New Zealand and the changing Asian balance

Further afield in the Asia–Pacific the basis for a strong Australia–New Zealand alliance relationship has perhaps been more uncertain, but remains full of possibilities nonetheless. In part because Australia has kept shaping its defence force for the potential demands of contingencies in East Asia, where it might well be called on to collaborate with its superpower ally the United States, and because New Zealand has not been doing so, the prospects would seem to look good on paper for divergent behaviour in the event of a major security crisis in East Asia.

The first major foreign policy challenge for the incoming Howard government in 1996 was the Taiwan Strait crisis between Washington and Beijing: Canberra sided with its ANZUS ally. In the years since, Bush administration officials, including one-time Deputy Secretary of State Richard Armitage, have gone to some length in public to remind Australia that its help would be expected in the event of another crisis in the Taiwan Strait. But as Australia's relationship with a rising China has become increasingly valuable economically (and more generally as well), such a choice has become increasingly painful to contemplate. During an August 2004 visit to Beijing, Foreign Minister Alexander Downer opined that ANZUS would not require Australia to go to America's assistance in such a crisis.[30] Both he and Prime Minister Howard have repeatedly indicated Australia's opposition to any attempts to contain China. While some of the heat may well have departed the Taiwan issue, the bubbling over of Sino–Japanese tensions in recent years portends an even graver choice for Australia given the closeness of its ties with all major parties—Japan and its superpower supporter the United States, and China itself.

Traditionally one might have been tempted to contrast the Australian predicament here with New Zealand's freedom from any alliance entanglements. The curse of being an alliance free rider (as New Zealand has sometimes appeared to be) is also the blessing of avoiding alliance entrapment. To some extent this is a valid comparison, but the two countries are perhaps converging a little more than some may think. On the one hand there are Australia's attempts to extend its relationship with China and to also retain its hearty alliance with the United States. Canberra's commitments in Afghanistan and Iraq have been welcome in this context because they allow the US alliance to be advanced in a part of the world where Sino–American strategic competition is less palpable. As a result, Australia can afford to play for some wriggle room in East Asia. On the other hand, New Zealand is coming in from the cold to some extent in Washington's calculations, again partly thanks to its own commitments in the Middle East and Central Asia, but at the same time values very much its own warm relationship with Beijing.

Moreover, Australia and New Zealand are watching very closely the emerging architecture in East Asia which may betray the shape of the changing regional balance of power. Both have been negotiating free-trade agreements with China and both attend the East Asia Summit to which Washington is not invited. While this fledgling process may or may not lead anywhere, Wellington and Canberra both signed ASEAN's Treaty of Amity and Cooperation (TAC) as an entry condition, although it must be said that the Howard government did so much more reluctantly. The two Australasian countries have common interests in the peaceful regional management of the simultaneous integration of a re-emerging China, a rising India and a more assertive Japan. Both fear being left out should a more exclusive, East Asian, regional model take shape—and the links between Closer Economic Relations (CER) and the ASEAN Free Trade Area (AFTA) are important here for their wider, non-economic significance. Hence while their respective abilities to contribute to an East Asian crisis are quite different in defence capability terms, they have some close parallel interests in what might be called 'forward diplomacy'.

Indeed there are other reasons to consider the Australia–New Zealand alliance from a wider perspective than traditional defence calculations. In 2001 Wellington provided significant support to Australia in processing many of the asylum seekers who had been rescued by the Norwegian vessel, the MV *Tampa*. As some Pacific states face the prospects of submersion due to sea-level rise, Australia and New Zealand have a common interest in generating common policies on resettlement from such regional countries. For many years New Zealand has offered employment access for citizens of Samoa, Tonga and Fiji. A common labour mobility approach towards Melanesian states may offer a safety valve for these quickly growing countries without which more serious internal security problems may develop. The spread of HIV/AIDS in parts of the Pacific, which will place a severe governance strain on some regional countries (especially in PNG), will require continuing trans-Tasman consultation. The growing pressure on maritime resources, especially fisheries, is being felt in Australian and New Zealand waters, and the development of new patrol boats and associated capabilities by the two countries can be used for mutual benefit. Along with important defence collaboration—including a Status of Forces Agreement, active since May 2005—these trends point in the direction of what might become Closer Security Relations (CSR) between Australia and New Zealand. This might in turn be something of a model for the development of Australia's relations with other regional partners as alliance relationships expand from their traditional defence and intelligence foundations.

Conclusion: explaining Australasian alliance cooperation

This chapter began by considering the Australia–New Zealand alliance relationship as one of the three (original) legs of the tripartite ANZUS Treaty. The ensuing analysis might suggest, however, that there is an inverse relationship between the energy Canberra and Wellington devote to their own bilateral defence relationship and to their respective relations with major external allies, especially the United States. This shows up in at least three episodes when there was considerable concern about New Zealand's and/or Australia's relations with that great and powerful friend: (1) with the Canberra Pact in 1944; (2) the stimulus to focusing on the immediate neighbourhood following Britain's withdrawal from East of Suez and

Washington's Guam Doctrine; and (3) the aftermath of New Zealand's ANZUS crisis with the United States in the mid-1980s. The experience of the 'war on terror' period may be an exception to this rule.

An argument can also be made that there is a proportional relationship between the health of the trans-Tasman alliance and the degree to which both powers are focusing on security in the South Pacific. This in turn links in with the previous proposition, because there has been a tendency for New Zealand and Australia's alliance relations with the United States (and earlier with Britain) to emphasize commitments *beyond* the Pacific. Certainly the recent era of cooperative commitments to Bougainville, East Timor and the Solomon Islands has highlighted the significant closer regional foundations of alliance relations between the two countries.

Again, however, we should be wary of making iron-clad rules. Strong interests on both sides of the Tasman in Pacific security affairs—as we are seeing currently—do not mean that there are identical views emanating from Canberra and Wellington. There is a sense of competitiveness in their relationship which goes beyond the rugby field and has deep historical foundations. As Corner has observed, Richard Seddon (New Zealand's premier from 1893 to 1906) 'regarded the South Pacific as New Zealand's special sphere, not Australia's'.[31] In his recent study of the relationship, Rolfe notes the continuing symbolism of New Zealand's decision in 1901 not to take up the option to join the Australian Federation.[32] Aside from personal preferences, the effect of peculiar geographies, histories and cultures should not be underestimated. Yet the two countries have now moved into an era where they seem quite comfortable in acknowledging these differences, and in seeing how these might encourage complementary (rather than unitary) strategic entities. Their alliance is probably the better for this realization.

Notes

1 J. Rolfe, 'Australia–New Zealand relations: allies, friends, rivals', in Asia–Pacific Center for Security Studies, *Asia's Bilateral Relations*, Honolulu, HI: APCSS, 2004, p. 2.
2 P. Edwards, *Crises and Commitments: The Politics and Diplomacy of Australia's Involvement in Southeast Asian Conflicts, 1948–1965*, Sydney: Allen & Unwin, 1992.
3 H. Bull, 'Australia–New Zealand defence cooperation', in K. Keith (ed.) *Defence Perspectives: Papers Read at the 1972 Otago Foreign Policy School*, Wellington: Price Milburn, 1972, pp. 103–4.
4 A. Burnett, *The A–NZ–US Triangle*, Canberra: Australian National University, Strategic and Defence Studies Centre, 1988, p. 117.
5 J.A. Nockels, 'Australia–New Zealand defence cooperation in the Asia–Pacific region', in D. Ball (ed.) *The ANZAC Connection*, Sydney: George Allen & Unwin, 1985, pp. 82–90.
6 Quoted in Bull, 'Australia–New Zealand defence cooperation', p. 108.

7 D. Ball, 'The security relationship between Australia and New Zealand', in Ball, *The ANZAC Connection*, pp. 38–39.
8 Nockels, 'Australia–New Zealand defence cooperation in the Asia–Pacific region', p. 86.
9 I. McGibbon, 'New Zealand's defence policy from Vietnam to the Gulf', in B. Brown (ed.) *New Zealand in World Affairs, Vol. 3, 1992–1990*, Wellington: Victoria University Press, 1999, pp. 111–42.
10 P. Edwards, *Arthur Tange: Last of the Mandarins*, Crows Nest, NSW: Allen & Unwin, 2006, pp. 193–7.
11 P. Dibb, *Review of Australia's Defence Capabilities: Report to the Minister for Defence by Mr Paul Dibb*, Canberra: Australian Government Publishing Service, 1986.
12 McGibbon, 'New Zealand's defence policy from Vietnam to the Gulf', p. 116.
13 Ibid., p. 125.
14 Rolfe, 'Australia–New Zealand relations: allies, friends, rivals', p. 5.
15 G. Keating, *Opportunities and Obstacles: Future Australian and New Zealand Cooperation on Defence and Security Issues*, working paper no. 391, Canberra: Strategic and Defence Studies Centre, Australian National University, 2004, p. 4.
16 P. Jennings, 'Achieving closer defence relations with New Zealand', in R.A. Hall (ed.) *Australia–New Zealand: Closer Defence Relationships*, Canberra: Australian Defence Studies Centre, 1993, p. 51.
17 S. Hoadley, 'Trans-Tasman relations: CER and CDR', in Brown, *New Zealand in World Affairs, Vol. 3*, p. 180.
18 Ball, 'The security relationship between Australia and New Zealand', p. 37.
19 R. Thakur, 'Closer defence relations: costs and benefits to New Zealand', in Hall, *Australia–New Zealand: Closer Defence Relationships*, pp. 107–8.
20 Jennings, 'Achieving closer defence relations with New Zealand', p. 50.
21 Ball, 'The security relationship between Australia and New Zealand', p. 34.
22 R. Adams (ed.) *Peace on Bougainville—Truce Monitoring Group*, Wellington: Victoria University Press, 2001.
23 M. Bradford, 'Why have New Zealand and Australia drifted apart', in B. Brown (ed.) *New Zealand and Australia—Where are We Going?*, Wellington: New Zealand Institute of International Affairs, 2001, pp. 27–8; and R.G. Patman, 'Globalisation and trans-Tasman relations: integration or divergence', *Australian Journal of International Affairs*, vol. 55, no. 3, 2001, p. 398.
24 P. Dibb, D.D. Hale and P. Prince, 'Asia's insecurity', *Survival*, vol. 41, no. 3, 1999, p. 18.
25 Keating, 'Opportunities and obstacles: future Australian and New Zealand cooperation on defence and security issues', p. 6.
26 F.H. Corner, 'New Zealand and the South Pacific', in T.C. Larkin (ed.) *New Zealand's External Relations*, Wellington: New Zealand Institute of Public Administration, 1962, p. 135.
27 NATO, 'Secretary General discusses security cooperation in New Zealand', *NATO Update*, 24 March 2005.
28 United States Department of Defense, *Quadrennial Defense Review Report*, 6 February 2006, p. 7.
29 C. James, 'Trends in New Zealand', paper for Australia–New Zealand Leadership Forum, Auckland, 5 May 2006.
30 The Hon. Alexander Downer MP, Minister for Foreign Affairs, Australia, media conference transcript, Beijing, 17 August 2004.
31 Corner, 'New Zealand and the South Pacific', p. 136.
32 Rolfe, 'Australia–New Zealand relations: allies, friends, rivals', p. 2.

10 Australia–Singapore

Ron Huisken

Singapore, self-governing since 1959, emerged as a sovereign state on 9 August 1965. As Britain's largest military base in what was then called the Far East, Singapore had, however, figured quite prominently in Australia's security and defence thinking for decades prior to 1965. This account takes the position that any sensible perspective on the evolution of the security relationship between Australia and Singapore should look back to 1941 and the Japanese invasion and occupation of the Malay Peninsula.

The Australia–Singapore defence relationship falls broadly into two eras. The first, 1945–75, was defined by a prolonged but generally graceful process of decolonization, by communist insurgency and wider strategic concerns about communist expansion, and by the creation of the post-colonial political map of Southeast Asia. The second era, 1975 to the present, has been defined by the economic and political maturation of Southeast Asia and by a sustained, if uneven, transformation in the character of Australia's relationship with this region generally and perhaps with Singapore in particular.

The Second World War

Australia's first diplomatic representative in Southeast Asia was a single officer assigned to Singapore in 1941 as the prospect of war in the Pacific became more urgent. Almost, coincidentally, in an act of unthinkable independence, Australia defied London and Winston Churchill to unilaterally redirect its 8th Division (then at sea en route to the Middle East) to Singapore. The division had barely three weeks to settle in before being fully engaged alongside British and other Commonwealth forces in a futile effort to halt the Japanese advance down the Malay Peninsula toward Singapore in January/February 1942 and ultimately beyond into the Dutch East Indies. Some 2,000 Australians were killed in this campaign and more than 15,000 became prisoners of war. Many thousands of Australians therefore shared with the residents of Singapore the cruel hardships of Japan's military occupation for the next three and a half years. The bond that emerged from this experience, while certainly complex, was strong and overwhelmingly positive.

The Malay Emergency

Australian military personnel still in Singapore when Japan surrendered in August 1945 were quite promptly repatriated as Australia transitioned as quickly as it could from wartime mobilization. Australian policy toward Southeast Asia was buffeted by contradictory impulses. On the one hand, despite the shocks and disappointments of 1941–2 and the clear signals from postwar Britain that it had neither the means nor the will to restore the pre-war status quo, Australia still drew great comfort from a renewed British presence in Malay and Singapore—which remained a reassuringly distant first line of defence against whatever new perils might emerge from Asia. On the other hand, however, Australian policymakers were conscious that powerful forces were arrayed against colonialism—Washington for one, nationalism for another. Moreover, many of them believed that this practice should pass into history and that it would be wrong as well as short-sighted for Australia to support its perpetuation anywhere. Australia therefore found itself supporting Indonesia's independence from the Dutch while quietly relieved about the resumption of British rule in its territories on the Malay Peninsula and in Borneo and, indeed, disposed to prolong it.

In June 1948, the Malayan Communist Party began its campaign to achieve its political objectives through military means and a state of emergency was declared in Malaya and Singapore. The Emergency, as it came to be termed, endured officially until 1960, although counterinsurgency operations declined to very modest levels after the mid-1950s. From 1948, Britain routinely engaged Australia and New Zealand in discussions on the security of the Malayan area. Australia faced almost immediate pressure from the United Kingdom for a military contribution to the Emergency. Canberra, however, prevaricated, relishing neither the human and financial costs nor the risk of having nascent nationalist sentiments in the area directed against Australia. In addition, it was apparent even in these early years that the British commitment was no longer indefinite. An enduring strand of calculation in Australian assessments therefore became not inadvertently triggering a premature drawdown of British forces because London believed or could argue that British forces were no longer essential to the security of these colonial territories.

What Britain desired from Australia, above all, was ground troops, yet Canberra parried these requests for some seven years. In 1950, Australia agreed to deploy military transport aircraft (C-47s) and a squadron of *Lincoln* bombers (a four-engine heavy bomber from the Second World War) to Singapore for use in counterinsurgency operations. The C-47s left in 1952 but the *Lincoln* bombers stayed until 1958 when they were replaced by jet aircraft (*Canberra* bombers and F-86 fighters) and their base moved to Butterworth in Malaya.

The first Australian ground forces arrived in Malaya in October 1955, and comprised an infantry battalion of about 800 men, a field artillery battery and an airfield construction team tasked to upgrade the Butterworth base to jet-age standards. The total number of personnel was less than 1,400—the ceiling imposed by Canberra. This commitment—a battalion of infantry and a changing mix of engineers, artillery, pilots, aircraft maintenance crews and special forces—was sustained for the next 18 years; that is, until 1974.

Although Malaya achieved independence in 1957 and the Emergency officially ended in July 1960, Australia continued to deploy its infantry battalion in that country. In 1961–2, having successfully ousted the Dutch from West Papua, Indonesia registered its political objections to plans to incorporate British territories in Borneo along with Singapore into the new Federation of Malaysia. Then, in January 1963, Indonesia's foreign minister signalled Jakarta's determination to 'confront' this new entity. Later that year, Indonesian forces began border incursions into Borneo. Britain promptly deployed additional troops to Sabah and Sarawak in Borneo and again pressured Canberra and Wellington to contribute to this new campaign.

Konfrontasi, as it came to be called, posed an even more acute policy dilemma for Australia than the Malay Emergency. Combating an indigenous communist insurgency was one thing, engaging the forces of its most important neighbour quite another. Canberra again parried British requests for assistance, insisting that it would get involved only if the need was unambiguous. By this time, Britain had some 8,000 troops in Borneo and another 20,000 on the Malay Peninsula. Canberra relented in April 1964, to the extent of dispatching some combat-support capacities to Borneo— notably some 120 army engineers. The need for an Australian combat contribution became much harder to deny when Indonesian commandos and paratroopers landed in West Malaysia in August–September 1964. Finally, in February 1965, Australia sent its infantry battalion from Butterworth, together with a Special Air Service (SAS) squadron, to Sarawak. The attempted coup in Indonesia in October 1965, and the bloody purge of communists that followed, left all concerned rather confused about the outlook for *Konfrontasi*. As it happened, it was called off but this did not become reliably clear until mid-1966. Australian forces in Sarawak were withdrawn in November 1966, having lost 15 personnel over the 20-month deployment.

Australia's infantry battalion returned to Butterworth, but not for long. In July 1967, Britain made its long-anticipated announcement that it would withdraw all its forces from Malaysia and Singapore by the mid-1970s at the latest. This was followed shortly thereafter by signals from Washington that it intended to wind down its commitment in Vietnam, reviving concerns in Canberra that it could be exposed in the region, and specifically in Malaysia, with obligations and expectations that exceeded its means. In a precautionary move, Canberra divided its military assets between Malaysia and Singapore, leaving two squadrons of *Mirage III* fighters at Butterworth, but relocating the infantry battalion to Singapore in 1969–70.[1] In practice, regular training with Singapore's fledging air force meant that a fleet of *Mirage III*s (half a squadron) was essentially based permanently in Singapore. This configuration of military assets was committed to the Five Power Defence Arrangements (FPDA) agreed upon in 1971.

When Labor came to power in Australia in 1972, it fulfilled its election promise to bring Australian troops home from Vietnam and Singapore. The infantry battalion in Singapore returned to Australia in December 1973. This brought to an end an 18-year deployment of ground forces in the region, except for a rifle company (roughly 100 personnel) to provide security for Royal Australian Air Force (RAAF) aircraft at Butterworth, which continues to be deployed to the present time.

Over time, the growth of the Malaysian and Singapore armed forces (with attendant pressures on space at air bases in particular), growing confidence that the outcome in Vietnam would not fundamentally destabilize the region, together with the optics of the Australian military presence in terms of sovereignty and independence, led to an essentially consensual determination to terminate the permanent deployment of RAAF aircraft. One of the two *Mirage III* squadrons was withdrawn in August 1983. The following year, Canberra announced that it intended to replace the permanent basing of combat aircraft at Butterworth with rotational deployments from Australia (totalling about 16 weeks a year) of F/A-18 *Hornets* (and occasionally F-111s) when these aircraft entered service later in the decade. The last squadron of *Mirage III* fighters left Butterworth in 1988. At the present time, in addition to the rotational deployment of fighters, RAAF P-3C *Orions* operate out of Butterworth on surveillance operations in the Indian Ocean, sharing the 'product' with Malaysia and Indonesia. This arrangement was agreed to in 1980 and underpins the permanent deployment of the rifle company in Malaysia. In the gaps between the presence of RAAF aircraft, this company engages in training and exercise activities with the Malaysian Army.

Singapore's armed forces in Australia

Although Australia, like the United Kingdom, had never envisaged Singapore becoming an independent state, this became a reality in 1965 when Singapore was expelled from the Malaysian Federation after just two years. Among other things, racial and religious schisms precluded a truly level playing field that could allow the principle of a Singapore politician also becoming the leader of Malaysia. The rough coincidence of *Konfrontasi*, Singapore's split from Malaysia, and Britain's decision to withdraw from the region militarily briefly made Southeast Asia an issue in the global strategic calculations of the major powers—particularly given the US view that the loss of Vietnam would result in the domino-like expansion of communism throughout the rest of Southeast Asia. The United States had focused on Sukarno's Indonesia and, despite its rapidly escalating involvement in Vietnam, had indicated its resolve to confront Indonesia with force if it pressed *Konfrontasi* too far. Singapore's leader, Lee Kuan Yew, not least because of his passionate denunciations of American imperialism, was seen in 1964–5 as possibly being attracted to linkages to Communist China. Moreover, the announcement of Britain's intent to withdraw from the region militarily, although it came after it had been confirmed that Sukarno had effectively been sidelined and *Konfrontasi* abandoned, was viewed darkly in Washington as reinforcing the fact that the United Kingdom had declined to commit forces to Vietnam.[2]

As we saw earlier, Australia found these swirling developments rather unsettling and, in fact, viewed the redeployment of its infantry battalion from Malaysia to the new state of Singapore as a useful means of lowering its profile. Shortly afterwards of course, in 1971, Australia went the other way by joining the FPDA as unambiguously the most powerful of the regional participants. The FPDA was Britain's response to regional pressure (especially from Singapore and Australia, and presumably echoed by Washington) to delay the withdrawal of its forces and to alleviate the concerns associated with the implementation of its decision to withdraw.

Singapore's security priorities

As it happened, essentially from the moment when Singapore achieved full independence in 1965, Lee Kuan Yew was careful to make it very clear that the micro-state's strategic orientation would place it in the Western camp. Given the circumstances surrounding its birth, an intense preoccupation with security and defence was to be expected. In addition, the leaders of the new state recognized that the armed forces could play an essential role in the long-term task of inculcating a sense of nationhood among the mixed-race (but predominantly Chinese) community of traders that found themselves labelled 'Singaporeans'.

The strong priority given to national security was amply reflected in Singapore's early decision to look to Israel for guidance on building a viable defence force. This effort quickly came into conflict with the absence of ground, sea and airspace in which to train. Weapons acquisitions from the United States developed into long-term access arrangements, especially for advanced pilot training. For ground forces, Singapore's primary partner turned out to be Taiwan—a relationship that has endured despite Beijing's occasional less-than-diplomatic opposition. Australia was also attractive to Singapore in this regard owing to its relative proximity and the general familiarity with the Australian armed forces that had been built up during the 1950s and 1960s. Furthermore, Singapore's circumstances—a small, predominantly Chinese, state with very large Malay-Muslim neighbours—resulted in a high value being attached to linkages (particularly security connections) beyond its neighbourhood. It is no accident, for example, that Singapore has been more protective of the FPDA and more eager to expand the activities these arrangements support than any other participant.

After some initial hesitation, Australia agreed in 1980 to allow Singapore's ground forces to train and exercise at Australian Defence Force (ADF) facilities—specifically the Shoalwater Bay training area in Queensland. Once the precedent was set, Australia and Singapore went on to agree to several arrangements that broke new ground for Australia and which remain in place as key strands of the bilateral defence relationship. In 1990, a Memorandum of Understanding transformed *ad hoc* access for ground force training at Shoalwater Bay into arrangements that allowed heavy equipment to remain pre-positioned as troop formations cycled through the training area. A few years later, agreement was reached to also allow the Singapore armed forces (SAF) to conduct unilateral exercises at Shoalwater Bay, with ADF personnel merely observing. In recent times, some 6,500 SAF troops cycle through Shoalwater Bay annually, usually in brigade-sized formations.

Similarly, in 1981, agreement was reached on the establishment of the SAF's flying training school at the RAAF base Pearce, near Perth in Western Australia. This arrangement, which now involves some 280 Singaporeans at any one time, has also put down roots. The current agreement runs to 2018 and Singapore would reportedly be pleased to extend this date to 2028.

The third and most recent of the activities of this kind, confirmed in a treaty-level agreement in October 1996, provided for the basing of SAF helicopters at the ADF Army Aviation Centre (at Oakey in Queensland) initially for the period up to December 2012. This arrangement has been operational since late 1998 and now involves up to 12 helicopters and 130 Singaporean personnel and dependents. Singapore's helicopter squadron conducts conversion training as well as the development and maintenance of operational capabilities. The mix of helicopter types deployed at Oakey can be varied in consultation with the Australian Army.

In the background of these concrete milestones in the development of the bilateral defence relationship, Singapore has consistently been forthcoming in supporting Australia's defence engagement initiatives in Southeast Asia. This program flourished during the 1980s and into the 1990s as an essential backdrop to building toward the self-reliant defence of Australia. This aspiration was seen as infeasible (except in the context of a broader posture of actively seeking security 'with' Australia's Asian neighbours rather than vaguely imagining the task to be security 'from' them). Again, Singapore's broad policy interests in sustaining the engagement of outside powers with Southeast Asia created a predisposition to support Australian initiatives and thereby, indirectly, to encourage others to do so.

Intelligence: intersection, controversy, collaboration

Collaboration in the collection and/or use of intelligence information is seen, quite properly, as symptomatic of an unusually high degree of political and military confidence between states. At the same time, it is an arena fraught with risk of suspicion and controversy, not least because protecting sources and leaving technical capabilities ambiguous makes 'clearing the air' (of any misgivings that may arise) inherently difficult.

An early interaction between Australia and Singapore in the intelligence field flowed from Britain's decision in 1967 to withdraw militarily from East of Suez. Britain operated a signals intelligence facility in Singapore which, from 1968, was progressively taken over by Australia's Defence Signals Directorate (DSD). The withdrawal of Australian troops at the end of 1973 left this operation untenably exposed and it appears to have been mutually decided by the two governments that Singapore should inherit the facility. Australia had, by that time, set up a replacement capability at Shoal Bay near Darwin.[3]

During the 1980s, a small and rather basic operation monitored Soviet naval vessels transiting the Malacca Strait from Singapore. Officially known as the Australian New Zealand Military Intelligence Staff, it involved Australian and New Zealand photographers working from a launch provided by the US embassy.[4]

During the late 1980s and early 1990s, Singapore's military personnel based in Australia appear to have had a surge of testosterone. Occasional reports surfaced of SAF endeavours, particularly surveillance and photography (from the air), deemed by Australia to be beyond the bounds of the agreements governing their presence in Australia. An Australian Security Intelligence Organisation (ASIO) annual report in the early 1990s referred to an ASEAN country (identified informally as Singapore) being unusually 'aggressive' in gathering intelligence in Australia. These frictions naturally laced speculation about an episode from the early 1980s: the suspicion in DSD that Singapore had 'recruited' one of its operatives. Academics learned that an individual had been arrested in 1981 but ultimately not prosecuted, leaving open the possibility that the real culprit remained unidentified. The speculation surrounding this affair resurfaced in 2001 in the context of a *SingTel* bid to acquire *Optus*, including nominal control of a communications satellite of importance to Australia's defence.[5]

The Australia–Singapore intelligence relationship survived these frictions and continued to develop, notably through the mechanism of regular exchanges between assessment agencies. These international exchanges are conducted with a number of regional states, with the depth and candour of the exchange calibrated to reflect the quality of the wider relationship and the value of the intelligence which the other side is prepared to share. It would be reasonable to assume that Australia's exchanges with Singapore have become the most candid and rewarding of all those conducted with ASEAN states. This trend will have been spurred by the high priority both countries assigned to combating Islamic extremism in the region after the 11 September 2001 terrorist attacks on the United States, and facilitated by Singapore's progressively closer formal defence ties with the United States (which allows shared US–Australia intelligence to be more readily used in discussions with Singapore).

In the immediate aftermath of 11 September 2001, the US intelligence community released information on the possible dimensions of the al Qaeda network, indicating that cells could exist in as many as 60 countries and allowing the inference that, if there was to be a second front beyond Afghanistan, it could well lie in Southeast Asia. This possibility received dramatic confirmation when material uncovered in Afghanistan following the fall of the Taliban pointed to active preparations for coordinated bombing attacks on Western embassies in Singapore, including those of the United States, United Kingdom and Australia. The material from Afghanistan was sufficiently specific and timely to enable Singapore to preempt this operation, but it still propelled Singapore toward a stance on terrorism within Southeast Asia that was well ahead of the other ASEAN states. A year later, the bombing in Bali did the same for Australia, providing a further enduring impulse for intensified intelligence sharing with Singapore and a number of other ASEAN states.

The Five Power Defence Arrangements

We have seen how Australia ended up maintaining a continuous military presence in Malaya and then Malaysia/Singapore for nearly 25 years. We have also seen that Australia remained cautious throughout this period, placing the highest premium on delaying the inevitable British decision to withdraw and resisting continuous pressure, particularly from Britain, to expand its own commitment. A persistent Australian concern was to avoid a commitment of Australian forces that might incline London to persuade itself that it could now responsibly pull out.

Australian forces had been deployed in Malaya under the Anglo–Malayan Defence Arrangement. The British withdrawal from 1967 was deliberately gradual so as to ease any economic disruption and to minimize any adverse ramifications in political and security, as well as economic, terms. Australia supported this thinking by also keeping its commitment stable, apart from relocating its army battalion from Malaysia to Singapore in 1969. The prospect, attractive to all the players (Australia, New Zealand, Malaysia and Singapore), of retaining some form of British engagement beyond the withdrawal of its military assets, and the need for a new political instrument to support the deployment of Australian and New Zealand forces, gave rise in 1971 to the Five Power Defence Arrangements (FPDA).

The FPDA was an executive agreement (not a treaty) embodying a relatively soft undertaking to consult in the event of external aggression or threat of attack against Malaysia or Singapore. Whether this undertaking extended to East Malaysia (Sabah and Sarawak) was left deliberately vague. The core capability established to give substance to the FPDA was the Integrated Air Defence System commanded by an Australian and centred on the Butterworth airbase in Malaysia. The FPDA was clearly perceived by all concerned to be a bridging arrangement pending the development of defence capabilities in Malaysia and Singapore and, perhaps, of alternative regional security structures. In the event, of course, the FPDA proved to be sufficiently inoffensive to survive to the present day even though, for significant periods, its benefits appeared decidedly modest. Since the early 1990s, however, the arrangements became the vehicle for military activities that were both significantly more substantive and responsive to changing perceptions of the principal challenges to regional security.

Singapore, which recognized from its earliest days as an independent state the strategic value of security connections beyond its immediate neighbourhood, has consistently been both the most protective of the FPDA members and politically bold in seeking to develop the activities engaged in under the auspices of these arrangements. The arrangements remained relatively dormant in their first decade, although they played a positive role (then and since) in helping to contain the periodic political spats between Malaysia and Singapore. The limited regime of air exercises was supplemented in 1981 by modest land and naval exercises, but the more significant developments came later in the decade.

The context at that time included Australia's first full articulation of its 'Defence of Australia' posture in the 1987 White Paper, including the innovative practice of pro-actively providing regional governments with in-depth briefings on the thinking that lay behind this posture. The White Paper, like the Dibb Review that preceded it, did not place a high value on the FPDA. Furthermore, the date (1988) for the withdrawal of the last RAAF fighter squadron from Butterworth was drawing near, as was the withdrawal from Singapore of New Zealand's modest army contingent. In Southeast Asia, the success in securing Vietnam's withdrawal from Cambodia was balanced (particularly for Malaysia) by mounting evidence that the competing territorial claims in the South China Sea would evolve into a serious political and security issue.

Efforts within the FPDA to upgrade its exercises—both to make them more rewarding for participants and more relevant to contemporary circumstances—bore fruit with exercise *Lima Bersatu* in September 1988. This exercise set new standards in terms of scope (extending into the South China Sea) and in terms of coordinating air, land and sea forces. An FPDA naval exercise the following year—*Starfish*—similarly set qualitatively new standards in terms of complexity. This trend was sustained into the 1990s and in 1997 a further threshold was crossed when FPDA air and naval exercises were combined. In 2000, the FPDA political leadership agreed that army participation in the exercises should be further upgraded. Also in 2000 political confidence in the FPDA allowed for significant developments in the scope and complexity of its exercises to be reflected in the renaming and restructuring of its core institution, with the Integrated Air Defence System becoming the Integrated Area Defence System.

More recently, in 2004, FPDA defence ministers announced their agreement to include non-conventional threat scenarios—notably terrorism—in the exercise program. By this time, FPDA communiqués referred directly (and by historical standards, boldly) to enhancements in the military capabilities of participating states, and in the interoperability of these capabilities, as important contributions to regional stability.

The FPDA is now an important component of the fabric of security in Southeast Asia. Although its development was exceedingly slow and uncertain in its first two decades, the collective patience of the participants paid off. In Australia's case, in particular, it was appreciated only belatedly that there was a critical qualitative difference between defence engagement conducted through episodic visits and exercises and having the opportunity, through the FPDA, to be a player integral to the security agenda in Southeast Asia.

Conclusions

Broadly speaking, the defence relationship between Australia and Singapore has been on an unbroken, positive trajectory for nearly 60 years. This relationship has evolved from the days when Australia acted as deputy to the colonial power, through independence and Singapore's economic and political consolidation, into the present era of mature statehood in which the two countries engage comprehensively as equals.

Singapore's geographic and political context resulted in an enduring preoccupation with security which, in turn, accelerated the emergence of a defence force which the ADF regarded as a rewarding partner with whom to exercise and train. Moreover, Singapore has always attached a high value to strategic engagement with powers beyond its immediate region. This policy setting has been directed principally at the United States, but has been reflected also in the priority given to encouraging Australia's continued strategic engagement with the region, not least through the FPDA. Singapore was visibly responsive to Australian assessments throughout the 1970s and 1980s that the FPDA involved more costs than rewards and worked energetically to improve the balance.

At the present time, the defence relationship is mature, broad based and appears to have a secure future. This assessment derives in significant part from the fact that the defence relationship has not evolved in isolation but has been nestled securely in a broader framework of political, security and economic cooperation—a framework reflected in the Singapore–Australia Joint Ministerial Committee that has met every two years since 1997 and typically involves the Ministers for Foreign Affairs, Trade and Education. Defence collaboration seems likely in the future to extend beyond training, exercising and intelligence sharing into research and development and procurement. Broader strategic cooperation has also flourished. Australia and Singapore, together with Japan, are the prime movers in Asia for the Proliferation Security Initiative (PSI). Similarly, Singapore, together with Japan and to a lesser extent Indonesia, appear to have lobbied strenuously in

2004–5 to ensure that the inaugural East Asia Summit in December 2005 included India, Australia and New Zealand in addition to the core group of ASEAN, together with China, Japan and South Korea. The importance of this new forum remains uncertain, but Australia's participation sets an invaluable precedent for future developments in multilateral security processes, whether Asia-wide or more specifically in Southeast Asia.

All in all, in Australia's long and uneven journey toward partnership with its neighbours in Southeast Asia, Singapore has proven to be an asset out of all proportion to its size.

Notes

1 K.Y. Lee, *From Third World to First: The Singapore Story: 1965–2000*, pp. 62–4, 73, 430.
2 The foregoing discussion draws substantially on W.R. Louis, 'The dissolution of the British Empire in the era of Vietnam', address to the 116th annual meeting of the American Historical Association, San Francisco, CA, 4 January 2002.
3 J.T. Richelson and D. Ball, *The Ties That Bind: Intelligence Cooperation Between the UKUSA Countries*, London and Sydney: Allen & Unwin, 1985, pp. 192–3.
4 D. Ball, 'The security relationship between Australia and New Zealand', in D. Ball (ed.) *The ANZAC Connection*, Sydney: George Allen & Unwin, 1985, p. 51.
5 See R. Maynard, 'Singapore spy claims threaten telecoms deal', *South China Morning Post*, 10 August 2001.

Part 4
Washing up

11 Threats without enemies

Are Australia's alliances and alignments still relevant?

Christopher Chung

With the acceleration of globalization and the increased influence of non-state actors in international affairs, a new set of threats has emerged that sit alongside the traditional security agenda focused on interstate conflict. Conceptually located within the so-called 'new' or non-traditional security agenda, these threats are characterized by their transnational and intrastate effects, an emphasis on non-military responses and a reliance on international cooperation to address them. As Alan Dupont notes, non-traditional security threats are 'complex, interconnected and multi-dimensional' as well as 'moving from the periphery to the centre of the security concerns of both states and individuals'.[1] In this context, they raise important questions about Australia's traditional security arrangements, concluded primarily to deal with conventional security threats. Are they sufficiently flexible to address non-traditional threats? Have new approaches emerged and what are their characteristics? Is there a shared view between Australia and its partners on perceptions and priorities towards these 'threats without enemies'?[2] Taking Southeast Asia as its analytical focus, a region where Australia has abiding political, economic and security interests, this chapter argues that the increased prominence of non-traditional security threats such as drug trafficking, terrorism and illegal people movements has prompted a shift in the form and content of Australia's security arrangements. On the one hand, to remain relevant in a changed strategic environment the activities encompassed by traditional security arrangements have been broadened. On the other hand, new frameworks have been developed that are less formal in structure, more expansive in scope and broader in participation than traditional security arrangements.

The chapter begins by examining Australia's approach in its security arrangements to handle non-traditional security threats. Particular emphasis is given to the reorientation of the Five Power Defence Arrangements (FPDA) and new approaches to cooperation. The greater uncertainty and complexity of the post-Cold War security environment has prompted scholars to reflect on the relevance and adaptability of traditional alliances in the new millennium. Australia's experience in dealing with non-traditional threats in Southeast Asia provides a useful contribution to that reflection. This is the focus of the second section. To conclude the chapter, the issue of differing perceptions and prioritization of non-traditional security threats between Australia and its Southeast Asian neighbours is then discussed. Narrowing the gap in threat perceptions and prioritization is likely to yield benefits at both the political and operational levels, enhancing the effectiveness and efficiency of response strategies. This perspective underlies the remarks that close the chapter.

The Five Power Defence Arrangements: sustaining relevancy through reorientation

Concluded in 1971, the FPDA commits Australia, New Zealand, the United Kingdom, Malaysia and Singapore to immediately consult with each other if the two latter countries come under external attack or threat thereof. Focused from the outset on conventional security threats, the FPDA targeted the air defence of Malaysia and Singapore as a priority in recognition of their limited capabilities in this area. An Integrated Air Defence System was established in 1971, a key element of which—as detailed by Ron Huisken in the previous chapter of this volume—was the continued stationing by Australia of two squadrons of fighters (together with their support units and, periodically, an infantry company) at Butterworth air base in Malaysia. Air defence exercises began in 1972 while land and sea components were introduced in the early 1980s. Combined air and sea exercises have taken place since 1997, and tri-service joint exercises were launched in 2000.[3] Since then the FPDA's emphasis on joint and more complex conventional security exercises has deepened, including the addition of a logistics element. More recently, the defence ministers endorsed the launch of a new major joint exercise, *Suman Protector.*

The FPDA provides more than an opportunity for regular inter-military training to improve understanding of each other's equipment, tactics and communications procedures. At a fundamental level, it has helped attenuate tensions between Malaysia and Singapore, a not inconsiderable achievement. Bilveer Singh notes that 'Malaysia is perhaps the most conspicuous factor in Singapore's security calculations'.[4] Informing this outlook is the qualitative and quantitative improvements in the Malaysian armed forces over the past 20 years, as well as tensions associated with Singapore's vulnerability to water supply disruption by Malaysia and contested sovereignty over Pedra Branca/Pulau Batu Putih, a rocky feature atop of which sits a lighthouse.[5] While Singapore's sustained investment in advanced weapons, systems and training, and its expressed willingness to use a military option if necessary may have moderated Malaysia's actions, so too has the FPDA. In particular, since its inception it has facilitated communication between the two militaries, despite periods of cool political relations.

Over time, the relevance of the FPDA and its utility to the membership has come under closer scrutiny. Impetus for this included the end of the Cold War, changes in the regional strategic environment and greater political recognition of non-traditional security issues. While traditional security issues such as maritime territorial disputes remain an enduring feature of Southeast Asia's strategic environment, the rise of non-state actor-based threats such as terrorism and the proliferation of weapons of mass destruction (WMD) or their component parts highlighted the narrow focus of the FPDA and its exercise scenarios.

Recognizing this, defence ministers agreed on the need to reorient the FPDA if it was to remain relevant in contributing to the security of the subregion. In 2003 the ministers agreed to exercises involving asymmetric and non-conventional threat scenarios and to the involvement of non-military agencies.[6] As then Australian Defence Minister Robert Hill noted: 'The capacity to respond to non-conventional threats will make the FPDA more relevant to a security environment where threats include terrorism, breaches of exclusive economic zones, smuggling, piracy and illegal fishing.'[7] The first FPDA exercise focusing on piracy and maritime terrorism took place in the South China Sea in October 2004, with a second in September 2005. Building on these exercises, in September 2006 Singapore hosted exercise *Bersama Padu* (meaning 'together united' in Malay) involving 21 ships, 85 aircraft, one submarine, diving teams, defence ground support personnel, Singapore's Maritime and Port Authority, Police Coast Guard, immigration authority and customs service.[8] Venturing further into the non-traditional security realm, the 2006 meeting of FPDA defence ministers agreed to explore cooperation on humanitarian assistance and disaster relief.[9] Within this context, Malaysia's Deputy Prime Minister and Minister of Defence Najib Tun Razak proposed the establishment of a regional humanitarian relief coordinating centre—an idea supported by the other members.

The FPDA has undergone an evolutionary shift to now encompass both traditional and non-traditional threats. In that sense, it usefully demonstrates Dupont's notion of coexistence of the two security agendas.[10] The by-product is an FPDA that is more in tune with the diverse range of contemporary regional security threats, catalyzing a reaffirmation by the membership's defence ministers of its relevance in the new millennium.

Framework-type arrangements

Complementary to the approach of adapting and broadening existing security mechanisms is another that can be categorized as framework arrangements. Under this approach, an umbrella agreement or other broad-based mechanism forms the basis for cooperation on traditional and non-traditional security issues. Both formal and informal framework-type arrangements have emerged, as illustrated below.

Formal instruments

Australia has engaged in new framework security arrangements that explicitly cover both traditional and non-traditional threats, and have a strong emphasis on capacity building and intelligence/information sharing. Two examples illustrate this. The first example is the security treaty between Australia and Indonesia—the so-called 'Lombok Agreement' signed on 13 November 2006 by the respective foreign ministers.[11] The treaty's provisions cover nine areas and forms of cooperation. Two aspects are striking. The first is its strong emphasis on non-traditional security issues. Of the nine areas of cooperation identified, only one focuses on traditional defence cooperation. The second is the structure of the instrument itself. Rather than being prescriptive, it is outcomes focused and establishes a broad-based agenda for action. In the words of Australian Foreign Minister Alexander Downer, 'existing and future MOUs on such issues as counter-terrorism, defence cooperation and police cooperation will operate within the overarching framework of the treaty-level agreement and be guided by the principles enunciated within'.[12]

The second example is a status of forces agreement between Australia and the Philippines on which discussions commenced in 2002. Following its expected ratification in 2007, the agreement will allow joint military exercises to be conducted in the Philippines similar to the arrangement Washington has with Manila. It will also enable joint sea patrols, transfer of surveillance technology, long-range reconnaissance training and the supply of small watercraft to help the Philippines military patrol rivers and marshlands in Mindanao in the fight against terrorism.[13]

Memoranda of Understanding

Canberra has concluded both regional and bilateral Memorandum of Understanding (MOU) arrangements, especially in the area of counter-terrorism cooperation. Regionally, the focus centres on the ASEAN–Australia Joint Declaration for Cooperation to Combat International Terrorism signed in July 2004. Among its provisions are enhanced cooperation and liaison among the parties' law enforcement and security agencies in order to bolster counterterrorism regimes, improved intelligence and information sharing, strengthened capacity-building efforts through training and education, and assistance on border and transport security measures.

By 2006 Australia had signed 12 separate bilateral MOUs on counter-terrorism cooperation with Asia–Pacific countries.[14] In Southeast Asia, they include Cambodia, Indonesia, Malaysia, Thailand and the Philippines. Building on the MOU with the Philippines, and following discussion between the defence ministers, in July 2005 military, police and intelligence officials of the two countries met to consider how they could best cooperate in the maritime and law enforcement domains and to conduct information exchanges. Concern about possible attacks in the southern Philippines against ships carrying Australian exports to Northeast Asia, including liquefied natural gas tankers, may have prompted this closer cooperation.[15]

Some government agencies have concluded MOUs in their own right with regional counterparts. The Australian Federal Police (AFP), for instance, has concluded MOUs with Indonesia (2002), Thailand (2003), the Philippines (2003) and Vietnam (2006). They provide for cooperation and information sharing between law enforcement agencies on terrorism, piracy, people smuggling and trafficking, drug and arms trafficking and economic crime such as money laundering and identity fraud. The in-country placement of AFP liaison officers augments these arrangements.

The Proliferation Security Initiative

Launched in 2003, the Proliferation Security Initiative (PSI) can be characterized as a 'community of like-mindeds', with a shared goal of preventing the spread by air, sea or land of WMD, their delivery systems and component materials between states or non-state actors of proliferation concern. More than 75 countries currently support the PSI but only some have openly declared so and there remain doubts about the commitment of others.[16]

Australia's support of PSI has been unwavering and openly declared since the initiative's inception. In the words of Foreign Minister Downer, 'Australia is proud to be a key driver of the PSI, a practical and informal arrangement among countries to cooperate with each other, as necessary' on interdicting illicit WMD trade.[17] Giving effect to this, Australia hosted and chaired the second PSI plenary meeting in Brisbane in July 2003 and a further meeting of legal and operational experts in Sydney in December 2004. Australia has hosted two multilateral PSI exercises: *Pacific Protector* in the Coral Sea in September 2003 and *Pacific Protector 06* in Darwin in April 2006. It also participated in the two PSI exercises held in Asia to date: *Team Samurai* hosted by Japan in 2004 and *Deep Sabre* in Singapore in 2005.

In justifying the Australian government's strong support of the PSI, Downer argued that:

> There has to be room in our non-proliferation agenda for a greater variety of measures and fresh thinking. For this reason, Australia, while continuing to support and engage in non-proliferation forums, has wholeheartedly joined the Proliferation Security Initiative. .... In a time of high demand and limited resources, a results-oriented approach is what is needed.[18]

Reinforcing this viewpoint, he noted separately: 'Gone are the days when Canberra Commission-style talk-fests are an acceptable or effective counter-proliferation outcome. This Government is about taking the next steps—

practical actions that make a difference.'[19] It is difficult, however, to assess how much of a difference PSI actions have made. The exercises have been conducted under controlled scenario scripts that do not include surprises to test flexibility and lateral thinking in command, communication and field operations. And while senior US officials claim 11 successful intercepts have been made since the PSI was launched, the details are vague.[20] This hampers independent evaluation of the claim.

Capacity development

Capacity development by Australia with regional countries has taken several forms, focused on niche areas and with a strong counterterrorism focus. At a country level, Australia has launched a four-year, A$10 million program with Indonesia to enhance law enforcement capabilities, establish a financial intelligence unit and tighten travel security screening. The Philippines has received a three-year, A$5 million package focused on strengthening law enforcement capabilities and border and port security. On a military level, the Australian Special Air Service (SAS) reportedly provided training, logistical and operational support to the armed forces of the Philippines in the southern Philippines as part of efforts to track and neutralize terrorists in the area, as well as participating in hostage recovery exercises.[21] In a similar vein, the Australian Defence Force (ADF) undertook counterhijack and hostage recovery training with specialist units of the Indonesian military and an exercise with Singapore on handling chemical, biological and radioactive threats.[22]

Strengthening counterterrorism capability has also underlain the placement of AFP advisors in Indonesia, Malaysia and the Philippines. In the wake of the February 2004 *Superferry 14* bombing in Manila Bay, the AFP's offer of technical, forensic and investigative assistance was quickly accepted by the Philippines National Police.[23] Other AFP initiatives in the Philippines include implementing a A$3.7 million joint project with the Australian Agency for International Development (AusAID) to enhance the capabilities of local law enforcement agencies in counterterrorism intelligence and investigation, bomb investigation techniques, forensic analysis and establishing a computer-based case management and intelligence system.[24]

Australia is also helping Burma in addressing non-traditional security threats. Over the next five years A$15 million will be channelled through the development assistance program to support prevention, treatment and care activities as part of a six-nation initiative to help fight HIV/AIDS, tuberculosis and malaria in Burma. It currently has the second highest incidence of HIV/AIDS in Asia, while tuberculosis and malaria are the leading causes of illness.[25] In the counterterrorism area several initiatives have been launched with Burma within the framework of programs offered to officials of ASEAN member states. The Australian Department of Immigration and Multicultural Affairs has provided training to Burmese officials on immigration intelligence while the Australian Transaction Reports and Analysis Centre (AUSTRAC), the Federal government's cash transactions reporting centre, has helped strengthen Burma's capability in tracking suspected terrorist financing. The Australian Nuclear Science and Technology Organisation (ANSTO) has helped in monitoring radioactivity and detecting the illegal use of nuclear material. Burmese officials have attended Australian-run courses on major investigation management, post-blast incident management and the international management of serious crime. They have also attended courses at the Jakarta Centre for Law Enforcement Cooperation (JCLEC), an initiative co-sponsored by Australia and Indonesia. These activities have helped build the contacts, knowledge and confidence among officials, all of which are useful for effective daily operations and critical for rapid action before or after a terrorist attack.

JCLEC represents a major Australian capacity-building initiative that provides research and educational and training programs in law enforce-ment, security and anti-corruption for officials from the region. Established in 2004, Canberra's commitment to the JCLEC includes funding of A$36.8 million over five years, appointment of an Australian as director of studies and the provision of course leaders. Indonesia hosts the JCLEC and shares management responsibility for it. Counterterrorism training, including investigations management, criminal intelligence, forensics, financial inves-tigations and communications, is a primary focus of JCLEC activities. Since its opening, more than 1,100 students from around the world have attended its courses.[26]

Cooperation with regional countries on port security has exhibited strong progress. The Australian Office of Transport Security within the Depart-ment of Transport and Regional Services (OTS/DOTARS) has liaison offi-cers in Jakarta and Manila. Working in conjunction with AusAID, OTS/DOTARS implemented a A$3.5 million capacity-building project in the Philippines focused on strengthening compliance with the International Maritime Organization's International Ship and Port Facility Security Code (ISPS Code), building a national framework for port security and improv-ing the security of local ports in the Sulu archipelago.[27] Australia has also supported capacity-building workshops in Indonesia, Thailand and Viet-nam to assist them in complying with the ISPS Code.[28] APEC's Secure Trade in the APEC Region initiative, launched in 2002, focuses on improv-ing maritime, aviation and supply chain security, passenger information management systems, capacity building and project planning. Within this process, OTS/DOTARS has targeted cooperation against piracy and com-pliance with ISPS requirements as priority activities. Through new funding in the 2006–7 Australian Federal Budget, explosives and drugs trace detec-tion technology will be installed in high risk ports in Indonesia, Malaysia, the Philippines and Thailand.[29]

Border control cooperation has taken several forms. In 2005 the Aus-tralian Customs Service worked with regional counterparts to improve border controls around the Sulu and Sulawesi seas. Building on this experience, the 2006–7 Australian Federal Budget allocated in excess of A$7 million over three years to help other countries strengthen their border controls. Particular emphasis is given to training in intelligence analysis, ship search, identification of chemical precursors (explosives and drugs) and commodities, passenger control and counterterrorism awareness.[30]

Combating people smuggling and trafficking is a further element of border control. In the wake of just over 6,600 people arriving illegally by boat from Indonesia during 2000 and 2001, the Australian Foreign Minister and his Indonesian counterpart convened a regional ministerial conference on people smuggling, trafficking in persons and related transnational crime in Bali in February 2002. From this emerged the Bali Process, an ongoing effort involving 50 countries within and beyond the Asia–Pacific and multilateral institutions such as the Asian Development Bank, the World Bank, the UN Office on Drugs and Crime, and Interpol. Its objectives include developing more effective information and intelligence sharing, improving cooperation among regional law enforcement agencies, strengthening cooperation on border and visa systems to detect illegal movements and placing greater emphasis on tackling the root causes of illegal migration. On the Australian side, the process is led by the Department of Foreign Affairs and Trade (DFAT) through its ambassador for combating people smuggling and trafficking, coordinating inputs from the AFP, Customs, the Attorney General, and Immigration. Numerous capacity-building activities and workshops have been held throughout Asia, involving foreign affairs, justice, police and immigration ministries from the region. Strengthened cooperation between Australian and Indonesian police, immigration and foreign affairs agencies has been a notable development since the launch of the process.

More recently, Australia committed A$21 million over five years to help judges and prosecutors in Burma, Cambodia, Laos and Thailand receive training and access to specialist advice and reference materials to help combat people trafficking. In addition, the ASEAN Secretariat will receive assistance on people trafficking issues and access to relevant research.[31] This builds on a 2003 commitment by the Australian government to provide more than A$20 million over four years to strengthen anti-people trafficking measures.[32]

Alliance reflections and Australia's Southeast Asian experience

As Bill Tow discusses in Chapter 2 of this volume, questions about the future relevance, shape and coverage of alliances have been the subject of considerable debate. In a thoughtful contribution to that discourse, Kurt Campbell argues that the key question is not whether alliances are dead, but how they are adapting to new demands and conditions.[33] In that context, Australia's experience in Southeast Asia offers a useful contribution about the structure and content of security arrangements in the new millennium.

Some scholars argue that while alliances will remain relevant, their nature and purpose will be different in the future. Campbell suggests that greater reliance will be placed on those *ad hoc* coalitions which can be assembled quickly and whose membership extends beyond traditional associates of the United States.[34] In his view, a typology of future US alliances is emerging, categorized as a new nuclear family, new friends and flings.[35] Strikingly, a common basis emphasized by Campbell in these structures is the new strategic environment engendered by the 'war on terror'.

That points to one of the evolutionary changes likely to characterize existing and future alliance arrangements: a mainstreaming of issues on the non-traditional security agenda. This contrasts markedly with the established focus of alliances on collective defence against traditional military threats. However, it is unlikely to simply be a case of 'in with the new security agenda, out with the old'; rather, both will have a place.

The Southeast Asian experience shows that adaptation of existing security arrangements is possible. The inclusion of non-traditional threats into the FPDA demonstrates how an existing security arrangement can evolve if the political will exists. Indeed, adaptation has re-energized the FPDA and its exercise regimes. Moreover, recent support by FPDA defence ministers to explore a role in humanitarian assistance and disaster relief indicates further engagement with the non-traditional security agenda.

Adaptation is also apparent in the other approaches being utilized by Australia in the region. Among the frameworks in use to structure security cooperation are bilateral treaties, MOUs, community of 'like-mindeds' and capacity-building projects. Together they represent a 'toolbox' of instruments available for use as appropriate to particular circumstances and partners. They also highlight that a broad range of 'tools' exist from which policymakers can select, going well beyond the 'coalition of the willing' arrangements identified by Campbell.

Military alliances have traditionally been limited in their composition to the armed forces in the context of confronting external threats to a nation's security. Australia's experience in Southeast Asia shows that, in addressing non-traditional security threats, the contributing members to security arrangements extend well beyond the military to include law enforcement, transport, customs, quarantine, immigration and financial-transactions tracking agencies. In some instances the military's role has been minimal; while in others it has been one actor among many—and often not in the lead role.

A characteristic of alliances such as the North Atlantic Treaty Organization (NATO) and the so-called 'San Francisco system' of bilateral alliances which the United States maintains in the Asia–Pacific is their longevity, with both arrangements established in the 1950s. This durability is unlikely to be replicated in the new approaches in which Australia is involved in Southeast Asia. The narrower focus of arrangements such as MOUs and capacity-building partnerships imbues them with a shorter lifespan. For example, MOUs are usually time bound and activity—or program—specific. While provision exists for their renewal, if it is judged that the MOU has fulfilled its purpose, that the threat for which it was established has diminished or new strategic or budgetary priorities emerge, the arrangement can be restricted, suspended or terminated relatively quickly. Further, while terrorism and other non-traditional security issues are of high concern, they do not fall within the category of existential threats or invoke collective defence—important factors for prolonged support of an alliance by its members. This is not to say that the above arrangements will be terminated any time soon, but it is to say that it is difficult to envisage their lifespan challenging the 50-plus years accumulated so far by NATO, for example.

In considering alliances, Bruno Tertrais poses a fundamental question: What does it really mean to be an ally in today's dynamic world without a single definitive threat?[36] The case of preemption in self-defence presents an interesting example. On the one hand, in 2002, as part of prosecuting the 'war on terror', Prime Minister Howard argued a case for launching a preemptive attack against terrorist groups in the region to defend the country's national interest. As he put it:

> It stands to reason that if you believed that somebody was going to launch an attack against your country, either of a conventional kind or of a terrorist kind, and you had a capacity to stop it and there was no alternative other than to use that capacity, then of course you would have to use it.[37]

Predictably generating anger in Southeast Asia about breaching sovereignty, neither Howard nor his senior ministers retreated in the wake of the regional reaction. On the other hand, Australia has worked assiduously in cultivating support at the bilateral and regional levels for counterterrorism measures. In this, a shared threat requiring cooperative responses has been a key message in Australia's efforts to broaden and deepen support among ASEAN members.

For Canberra, then, while different means contribute to the same end—that is, to secure Australia, its citizens and Australian interests—difficult decisions arise in balancing national and regional security agendas. In that context, Tertrais' question is particularly apposite. Complicating the calculus are differing perceptions and prioritization of security threats by Australia and its regional neighbours, all of which influence response strategies.

Mind the gap

Australia and Southeast Asia share common interests in a number of areas, as reflected in free trade agreements (concluded with Singapore and Thailand and under discussion with Malaysia and ASEAN) and bilateral security relationships.[38] Offsetting this positive element, however, is concern in

Southeast Asia arising from Australia's strong alignment with Western values, its close security alliance with the United States, including being perceived as the 'deputy sheriff' of the United States, and a more proactive military strategy.[39] The risk, in David Bolton's view, is that 'the substantial divide between Australian and Southeast Asian interests and values will continue to inhibit Australia's capacity to build cooperative security relations in the region'.[40]

Differences in the perception and prioritization of security threats are a manifestation of this. For Australia, 'defeating the threat of terrorism, countering the proliferation of WMD and supporting regional states in difficulty remain of the highest priority'.[41] They have underlain increases in budget allocations, personnel recruitment and outreach programs to Southeast Asian countries. As an example, in the 2006–7 Australian Federal Budget the AFP received an extra A\$25 million over four years to fund new training programs and increase the number of counterterrorism advisors working in its network of liaison offices in Asia.[42]

For many ASEAN countries, however, the above threats are not the highest priority. One Indonesian analyst remarks that:

> Indonesia is an easy target for criminals or transnational crimes [sic] organization. Their activities include illicit drugs, small-arms, and people trafficking, piracy, documents fraud, as well as money laundering. ... transnational crime is one of the most serious challenges to our national security, and must be put *at the top of our priority list* [emphasis added].[43]

In the maritime domain, there are obvious divergences in threat perceptions. Australia's maritime security agenda gives strong emphasis to the PSI and the threat of piracy and maritime terrorism. By contrast, Indonesia gives highest ranking to threats to its sovereignty, followed by arms smuggling.[44] It has hesitated at becoming a member of the PSI despite pressure from the United States: as Valencia succinctly puts it, 'WMD are simply not Malaysia's or Indonesia's chief concern'.[45] Like Indonesia, Malaysia's highest maritime security priority is threats to its sovereignty; this is followed by illegal migration, the environmental and fisheries impacts of oil spills, and threats to its fishermen, especially from Indonesian pirates.[46] Maritime terrorism, piracy against foreign ships, and arms smuggling all rank as lower priorities.[47]

Differences in threat perception and of collective identity within ASEAN's membership mean that outside powers such as the United States have had mixed influence on the security policy settings of individual countries. This ranges from enthusiastic support of US aid to wariness of the domestic political and sovereignty implications of aligning too closely with Washington. The same could be said in relation to Australia. Countries like Singapore and the Philippines have been supportive of Australia's contributions to regional counterterrorism efforts. Indonesia's reaction has been mixed. In some cases it has been in concert with Canberra, as in the establishment of the JCLEC and the Bali Process. At other times it has hesitated, to Canberra's disappointment. This includes the delayed enactment of antiterrorism legislation and not proscribing *Jemaah Islamiyah* as a terrorist organization.

ASEAN's intramural differences are also a factor. In the case of maritime terrorism, for example, Singapore has tended to link it with piracy to stimulate a heightened sense of threat requiring urgent countermeasures to be developed.[48] On the other hand, Malaysia and Indonesia have sought to decouple the two issues and take a low profile, nuanced stance, influenced in part by domestic politics and a suspicion of Western intentions.[49] This difference is also apparent in addressing the terrorism threat more broadly, with Singapore being more proactive and direct in introducing countermeasures.

In narrowing the gap between perceptions and priorities, greater acknowledgment needs to be given to the fact that Asian countries view security in broad terms, extending beyond the military dimension to include political, economic and socio-cultural elements.[50] This wider perspective underlies a wariness of single 'magic bullet' solutions, particularly in the context of the 'war on terror'. A comprehensive approach to non-traditional security issues is required if coherent and durable response strategies are to be developed. Acting on this is the shared challenge for political and policy elites in Australia and Southeast Asia.

Notes

1 A. Dupont, *East Asia Imperilled. Transnational Challenges to Security*, Cambridge and New York: Cambridge University Press, 2001, p. 2.
2 The term is borrowed from G. Prins (ed.) *Threats Without Enemies: Facing Environmental Insecurity*, London: Earthscan Publications, 1993.
3 D. Bristow, 'The Five Power Defence Arrangements: Southeast Asia's unknown regional security organization', *Contemporary Southeast Asia*, vol. 27, issue no. 1, April 2005, pp.7–8.
4 B. Singh, *Arming the Singapore Armed Forces. Trends and Implications*, Canberra papers on strategy and defence no. 153, Canberra: Strategic and Defence Studies Centre, Australian National University, 2003, p. 23.
5 Ibid., pp. 23–6.
6 Bristow, 'The Five Power Defence Arrangements', pp. 8–9.
7 Senator the Hon. Robert Hill, Minister for Defence, leader of the government in the Senate, Australia, media release, *Australia in Five Power Defence Exercise*, MIN154/05, 15 September 2005.
8 D. Boey, 'Current 5-nation war games most complex ever', *Straits Times*, 8 September 2006.
9 Ministry of Defence, Singapore, 6th FPDA defence ministers' meeting, 5 June 2006.
10 Dupont, *East Asia Imperilled*, p. 7.
11 *Agreement between the Republic of Indonesia and Australia on the Framework for Security Cooperation*, 13 November 2006.

12 The Hon. Alexander Downer MP, Minister for Foreign Affairs, Australia, *Signature of the Australia–Indonesia Agreement on the Framework for Security Cooperation*, media release FA124, 13 November 2006.
13 Philippine Sun Star report cited in S. Ulph, 'A new alliance in the Philippines', *Terrorism Focus*, vol. 20, no. 2, 31 October 2005.
14 C. Ungerer, 'Communication. Australia's policy responses to terrorism in Southeast Asia', *Global Change, Peace and Security*, vol. 18, no. 3, 2006, p. 193.
15 M. Richardson, 'Maritime attacks could damage our gas exports', *The Australian*, 12 July 2005; and M. Richardson, 'Australia and the Philippines expand cooperation in sea surveillance', *The Jakarta Post*, 4 July 2006.
16 M.J. Valencia, *The Proliferation Security Initiative: Making Waves in Asia*, Adelphi paper no. 376, Abingdon and New York: Routledge, 2005, p. 29.
17 The Hon. Alexander Downer, Minister for Foreign Affairs, Australia, 'Proliferation security initiative', media release FA70, 31 May 2005.
18 The Hon. Alexander Downer MP, Minister for Foreign Affairs, Australia, 'Weapons of mass destruction: the greatest threat to international security', speech at the Proliferation Security Initiative, Brisbane, 9 July 2003.
19 The Hon. Alexander Downer MP, Minister for Foreign Affairs, Australia, 'The threat of proliferation: global resolve and Australian action', speech to the Lowy Institute, Sydney, 23 February 2004.
20 Valencia, *The Proliferation Security Initiative*, p. 8.
21 G. Sheridan, 'SAS in hunt for Asia's terrorists', *The Australian*, 14 October 2006; and M. Dodd, 'Forces build regional links', *The Australian*, 15 August 2006.
22 Dodd, 'Forces build regional links'.
23 Australian Federal Police, *Annual Report 2004–05*, Canberra: Australian Federal Police, p. 20.
24 Ibid., pp. 21, 65.
25 The Hon. Alexander Downer MP, Minister for Foreign Affairs, Australia, 'Australia helps found new fund to fight diseases in Burma', media release AA 06 51, 18 August 2006. The other donors are the European Commission, the Netherlands, Norway, Sweden and the United Kingdom.
26 Australian Federal Police, *Annual Report 2005–06*, Canberra: Australian Federal Police, 2006, p. 5.
27 The Hon. Warren Truss, MP, 'Address to the Port and Maritime Security and Counter-Terrorism conference 2006', 18 May 2006; and Australian Agency for International Development, 'Fact sheet: Aid activities in the Philippines', Canberra: Australian Agency for International Development, 2006.
28 A. Bergin and S. Bateman, *Future Unknown: The Terrorist Threat to Australian Maritime Security*, Canberra: Australian Strategic Policy Institute, 2005, p. 65.
29 Australian Government, Attorney General's Department, 'Security environment update', Canberra: Attorney General's Department, 9 May 2006.
30 Ibid.; and Australian Government, Attorney General's Department, 'Customs border protection capability strengthened', press release, Minister for Justice and Customs, Senator the Hon. Chris Ellison, 9 May 2006.
31 The Hon. Alexander Downer MP, Minister for Foreign Affairs, Australia and Senator the Hon. Chris Ellison, Minister for Justice and Customs, 'Australia increases commitment to combating people trafficking in Asia', media release AA06 061, 15 September 2006.
32 On this earlier commitment, see the Hon. Alexander Downer MP, Minister for Foreign Affairs, Australia, joint media release, 'Australian government announces major package to combat people trafficking', 13 October 2003.
33 K.M. Campbell, 'The end of alliances? Not so fast', *Washington Quarterly*, vol. 27, no. 2, Spring 2004, p. 153.
34 Ibid.

35 Ibid., p. 158.
36 B. Tertrais, 'The changing nature of military alliances', *Washington Quarterly*, vol. 27, no. 2, Spring 2004, p. 148.
37 Cited in B. Burton, 'Howard unmoved by "preemption furor"', *Asia Times Online*, 3 December 2002.
38 Existing bilateral relationships include Malaysia, Singapore, Thailand and the Philippines. New ones are being forged with Cambodia, Brunei, Laos and Vietnam.
39 D. Bolton, *The Tyranny of Difference: Perceptions of Australian Defence Policy in Southeast Asia*, Strategic and Defence Studies Centre, working paper no. 384, Canberra: Strategic and Defence Studies Centre, Australian National University, 2003, pp. 2–7.
40 Bolton, *The Tyranny of Difference*, p. 8.
41 Commonwealth of Australia, *Australia's National Security. A Defence Update 2005*, Canberra: Department of Defence, 2005, p. 2.
42 Australian Government, Attorney General's Department, 'Security environment update'; and Australian Government, Attorney General's Department, 'Customs border protection capability strengthened'.
43 L.H. Subianto, 'Transnational security threats', *Indonesian Quarterly*, vol. 32, no. 3, 2004, p. 306.
44 Valencia, *The Proliferation Security Initiative*, p. 19.
45 Ibid.
46 Ibid.
47 Ibid.
48 J.H. Ho, 'The security of sea lanes in Southeast Asia', *Asian Survey*, vol. 46, no. 4, July/August 2006, pp. 564–5.
49 Ibid., p. 565.
50 This broader view of security is articulated in M. Alagappa, 'Asian practice of security: key features and explanations', in M. Alagappa (ed.) *Asian Security Practice: Material and Ideational Influences*, Stanford, CA: Stanford University Press, 1998, pp. 624–5.

12 Australia's changing alliances and alignments

Towards a new diplomatic two-step?

Pauline Kerr and Shannon Tow

Australia's security has long been intertwined with developments in the Asia–Pacific region. At differing points in time, Australian perceptions of the region have varied between that of threat and that of opportunity. Yet the enduring centrality of the region to Australia's security has induced it to become an adroit performer of a two-step dance—with its traditional security ally on the one hand, and its regional partners on the other. With the onset of the Cold War, Australia's sense of vulnerability was such that it turned towards the United States as its key security partner, despite its ongoing socio-cultural identification with Great Britain. Australia vigorously pursued and obtained a formal security alliance with the United States in 1951. During the Cold War and post-Cold War periods, Australia continued to strengthen this alliance and, simultaneously, to engage with different regional countries across a range of security and economic issues. Today, Australia realizes that its security and its economic wellbeing depends as much on China's behaviour as it does on the United States. Australia is bilaterally engaging with both countries with an intensity that is unprecedented.

Yet Australia's two-step dance, with its traditional security ally on the one hand and regional partners on the other, presumes that Canberra will be able to retain a significant degree of agency in managing these relationships. Recent developments, such as the East Asia Summit (EAS) however, suggest that there are strong trends of regional integration that could potentially dislocate Australia from this driving position. This prompts the question of whether Australia's past behaviour is therefore necessarily a reliable guide to the future. Will Canberra be able to maintain this two-step dance and, if so, in what form? This chapter seeks to address these questions by examining contemporary regional trends that are affecting Australia's perceptions of its security, by examining how Australia has thus far responded, and with what effect for its relationship with the United States.

This chapter argues that an important trend in the region is what can be understood as the 'politics of leadership' among the major powers: the United States, China, Japan and India. This is being driven by China's rise, Japan's efforts to retain a regional balance of power, and US efforts to reconcile regional structural change with its own global predominance. While the United States remains the global unipolar power, an increasingly multipolar order appears to be emerging at the regional level. Australia has responded to the politics of leadership by deepening its bilateral relations with each of the key regional players. Accordingly, Australia is acting 'as if' a multipolar regional system exists. This posture is driven by its efforts to maximize security and economic advantages, to avail itself of Asia's economic dynamism, and to appear to be even-handed with regard to the leadership politics among the major powers. This approach confirms the Howard government's view that pragmatic bilateral relationships provide Australia with influence to shape the regional architecture to its own advantage.

Yet the Howard government's approach, while having certain virtues, is nonetheless potentially unsatisfactory for establishing Australia's credentials as an influential *regional* player. New regionalist projects, such as the EAS, have presented the Australian government with powerful countertrends to its bilateral approach. To some extent, the Howard government has been forced to modify this approach in order to avoid being marginalized as a second-tier member with diminished influence in the region. However, the government's modifications may not be enough to give it the agency it seeks. If Australia were to be marginalized, its utility to the United States would be diminished and US–Australia relations could suffer. If that happened, then Australia's value to the region, as a means of keeping the United States engaged, could be further undermined. The end point of this logic is that Australia could end up being marginalized by both the region and the United States.

The first part of this chapter will address the changes that have recently occurred in regional order. It will subsequently examine Australia's responses to these trends and how the Howard government has modified its approach accordingly. It will explore these responses in the context of Australia's bilateral relationships as well as in the context of regional institutions, including the Asia–Pacific Economic Cooperation (APEC) forum, the ASEAN Regional Forum (ARF), and most recently the EAS. Finally, it will outline the implications of Australia's changed approach for its bilateral alliance with the United States and offer some brief conclusions regarding the utility of this approach over the longer term.

The politics of regional leadership and Australia's responses

A significant dynamic in the Asia–Pacific region that influences Australia's security perceptions is what can be understood as the 'politics of leadership' which is being played out by the major powers—the United States, China, Japan and India—at the geostrategic, economic and regional institutional levels. China's rise and the economic dynamism of the region is causing the other major powers to consider their place in the region in unprecedented ways. China's growth rates have approximated at nine per cent per annum for more than 25 years. There are predictions that by 2040 China will surpass the United States to become the largest global economy.[1]

There is now a robust debate on the current and future nature of the relationships between the United States and the rising Asian powers. Offensive realists, such as John Mearsheimer, forecast an inevitable conflict between China and the United States at some yet undetermined time.[2] Liberal institutionalists, while not explicitly disagreeing with Mearsheimer, argue that China is learning new habits and demonstrating its international institutionalism credentials by participating in regional and global institutions in an interdependent economic system.[3] But regardless of their positions, most scholars would agree that regional great powers are increasingly trying to establish their leadership credentials and to attract other countries as at least non-committed hedgers, if not active supporters.

China has been particularly active in cultivating such support. Since 1979, China has undergone staggering economic growth and used this to concomitantly increase its regional influence. Its success in doing so has been largely contingent on its ability to persuade Southeast Asian countries, as well the United States and Japan, that it is essentially a peaceful power that does not seek to revise the status quo. Its increasingly proactive participation in multilateral regional forums and initiatives, such as the signing of the Treaty of Amity and Cooperation (TAC) in October 2003 and the ASEAN Code of Conduct on the South China Sea in November 2002, are illustrative of some of the initiatives it has taken to achieve this objective. China has also signed a series of bilateral agreements with individual Southeast Asian countries as part of its 'new security concept'.[4] It has done so in order to reassure these states that it does not seek to dislocate the United States from the region. While China is eager to garner increased regional support, its concerns relating to a resurgent and remilitarized Japan render it more accepting of the United States as an important constraining influence.

The United States' own views of China's rise in the region, however, are multifaceted and frequently vary depending on the particular government agency. In its 2006 Annual Report to Congress, the US Department of Defense noted that 'China has the greatest potential to compete militarily with the United States and field disruptive military technologies that could even over time offset traditional US military advantage'.[5] US Deputy Secretary of State Robert Zoellick was representative of the State Department's more moderate view of China, when he stated in 2005 that he hoped China would become a 'stakeholder' in the region.[6] While more moderate, Zoellick's speech still highlighted Washington's expectations that China become a party to, and actively support, the US-led global order. Yet these statements are also suggestive of the Bush administration's ambiguous stance relating to how much influence it is willing to concede to China at the regional level.

This sense of caution regarding China's current and future behaviour is also shared by most Japanese officials. As a key player in the politics of regional leadership, Japan is frequently seen to be pursuing closer alliance relations with the United States to balance against China. Its insinuated support for Taiwan is also said to be motivated by China's rise. Certainly the fluctuating Sino–Japanese relationship—focused on the 'wars of history' and competing claims in the East China Sea—is one dimension of the politics of leadership that takes place in the region. Another dimension is the economic competition between the two countries that is observable in the rush towards preferential trade agreements with the ASEAN countries. In response to China's recent efforts to cultivate a series of bilateral free trade agreements, for instance, Japan proposed a regional multilateral free trade area in August 2006.

Increasingly, the rise of India is also affecting the regional power equation. While the Sino–Indian relationship is warming, there is evidence to suggest that both Japanese and US policymakers regard India as a potentially important balancing force. The Bush administration's efforts to forge a 'strategic partnership' with India are illustrative. Washington and Tokyo's views relating to India as an important balancer are reinforced by India's still outstanding border disputes with China. India's aims for leadership in South Asia are also often frustrated by Beijing. For example, China continues to foster close relations with Myanmar and has constructed intelligence collection facilities in the Andaman Sea. China also provides ongoing support to Pakistan, including material support for its nuclear deterrent against India.

The regional powers' jostling for leadership is evident not only in their relationships with each other but also in their dealings with other countries that they wish to influence. The United States is the most experienced leader but also the most complacent, usually relying on other smaller countries to 'need' the US presence as insurance against the unknowns of Japan and China. Japan's leadership credentials are limited to its economic prowess as the third largest world economy and as the leading source of regional investment and capital. This is primarily because Tokyo continues to battle with others' perceptions of its militarist past and as a state that cannot be a 'normal' military power. China too is inexperienced as a leader and ambivalent about what such leadership should connote. This ambivalence derives from a fundamental dilemma which Beijing faces as China continues to develop. On the one hand, China must remain focused on its internal development and foster a stable regional environment to facilitate its ongoing economic growth. It is this ongoing economic growth that allows it to exercise regional influence. It is also learning from observing the United States that hegemony and unilateralism can engender strong 'soft balancing' tendencies on the part of other countries. Simultaneously, however, China must also *appear* strong. As Robert Gilpin has observed, cultivating the reputation for power is equally as important as developing material capabilities.[7]

Without this visible demonstration of power, Japan and the United States could also cause China to appear weak in the eyes of smaller Southeast Asian countries and indeed its own population.

Yet it is because of the various flaws in the leadership credentials of each of these major powers that they continue to compete in the politics of leadership. The significance of this is that it reveals a new development in the evolution of regional order. With four major powers now vying for positions of leadership, the Asia–Pacific is increasingly evolving into a regional multipolar order rather than a unipolar one dominated by the United States.

Australia's responses

Australia's primary response to these developments has been to both broaden and deepen its relations with all four countries. As Prime Minister Howard explained in his September 2005 address to the Asia Society, 'one of the hallmarks of Australia's policy in the past decade has been our capacity, simultaneously, to deepen relations with the United States, whilst expanding our relations with *many* nations in the Asia Pacific region' [emphasis added].[8] Clearly, the Howard government believes that it can legitimately manage a series of 'special relationships' with multiple regional actors.[9]

As Paul Dibb notes in Chapter 3 of this volume, the Howard government maintains that its relationship with the United States remains the most integral to Australia's national security. It has differentiated its relationship with the United States from that of other countries by emphasizing the binding force of shared values between the two countries. Australia has also emerged as a staunch supporter of the US-led 'war on terror', conducted under the auspices of ANZUS. While Australia's military contributions to 'coalitions of the willing' in Iraq and Afghanistan are limited, Canberra's diplomatic support for these missions is highly valued by the United States as lending a degree of diplomatic legitimacy. Strong diplomatic support, coupled with Howard's close personal ties with US President George W. Bush, signal confirmation of Australia's ongoing security relationship with the United States. Apart from being Australia's closest security ally, the United States is also one of Australia's most important longstanding economic partners: for example, it continues to be Australia's largest source of foreign direct investment.[10]

At the same time, as Michael Wesley observes in Chapter 5, Australia's relationship with China is widening and deepening. In line with Prime Minister Howard's view that China is 're-shaping Asia and the world',[11] Australia's trade with China has quadrupled in the last decade.[12] Such is its desire to increase the economic relationship that Australia is the second developed country to begin negotiations with China on a free trade agreement. Yet even without a free trade agreement, China has become Australia's second largest export market after Japan.[13] The Sino–Australian relationship is an increasingly dynamic one and goes beyond the obvious mutual economic complementarities of which each is taking advantage. Australia is more optimistic than its US ally regarding China's current and future behaviour. On the thorny issue of Taiwan, Australian Foreign Minister Alexander Downer is 'optimistic' that both sides will exercise restraint, not least because each side has 'so much at stake economically'.[14] Howard advised his audience at the Asia Society that 'to see China's rise in zero-sum terms is overly pessimistic, intellectually misguided and potentially dangerous. It is the negation of what the West has been urging on China now for decades'. As he went on to make clear, the relationship is built on 'shared goals' and is not 'obsessed by those things that make us different'.[15] The United States is observing Australia's relationship with China with interest. According to one Australian foreign policy scholar, Washington has 'noted Australia's refusal to support the United States in opposing the European Union's relaxation of the arms embargo to China [and] Foreign Minister Downer's ambiguous interpretation of Australia's obligations in a Taiwan contingency'.[16]

As Des Ball and Brendan Taylor detail in Chapter 4 of this volume, Australia is also deepening its relations with Japan, putting aside several decades of fear regarding resurgent Japanese militarism. The Trilateral Strategic Dialogue (TSD) between Japan, the United States and Australia has already been elevated to ministerial level, underscoring Downer's comments that 'Japan remains a strong ally of both the United States and Australia'.[17] Australia was willing to invest in this dialogue, despite its own apprehensions that China might perceive it as part of a US-led containment plot. Beyond the TSD, other defence connections with Japan have included protection by the Australian Defence Force (ADF) of Japanese personnel undertaking reconstruction in Iraq's Al Muthanna province. In August 2006, Downer proposed a new formal security agreement between Australia and Japan that would include joint exercises and training between the two defence forces and build on existing humanitarian cooperation and peacekeeping operations. Australia has also vigorously supported Japan's membership of the UN Security Council. Australia's economic relationship with Japan is additionally poised to develop further if the 2005 feasibility study for an Australia–Japan free trade agreement reveals that such an agreement would be mutually advantageous.[18]

And as Sandy Gordon discusses in Chapter 6, India is the latest country to be added to Australia's list of major trading (and potentially strategic) partners. India is the world's second-fastest growing economy next to China. With growth rates of eight per cent per annum, India is now Australia's sixth biggest export market.[19] In May 2005, the Indian and Australian trade ministers agreed to negotiate a Trade and Economic Framework.[20] Australia's economic relationship with India could be further enhanced if, when it hosts the 2007 APEC Summit, Australia chooses to invite India.[21] Australian foreign policy has traditionally neglected India due to the relative distance between India and Australia's major population centres on the Australian eastern seaboard. Yet Canberra's increasing engagement with that power underscores Australia's approach to its regional relationships. Rather than placing all its eggs in one basket, Australia has sought to diversify its ties in the region, so as to continue to capitalize on the unique security and economic benefits that each potential 'leader' provides amidst emerging multipolarity.

Explaining Australia's responses

Australia has diversified its relations with the region's major powers, deepened and widened its bilateral arrangements, and concentrated on achieving material outcomes for several reasons. First, such an approach enables Australia to maximise its economic and security benefits. Australia seeks to capitalize on Asia's rapid growth, but the 1997 Asian financial crisis also underscored the importance of economic diversification. Indeed, Australia's European and American markets are widely credited as having allowed Australia to be less adversely affected. With regards to security, Australia's diversification approach has allowed it to tread a fine line between supporting the US alliance whilst not ignoring the importance of working with other regional powers to realize Australia's national interests. In fact, the Howard government regards its approaches to both the United States and regional powers as mutually reinforcing. Whereas Australia's relationship with the United States is perceived as granting it greater leverage in engaging with countries in East Asia, so too do Australia's relationships within, and specialized knowledge of, the region provide it leverage within the alliance. By adopting a diversification approach, Australia is therefore able to garner greater influence in its respective relationships and maximise its security and economic benefits.

These fallback options, and the leverage they subsequently garner, also enable Australia to stay outside the politics of leadership on specific issues, should it so choose. In part, Australia's stable bilateral relationship with the United States has assisted it in not necessarily having to choose sides between China and Japan. Likewise, Australia's strengthened relationship with China is also being heeded by US officials. In 2001, former US Deputy Secretary of State Richard Armitage visited Australia expounding that, in the event of a Taiwan crisis, Australia would be expected to provide support for US troops. The United States has remained sensitive to Australia's stance on the Taiwan issue, as evidenced by reactions to Downer's statements in 2004 that ANZUS would not necessarily be invoked in such a crisis.[22] More recently, however, US officials have adopted a softer line and have not voiced such stark demands.

Like the ASEAN states, Australia has adopted this diversification approach so as to shape the region in ways that suit its own interests. As the prime minister stated in his 2005 speech at the Lowy Institute for

International Policy: 'Australians can shape our environment and our destiny, and not simply be takers of trends set elsewhere.'[23] Australia is particularly intent on preventing its marginalization in the region in the light of Asia's rapid growth. According to some scholars, Australia is already marginalized to the point that it is losing its relative influence. In his book *Australian Finds Home,* for instance, Graeme Dobell observes that the gap in wealth and strategic capabilities between Australia and regional states has closed or has increasingly narrowed, thereby forcing the Howard government to adjust Australia's regional foreign policy to these changed circumstances.[24] Through its strong bilateral relationship with the United States, Australia hopes to gain greater leverage in its relations with Asian countries. The Howard government therefore does not use the alliance to separate itself from the region, but rather as a means of gaining greater leverage and as an alternative basis for relating with core ASEAN members and Japan.

The efficacy of Australia's responses

Australia's strong emphasis on bilateral arrangements that produce substantive practical outcomes has enabled the Howard government to maintain its strong record of economic growth and to build relations with countries that hold differing value systems. However, the Howard government's emphasis on strong bilateral relationships also appears to have simultaneously undermined its efforts to gain greater influence over the future shape of the regional order. Leverage-seeking strategies, such as used by Australia in its efforts to counterbalance the US alliance through its various relationships with East Asian countries, are an effective form of influence in a bilateral context.

Yet, increasingly, the politics of leadership are also being played out at the multilateral level and in regionalist projects. Since the 1997 Asian financial crisis and widespread dissatisfaction with the US response to that event, there has been a profusion of regional multilateral forums that are dedicated to a range of security issues—narrowly and broadly defined—and economic development. In addition, there has emerged a robust dialogue regarding a new form of regionalism based on establishing security and economic 'communities' throughout Northeast and Southeast Asia. This has been officially encapsulated in the notion of an 'East Asian Community'. These initiatives are primarily ASEAN-driven. They are consistent with the politics of leadership, however, in that they reaffirm the credentials of rising Asian powers to exercise a leadership position in the region vis-à-vis the United States, and to further their own regional influence within regionalist projects. Regionalist projects enable the great powers to compete for leadership credentials, yet without giving rise to perceptions of revisionism and thereby alienating lesser powers. Middle powers, such as Australia, have traditionally been *able* to exercise influence in multilateral forums, but this is predicated on their actual willingness to engage with these initiatives.

Until very recently Australia's approach to this regionalism dynamic has generally been to explicitly declare its ongoing preference for bilateralism based on achieving substantive and practical outcomes. Yet this approach misses the point that all the regionalist projects—forums and communities—have two agendas. The first is the one that Prime Minister Howard alludes to: measurable material outcomes, or 'substance'. Such substantive outcomes may include the potential benefits of low or zero tariffs as part of a region-wide free trade agreement. Regional security arrangements that produce transparent defence budgets and help ameliorate regional security problems, such as nuclear proliferation from North Korea, are illustrative of some of the more substantive and concrete security benefits that may ensue.

The other less explicit but equally important role of multilateral forums and regionalist projects is to provide an avenue for diplomatic signalling. A country may demonstrate support for a regional multilateral forum, perhaps to signal that it identifies with other participants of the forum and has commonly held interests or principles. These interests and principles may range from support for the status quo, preservation of territorial integrity, or certain pan-regional ideals. Signals may also be sent in multilateral forums as a means of demonstrating support for a particular member's political objectives. These include assisting a major power in establishing its leadership credentials or including a particular power to signal that it should be more involved in regional affairs. Participation in regionalist projects also sends important signals that despite continuing political tensions, notions of regionalism and cooperation are still endorsed.

This explanation of a dual agenda goes some way towards reconciling the arguments maintained by the sceptics and the optimists of East Asian regionalism. In line with the sceptics, it acknowledges the importance of attaining substantive outcomes and the role that great power politics can play in shaping multilateralism. Yet it also acknowledges the liberal institutionalist arguments that regionalism and multilateralism are not necessarily incompatible with power politics and that within East Asia competition and cooperation coexist. In short, achieving substantive outcomes and diplomatic signalling as part of a larger great power political game can coexist with multilateralism.

Under the Howard government, Australia's approach towards regionalism has tended to place greater emphasis on the first objective: obtaining substantive material outcomes. As Howard said recently, 'we believe that what matters most for our regional engagement is the substance of relations between countries, more so than the formal architecture of any diplomatic exchange'.[25] For this prime minister, 'instruments ... [that] elevate results over process and form ... serve Australia well'.[26] Australia has supported regional dialogues and multilateral arrangements geared towards the realization of clear practical outcomes. Recent examples include the Proliferation

Security Initiative (PSI) and the Asia–Pacific Climate Change Partnership. This corresponds with the Bush administration's 'coalitions of the willing' approach—namely, that mission determines the members and not vice versa.

This is in direct contrast to Australia's approach to regional forums and community building under the Hawke and Keating Labor governments. During this period, Australia played an important instigative role in establishing the APEC forum and the ARF. Such was then Foreign Minister Gareth Evans' enthusiasm for regional multilateralism, as a feature of the regional architecture and as an instrument for shaping regional order to suit Australia's interests, that he was sometimes accused of subjecting the region to 'initiative overload'. Nonetheless, Evans' enthusiasm reflected his awareness that regional forums have a dual agenda—a material one and a diplomatic one—and that it is imperative that Australia participates in both.

If Australia gives preference to the first agenda, it sends an implicit signal that Australia has little confidence in efforts to forge a regional identity or in viable regional cooperation over the longer term. It is a vote of 'no confidence' in regionalist projects, which can be offensive to those who participate in the discourse and the practical efforts to institutionalize regionalism. By not endorsing the second agenda, the Australian government is also at risk of failing to acknowledge the importance of discourse and the diplomatic signalling practices that participation in regionalism conveys. All these factors work against Australia's stated objective to shape the region to its advantage.

The Howard government's often under-appreciation of the importance of this second agenda was suggested by the prime minister's 2005 remarks regarding the TAC. This document of codified regional principles has served as the basis for several regionalist initiatives in recent years. The prime minister argued that the TAC was representative of a 'mind-set that we've really got to move on from'.[27] His views were regarded as offensive by some of those countries who have already signed the TAC—not just the ten ASEAN states but also China, Japan and South Korea.[28] Malaysian Prime Minister Abdullah Badawi rebuked the Australian prime minister with his reply that members of the Asian community 'have a role to play and standards to uphold'.[29] Badawi's comments suggest that if Australia wanted to have a role in influencing the shape of the region, it had to uphold certain diplomatic standards predesignated by the ASEAN countries as integral to the regionalist project. It stands to reason that Australia's reluctance to engage in the second diplomatic agenda of regionalism has gone some way towards hindering its ability to cultivate a larger regional role.

Changes in the Howard government's approach?

There is some evidence that the Howard government is shifting towards combining the first and second agendas, at least in APEC and the ARF. After some neglect in the early part of its term, the Howard government is now elevating APEC as Australia's preferred regional forum. It regards APEC as an increasingly important driving force in shaping the region's institutional architecture. As the prime minister has observed, 'APEC has served us well as the pre-eminent regional institution and Australia remains strongly committed to ensuring that it remains responsive to emerging regional challenges'.[30] APEC is favoured by the government for several reasons. First, its emphasis on trade liberalization and economic cooperation ostensibly delivers Australia the substantive material outcomes that the Howard government desires. Second, it is one of the few regional forums that includes Australia and meets at the heads-of-government level and which, simultaneously, includes the United States. Accordingly, Australia is able to use this forum as an avenue through which to diplomatically signal its own regional credentials and the continued centrality of the United States to the emerging Asia–Pacific order. US participation is supported by some other regional states, such as Japan, which have a strong interest in retaining an offshore American presence in this part of the world. The United States likewise regards APEC as an important forum for diplomatically advancing its own objectives, including ongoing active economic engagement in the region and counterterrorism initiatives in Southeast Asia. With the support of these countries, Australia hopes to be able to pursue its aims of shaping an open and inclusivist regional order.

Yet, regardless of the Australian government's view, APEC's prospects are limited because of longstanding regional scepticism about realizing the forum's economic objectives across different sectors within a meaningful timeframe. Moreover, APEC's impotency during the Asian financial crisis, coupled with Washington's increasing preoccupation with Iraq and Afghanistan, have cast doubt on that institution's long-term viability and purpose. These doubts have been only further exacerbated by the increasingly diffuse nature of APEC's agenda. APEC's agenda has recently been broadened to encompass not only economic trade liberalization, but also issues including counterterrorism and avian flu. This broadening focus has not only led member countries to question APEC's institutional rationale, but has also distracted them from concentrating on trade liberalization objectives that were established at the forum's outset. Therefore, although Australia is emphasizing APEC's diplomatic agenda, the institution's capacity to remain viable is a matter of debate.

Australia's attempts to pursue a dual agenda—and its limitations in doing so—are also evident in Australia's recent support for the ARF. Until recently, the Howard government's support for the ARF has been based on the expectation that the institution should deliver material outcomes that ameliorated or even resolved existing regional security problems that were of concern to Australia. Yet, with each annual ARF meeting, no such resolutions were forthcoming. The ARF did not even demonstrate visible progress towards implementing those preventive diplomacy measures that were outlined in the 1995 ARF Concept Paper. Moreover, the prospects for the ARF's substantive change are not high. Yet, according to East Asian security scholar, Barry Desker, 'unless a new role is found for the ARF, it will be sidelined in the years ahead'.[31]

Notwithstanding its desire to see the ARF produce more concrete positive outcomes, Australia appears to appreciate the diplomatic importance of endorsing it as a regionalist project. As Downer said after the 2006 ARF meeting, 'the ARF is effective in helping to create an environment in the region even if you can't always expect it over night to solve problems'.[32] Moreover, from the Howard government's perspective, the ARF—like APEC—ties the United States into the emerging regional security architecture. Indeed, Washington also appears to be increasingly appreciative of the ARF's diplomatic value. In September 2005, the US Deputy Secretary of State, Robert Zoellick, stressed that ASEAN, Japan and Australia and others should work with the United States 'through the ASEAN Regional Forum and the Asia Pacific Economic forum'.[33] Increasingly, the United States regards the ARF as a way to signal to China its ongoing interests in, and commitment to, the region. The attendance of US Secretary of State, Condoleezza Rice, at the 2006 ARF meeting was another such signal.[34] The US comments and actions flow on from China's own efforts to use the ARF as a useful avenue through which to signal its new-found conversion to regional multilateralism and leadership capacity.

Ironically, Australia's (and the United States') increasing support for and use of APEC and the ARF as diplomatic instruments, largely result from the emergence of regional institutions and a regionalist idea that is potentially exclusive of these countries. The notion of an exclusively 'East Asian' regional grouping dates back to the mid-1990s. Yet the potential institutionalization of these ideas—in the form of the ASEAN-plus-three grouping and, more recently, the EAS—were suggestive of trends that were adverse to Australian interests and merited a more active Australian involvement in multilateralism. If Australia was to shape events in a way conducive to its own preferred notion of what constitutes regional order, engagement predicated on realizing merely 'substantive' outcomes or material benefits was no longer sufficient. Instead, Canberra increasingly perceived Asian multilateralism in political terms and sought to use these forums as instruments of diplomatic signalling. This is evident not only in the growing and changing nature of Australian support for more inclusivist regional institutions such as APEC and the ARF, but also by the nature of its participation in the potentially more 'exclusivist' EAS and the ways in which it has sought to shape this nascent institution's development.

The East Asia Summit: Australia as a second-tier member?

The idea of an EAS originates in a 2001 report by the ASEAN-led East Asian Vision Group, which identified it as one of the foremost long-term goals in the establishment of an East Asian Community. APEC's weaknesses in delivering on trade liberalization, as well as emergent trends towards greater regionalism in Europe and the Americas, furthered regional countries' drive for a more integrated East Asian Community. The inaugural meeting of the EAS took place in Kuala Lumpur on 14 December 2005. Some analysts have argued that, if successful, the EAS could potentially rival the European Union (EU) and the North American Free Trade Agreement (NAFTA) in stature.[35] Yet, what remains at issue is what actually constitutes an East Asian Community as embodied in the EAS. Who is a member and what does this membership connote?

With some resistance from Malaysia and China, the decision was made in March 2005 that membership should also be extended to India, Australia and New Zealand. Yet such membership was to be made contingent on the willingness of these countries to accede to the TAC. ASEAN's insistence that Australia sign the TAC before joining the EAS was illustrative of the distinct limits on Australia's negotiating capacity and its difficulties in shaping regionalism in a more integrated regional structure. Unlike APEC in the early 1990s, the EAS was an ASEAN-plus-three-led initiative and not one in which Australia played an integral instigative role. More important than the institution itself was what the EAS symbolized: a strengthened East Asian bloc that could potentially exclude Australia. Australia was invited into this summit on conditional terms, and not presumed an automatic candidate.

While Australia was eager to secure a place at the EAS, so as not to be excluded from the region, it was initially hesitant to sign the TAC. The Howard government had fundamental concerns relating to the TAC's ideological ramifications and its potential effects for Australia's own security. Unlike the ASEAN countries, Australia does not subscribe to the 1955 Bandung Principles of Non-Alignment and maintains a security alliance with the United States. Yet in July 2005, the Australian government reversed its previous decision, and agreed to sign this treaty on the basis of a series of negotiated understandings with the ASEAN countries. These understandings allowed Australia to adhere to the TAC without simultaneously prejudicing its pre-existing bilateral or multilateral obligations. As Downer stated at the time: 'It's as simple as that. Signing is the price we pay.'[36] While the Australian government remained a reluctant party to the TAC, Downer's comments are suggestive of a recognition that Canberra would have to engage with East Asia, to a large extent, on ASEAN's own terms.

From an Australian perspective, membership in the EAS is important, in part, for the material economic and security benefits that Australia is likely to derive. The EAS promises to facilitate greater flows of investment, create more opportunities for Australian business, and over time produce a free trade area extending from northern China to western India to New Zealand. Strategically, it has the potential to integrate security cooperation among East Asian states that will assist in controlling transregional threats such as avian flu, terrorism and environmental degradation. It could also assist in developing common regional solutions for potential flashpoints including the Korean Peninsula, the South China Sea or maritime security in the Malacca Strait. As energy demands in the region increase, cooperation on such issues will become more important. For these reasons the Howard government regards the EAS as an important opportunity, from which Australia should not to be excluded.

The EAS is also likely to confer certain diplomatic benefits. These include discouraging regional hegemony by any one of Asia's rising great powers— China, Japan, or India—by institutionally embedding ASEAN as the key driving force for regional integration. The EAS also signals to the United States that its membership—let alone its leadership—in the region cannot be taken as a given. Paradoxically, the EAS is likely to, and indeed has, commanded greater US attention on regional affairs. Yet Australia's own status as a full-fledged member of this summit is also important if it is to maximize these benefits and safeguard against its own exclusion.

Australia's potential for marginalization in the emerging East Asian order was further underscored by comments made during the inaugural meeting. Indeed, the possible second-tier status of Australia in this regional institution was alluded to by Chinese premier Wen Jiabao who observed that while Australia, New Zealand and India would be welcome to participate: 'The East Asia Summit should respect the desires of East Asian countries, and should be led by East Asian countries.'[37] Likewise, Malaysian Prime Minister Badawi suggested:

> You are talking about a community of East Asians, and I don't know how the Australians could regard themselves as East Asians. ... The East Asian community is a geographic definition. We are not talking about [Australia, New Zealand, or India] being a member of the community. We are talking about common interests. If the common interests are that we want to see stability and prosperity, and our friends are willing to contribute through such forums as the East Asia Summit, then certainly, they will be welcome.[38]

While Australia has been welcomed into the EAS by such countries as Japan and Singapore, this emerging differentiation between 'members' of the community and 'friends' underscores the 'relative decline thesis' in Australia's regional influence. Further East Asian integration—where Australia is not designated by regional countries as an East Asian state—could portend an even further weakening of Australia's influence.

Australia's vision of an East Asian Community: mixed signals

Australia has still made use of the EAS as an avenue through which to diplomatically signal its own preferred view of regional order and, in doing so, it hopes to condition the development of the summit along these lines.

First, Australia has consistently advocated that the EAS should be built on the basis of practical ties and not on the basis of ideology. As Downer has emphasized, 'an East Asian Community will emerge for practical reasons, not for ideological reasons'.[39] In many ways, this is a reaction to former Malaysian Prime Minister Mahathir's notion of the East Asian Economic Caucus (EAEC) geared towards unifying Asian countries to confront European or North American countries in international trading institutions. It is also closely linked to the 'Asian values' debate of the 1990s, during which period some Southeast Asian leaders argued that Asian countries possessed a particular set of communal values which differentiated them from Western countries. By divorcing the EAS and East Asian integration from ideological principles, Australia is able to avert difficult questions relating to its own identification with the region as a culturally Western country. As such, it can mitigate the likelihood that it will become a second-tier member of the forum because it is not, and does not distinctively identify itself as, East Asian. Moreover, it is able to maintain its alliance with the United States, yet still participate in a group that is nominally built on the basis of principles of non-alignment. By emphasizing the EAS' practical character, the Howard government is able to maintain its posture that Australia does not have to choose between its history and geography. Furthermore, an EAS built on practical ties supports Australia's preference for material outcomes.

Second, the Howard government has publicly emphasized that it regards the EAS as just one of many overlapping regional institutions in East Asia that could engender the formation of an East Asian Community. Such overlapping forums would certainly serve Australia's political interest in keeping the United States and all other major powers centrally involved. Australia would also be assured of augmenting its own 'voice' in regional affairs by preventing the marginalization of those forums in which its plays a more important role, rather than the second-tier position it is presently allocated in the EAS. Indeed, as indicated above, the Howard government has constantly reiterated the continued overriding importance of APEC and has gone so far as to emphasize that the EAS cannot replace APEC as the premier East Asian regional organization.[40]

Third, Australia does not anticipate that the East Asian Community will resemble that of the EU. As Downer has observed:

> Rather we expect to see the gradual evolution of an East Asian community that reflects the character of the region. This will entail growing economic integration through a web of free trade agreements which might eventually emerge into one regional FTA ... [and] a gradual strengthening of security cooperation in the region, particularly to counter trans-boundary threats.[41]

This envisioned feature would continue to support the Howard government's traditional preference for bilateralism.

Fourth, Australia's efforts to preserve bilateralism and to augment its strategic standing by promoting APEC and other non-exclusively East Asian regional organizations is underscored by the Howard government's strongly expressed view that the EAS is only in its early evolutionary stages and is not yet guaranteed. As Howard somewhat undiplomatically noted, 'I am very pleased that Australia is part of [the East Asia Summit] but I don't think we should get exaggerated views about its relevance at this point'.[42] In part, this is attributable to the government's concerns regarding the long-term viability of the institution to produce material outcomes. However, as already suggested above, it is also indicative of Australia's efforts to augment its own 'voice' by subscribing to the importance of other non-exclusively East Asian regional organizations in which the United States, Australia's security ally, plays an important role.

Hedging its bets

Notwithstanding the desire to have a voice in shaping the material and diplomatic regional architecture, Australia has continued to cultivate its own independent capacity for leverage in the region by maintaining strong bilateral ties with various regional partners. Australia believes it can command greater influence in a bilateral context (because of its mineral resources and security ties with the United States) than in a collective East Asian grouping (that evolves on an ideological basis). Australia assumes that it can make use of such bilateral relationships to build coalitions and garner greater influence within the EAS. To some extent, this was evidenced during the initial stages of determining the EAS' membership, in which countries such as Singapore, Thailand and Japan advocated a more open and inclusive regional architecture that included Australia, compared with China and Malaysia who sought a more distinctively East Asian grouping. During the latter part of 2005, Australia made use of its bilateral talks with China to encourage greater Chinese support for Australia's participation in this summit.[43]

Australia has also continued to cultivate its own independent capacity for exercising leverage in the region by maintaining its strong alliance with the United States. The Howard government has consistently maintained that '[Australia] would not be as engaged in Asian security matters was it not for this strong US alliance'.[44] The US alliance is regarded as 'enhanc[ing] the scope and effectiveness of our engagement with regional countries and institutions'.[45] For these reasons, Australia was markedly hesitant to sign the TAC, out of concern regarding its implications for Australia's alliance commitment with the United States and the potential political impact of Australia's membership on the Australian–US relationship. While the United States was initially apprehensive regarding the potentially exclusivist nature of the EAS, the Bush administration was reported as endorsing Australia's participation in that forum during Prime Minister Howard's visit to Washington in July 2005.[46] For Washington, one of the values of the US–Australian relationship is the insights that Australia's embedded place in the region provides the United States. Ironically, the logic of that observation is that if Australia's place in regionalism is diminished, then so too is its usefulness to Washington.

While Australia is indeed hedging its bets, as are many other regional countries, it is evident that the Howard government's own sensitivity to changing regional dynamics, and the weaknesses of its traditional approach, has informed Australia's own response to the EAS and to the East Asian Community-building process as a whole. Australia has increasingly engaged in regional multilateralism and made use of diplomatic signalling in order to shape the development of regional order in a way that is conducive to its own interests. The extent to which it will be successful in doing so, however, is debatable in view of current regional dynamics. While Australia seeks to shape regional order, other countries in the region must also be willing to let it do so. To a large extent, this will depend on how the 'politics of leadership' plays out over the longer term.

Conclusion

Australia faces a number of challenges in its ongoing efforts to perform a two-step dance with its regional partners and its traditional security ally, the United States. This is not necessarily because it will be confronted with any distinctly defined 'choice', as is often presented in the literature. Rather, it is because changes in the regional order could potentially make it increasingly difficult to fulfil the expectations of these partners. With the rise of three new Asian powers, Australia behaves increasingly as if it is in a multipolar regional order, and has sought to solidify its relationships with each of these countries. The emergence of these powers, coupled by their competitive pursuit for regional leadership credentials, has given rise to new integrative forces for an East Asian Community. This is most clearly manifest in institutions such as the EAS. Whilst diversifying its relationships, Australia has also had to modify its approach towards these regional forums in a way that is complementary to, rather than subsidiary to, its bilateral agenda. Increasingly, Australia has made use of these institutions not only as a way of securing material outcomes, but also as an avenue through which to engage in diplomatic signalling. It has sought to do so in order to shape the evolving regional order in a way that is conducive to its own preferred vision of East Asian regionalism. This vision is one in which there are multiple overlapping regional institutions, the United States remains a key player, and Australia retains a prominent position rather than second-tier status.

This is broadly compatible with Australia's alliance with the United States. Indeed, several regional powers also maintain relationships with the United States and regard that power as an important offshore balancer. It is important to note however that, as these Asian powers become stronger, the need for such an offshore balancer may diminish. In the wake of the Asian financial crisis, intensified European and American regionalism, and American preoccupations with the 'war on terror', Asian countries increasingly perceive the importance of developing regional solutions for regional problems. The United States, meanwhile, has recently applauded Australia's participation in the EAS. As a close US ally, Australia is likely to assist in shaping regional order in a way that is conducive to US interests and continued active US involvement in the region. Embedded within the region, Australia also provides a source of specialized knowledge that can, in turn, inform US policy. Australia will face difficulties in maintaining this two-step dance if it becomes unable to fulfill these objectives because of its own marginalization from the region.

Whether or not Australia will be able to prevent this marginalization is largely contingent on how the politics of leadership plays out over time. To assist in shaping regional order, Australia must be able to build coalitions of like-minded countries within these multilateral forums. Institutional dominance by any one power will render this a difficult task. So too will US inactivity, or collusion between the regional powers to exclude the United States. A variety of institutions in which Australia can exercise greater initiative is also likely to be helpful. In view of these considerations, Australian policymakers have a vested interest in continuing to support ASEAN as the driving force for regional integration. Australia should also encourage greater US participation in the region, and attempt to provide each of the major powers with a voice in regional affairs whilst denying them hegemony.

However, diplomacy is always an interactive process. While Australia has adapted its methods so as to be able to successfully maintain its two-step dance over the longer term, ultimately it will only succeed if its regional dance partners are willing to come to the table. If Australia fails, it will not be because the United States and the region are necessarily in juxtaposition with one another. Instead, Australia's ability to manage *both* its alliance and regional partnerships will rest on how well it is able to cultivate the receptivity of these regional countries to Australia's diplomatic signals.

Notes

1 D. Shambaugh (ed.) *Power Shift: China and Asia's New Dynamics*, Berkeley, CA: University of California Press, 2005.
2 J. Mearsheimer, 'The rise of China will not be peaceful at all', *The Australian*, 18 November 2005.
3 R. Foot, 'Chinese strategies in a US-hegemonic global order', *International Affairs*, vol. 82, no. 1, January 2006, pp. 77–94.
4 The 'New Security Concept' is a Chinese foreign policy initiative presented at various ASEAN-led regional meetings since 1996. It was designed to counter what Beijing perceived as outmoded Cold War bilateral alliance relations, such as represented by the US San Francisco system. Beijing envisions regional security instead to be based on a series of mutually beneficial relationships. China has

sought to implement this concept by forging a series of friendships and partnership treaties with a variety of Southeast Asian countries.

5 United States Department of Defense, *Annual Report to Congress: Military Power of the People's Republic of China 2006*, Washington, DC: Department of Defense, 2006.

6 US Department of State, 'Whither China: from membership to responsibility?', Robert B. Zoellick, Deputy Secretary of State, remarks to National Committee on US–China Relations, 21 September 2005.

7 R. Gilpin, *War and Change in International Politics*, Cambridge: Cambridge University Press, 1981, p. 33.

8 Prime Minister the Hon. John Howard MP, address to the Asia Society lunch, New York City, 12 September 2005.

9 D.M. Jones and A. Benvenuti, 'Tradition, myth and the dilemma of Australian foreign policy', *Australian Journal of International Affairs*, vol. 60, no. 1, March 2006, pp. 114–5.

10 T. Sutherland, 'America invests less despite FTA', *Australian Financial Review*, 11 August 2006.

11 Howard, address to the Asia Society lunch.

12 Ibid.

13 Ibid.

14 The Hon. Alexander Downer MP, Minister for Foreign Affairs, Australia, 'The Australia–Japan partnership—growing stronger together', speech to the Japan Institute for International Affairs, 22 March 2005.

15 Howard, address to the Asia Society lunch.

16 M. Kelton, 'Perspectives on Australian foreign policy, 2005', *Australian Journal of International Affairs*, vol. 60, no. 2, June 2006, p. 231.

17 The Hon. Alexander Downer MP, Minister for Foreign Affairs, Australia, 'Australia, the United States and the world', speech to the Victorian Branch of the Australian Institute of International Affairs, 5 July 2005.

18 A. Capling, 'The case for a bilateral trade arrangement with Japan', *The Australian*, 4 August 2006.

19 The Hon. Alexander Downer MP, Minister for Foreign Affairs, Australia, 'Speech to the Australia–India Chamber of Commerce', Chennai, 6 June 2005.

20 Ibid.

21 G. Sheridan, 'Howard must bat for India', *The Australian*, 5–6 August 2006.

22 M. Foley, 'Australian government under fire for foreign minister's comments on Taiwan', *Associated Press*, 20 August 2004.

23 Prime Minister the Hon. John Howard MP, address at the opening of the Lowy Institute for International Policy, Sydney, 31 March 2005.

24 G. Dobell, *Australia Finds Home: The Choices and Chances of an Asia Pacific Journey*, Sydney: ABC Books, 2000.

25 Howard, address to the Asia Society lunch.

26 Ibid.

27 P. Kelly, 'Howard Taught a lesson in Asia', *The Australian*, 27 April 2005.

28 Ibid.

29 Ibid.

30 Howard, address to the Asia Society lunch.

31 B. Desker, 'Is the ARF obsolete? Three steps to avoid irrelevance', *PacNet*, no. 37A, 27 July 2006.

32 The Hon. Alexander Downer MP, Minister for Foreign Affairs, Australia, transcript, 'Question and answer session at the Japan National Press Club', 1 August 2006.

33 Cited in A. Acharya, 'East Asian integration is test for big powers', *Financial Times*, 14 December 2005.

34 The Secretary of State was criticized strongly for missing the 2005 meeting. See, for example, R.A. Cossa, 'Condoleezza Rice's "unfortunate" decision', *PacNet*, no. 30, 22 July 2005.
35 M. Richardson, 'Australia–Southeast Asian relations and the East Asian Summit', *Australian Journal of International Affairs*, vol. 59, no. 3, September 2005, p. 359.
36 'Australia signs friendship pact', *Straits Times*, 11 December 2005.
37 'Australia says it's no junior partner in East Asia', *Agence France Presse*, 14 December 2005.
38 Cited in T. Colebatch, 'Summit gets a little bit higher for Howard', *The Age*, 15 December 2005.
39 The Hon. Alexander Downer MP, Minister for Foreign Affairs, Australia, 'Australia's engagement with Asia', speech to the Asialink chairman's dinner, Melbourne, 1 December 2005.
40 Prime Minister the Hon. John Howard MP, transcript, 'Doorstop interview', Regent Hotel, Kuala Lumpur, 13 December 2005.
41 The Hon. Alexander Downer MP, Minister for Foreign Affairs, Australia, 'Australia, Asia, and global drivers for change', speech at Future Summit 2006, Brisbane, 12 May 2006.
42 Howard, 'Doorstop interview'.
43 'Australia gets "positive" response from China on East Asia Summit: Howard', *Agence France Presse*, 19 April 2005.
44 Downer, 'Australia, Asia, and global drivers for change'.
45 The Hon. Alexander Downer MP, Minister for Foreign Affairs, Australia, Biennial Sir Arthur Tange Lecture in Australian Diplomacy, Canberra, 8 August 2005.
46 P. Hartcher and Cynthia Banham, 'Bush gives Howard the nod for summit', *Sydney Morning Herald*, 21 July 2005.

Selected bibliography

Adams, R. (ed.) *Peace on Bougainville—Truce Monitoring Group*, Wellington: Victoria University Press, 2001.

Alagappa, M. (ed.) *Asian Security Practice: Material and Ideational Influences*, Stanford: Stanford University Press, 1998.

Ayson, R. and Ball, D. (eds) *Strategy and Security in the Asia–Pacific Region*, New South Wales: Allen & Unwin, 2006.

Ball, D. (ed.) *Pine Gap*, Sydney: Allen & Unwin, 1988.

——, *The ANZAC Connection*, Sydney: Allen & Unwin, 1985.

Ball, D. and Kerr, P., *Presumptive Engagement: Australia's Asia–Pacific Security Policy in the 1990s*, Sydney: Allen & Unwin, 1996.

Bearce, D.H., Flanagan, K.M. and Floros, K.M., 'Alliances, internal information, and military conflict among member-states', *International Organization*, vol. 60, no. 3, July 2006.

Bergin, A. and Bateman, S., *Future Unknown: The Terrorist Threat to Australian Maritime Security*, Canberra: Australian Strategic Policy Institute, 2005.

Blackwill, R. and Dibb, P. (eds) *America's Asian Alliances*, Cambridge, MA: MIT Press, 2000.

Blustein, P., *The Chastening: Inside the Crisis that Rocked the Global Financial System and Humbled the IMF*, New York: Public Affairs, 2001.

Bolton, D., *The Tyranny of Difference: Perceptions of Australian Defence Policy in Southeast Asia*, working paper no. 384, Canberra: Strategic and Defence Studies Centre, Australian National University, 2003.

Boyce, P.J. and Angel, J.R. (eds) *Diplomacy in the Marketplace: Australia in World Affairs 1981–90*, Melbourne: Longman Cheshire, 1992.

Brenchly, F., 'The Howard Defence Doctrine', *The Bulletin*, 28 September 1999.

Bristow, D., 'The Five Power Defence Arrangements: Southeast Asia's unknown regional security organization', *Contemporary Southeast Asia*, vol. 27, issue 1, April 2005.

Brown, B. (ed.) *New Zealand and Australia—Where are We Going?*, Wellington: New Zealand Institute of International Affairs, 2001.

——, (ed.) *New Zealand in World Affairs, Vol 3, 1972–1990*, Wellington: Victoria University Press, 1999.

Burnett, A., *The A–NZ–US Triangle*, Canberra: Strategic and Defence Studies Centre, Australian National University, 1988.

Campbell, K.M., 'The end of alliances? Not so fast', *Washington Quarterly*, vol. 27, no. 2, Spring 2004.

Cha, V., *Alignment Despite Antagonism: The United States–Korea–Japan Security Triangle*, Stanford, CA: Stanford University Press, 1999.

Commonwealth of Australia, *Australian Aid: Promoting Growth and Stability. A White Paper on the Australian Government's Overseas Aid Program*, Canberra: AusAID, 2006.

——, *Advancing the National Interest: Australia's Foreign and Trade Policy White Paper*, Canberra: National Capital Printing, 2003.

——, *Defence 2000: Our Future Defence Force*, Canberra: Department of Defence, 2000.

——, *Australia's Strategic Policy*, Canberra: Department of Defence, 1997.

——, *Defending Australia: Defence White Paper 1994*, Canberra: Department of Defence, 1994.

——, *Australia's Strategic Planning in the 1990s*, Canberra: Department of Defence, September 1992.

Cook, I., *Australia, Indonesia and the World: Public Opinion and Foreign Policy*, Sydney: Lowy Institute for International Policy, 2006.

——, *Australians Speak: Public Opinion and Foreign Policy*, Sydney: Lowy Institute for International Policy, 2005.

Cossa, R., 'US Asia policy: does an alliance-based policy still make sense?', *Issues & Insights*, vol. 3, no. 1, September 2001.

Cotton, J. and Ravenhill, J. (eds) *Trading on Alliance Security: Australia in World Affairs 2001–2005*, Melbourne: Oxford University Press, 2006.

——, *Seeking Asian Engagement: Australia in World Affairs 1991–1995*, Melbourne: Oxford University Press, 1997.

Dibb, P., *Essays on Australian Defence*, Canberra papers on strategy and defence no. 161, Canberra: Strategic and Defence Studies Centre, Australian National University, 2006.

——, 'Is strategic geography relevant to Australia's current defence policy?', *Australian Journal of International Affairs*, vol. 60, no. 2, June 2006.

——, 'US–Australia alliance relations: an Australian view', *Strategic Forum*, no. 216, Washington, DC: Institute for National Strategic Studies, National Defense University, 2005.

——, *Australia's Alliance with America*, Melbourne Asia policy papers no. 1, Melbourne: University of Melbourne, March 2003.

——, *Review of Australia's Defence Capabilities: Report to the Minister for Defence by Mr Paul Dibb*, Canberra: Australian Government Publishing Service, 1986.

Dibb, P., Hale, D. and Prince, P., 'Asia's insecurity', *Survival*, vol. 41, no. 3, 1999.

Dobell, G., *Australia Finds Home: The Choices and Chances of an Asia Pacific Journey*, Sydney: ABC Books, 2000.

Dupont, A., *East Asia Imperilled. Transnational Challenges to Security*, Cambridge and New York: Cambridge University Press, 2001.

Edwards, P., *Arthur Tange: Last of the Mandarins*, Crows Nest, NSW: Allen & Unwin, 2006.

——, *Permanent Friends? Historical Reflections on the Australian–American Alliance*, Lowy Institute paper 08, Sydney: Lowy Institute for International Policy, 2005.

——, *Crises and Commitments: The Politics and Diplomacy of Australia's Involvement in Southeast Asian Conflicts, 1948–1965*, Sydney: Allen & Unwin, 1992.

Edwards, P. and Goldsworthy, D., *Facing North: A Century of Australian Engagement with Asia, Vol. 2*, Melbourne: Melbourne University Press, 2003.

Elson, R.E., *Suharto: A Political Biography*, Cambridge: Cambridge University Press, 2001.

Foot, R., 'Chinese strategies in a US-hegemonic global order', *International Affairs*, vol. 82, no. 1, January 2006.

Forrester, G. and May, R.J. (eds) *The Fall of Soeharto*, Singapore: Select Books, 1999.

Garnaut, R., *Open Regionalism and Trade Liberalisation: An Asia–Pacific Contribution to the World Trade System*, Singapore: ISEAS, 1997.

Gheciu, A., 'Security institutions as agents of socialization? NATO and the "New Europe"', *International Organization*, vol. 59, no. 4, October 2005.

Gilpin, R., *War and Change in International Politics*, Cambridge: Cambridge University Press, 1981.

Goh, E., 'The US–China relationship and Asian security: negotiating change', *Asian Security*, vol. 1, no. 3, December 2005.

Goldstein, A., *Rising to the Challenge: China's Grand Strategy and International Security*, Stanford, CA: Stanford University Press, 2005.

Goldsworthy, D. (ed.) *Facing North: A Century of Australian Engagement with Asia*, *Vol. 1*, Melbourne: Melbourne University Press, 2001.

Gordon, A., 'The search for substance: Australia–India relations into the nineties and beyond', Australian foreign policy papers, Canberra: Department of International Relations, Australian National University, 1993.

Greenwood, G. and Harper, N. (eds) *Australia in World Affairs 1966–1970*, Melbourne: F.W. Cheshire, 1974.

——, *Australia in World Affairs 1950–1955*, Melbourne: F.W. Cheshire, 1957.

Groennings, S., Kelley, E.W. and Leiserson, M. (eds) *The Study of Coalition Behaviour*, New York: Holt & Winston, 1970.

Gyngell, A. and Wesley, M., *Making Australian Foreign Policy*, Port Melbourne: Cambridge University Press, 2003.

Hale, D., 'China's growing appetites', *The National Interest*, issue 76, Summer 2004.

Hall, R.A. (ed.) *Australia–New Zealand: Closer Defence Relationships*, Canberra: Australian Defence Studies Centre, 1993.

Hanson, M. and Tow, W.T. (eds) *International Relations in the New Century: An Australian Perspective*, South Melbourne: Oxford University Press, 2001.

Harries, O., *Understanding America*, Sydney: The Centre for Independent Studies, 2002.

Harries, O. and Switzer, T., 'Loyal to a fault', *The American Interest*, vol. 1, no. 4, Summer 2006.

Harrison, S.S. and Kemp, G., *India and America After the Cold War*, report of the Carnegie Endowment Study Group on US–Indian Relations in a Changing International Environment, Washington, DC: Carnegie Endowment for International Peace, 1993.

Hastings, P., *New Guinea: Problems and Prospects*, Melbourne: Cheshire/Australian Institute of International Affairs, 1969.

Hawke, B., *The Hawke Memoirs*, Melbourne: Mandarin, 1996.

Ho, J.H., 'The security of sea lanes in Southeast Asia', *Asian Survey*, vol. 46, no. 4, July/August 2006.

Hosono, S., 'Towards a comprehensive strategic partnership between Australia and Japan: Japan's perspective', *Australian Journal of International Affairs*, vol. 60, no. 4, December 2006.

Hudson, W.J. (ed.) *Australia's New Guinea Question*, Melbourne: Nelson/Australian Institute of International Affairs, 1975.

Huntington, S.P., *The Clash of Civilizations and the Remaking of World Order*, New York: Simon & Schuster, 1995.

——, 'The clash of civilizations?', *Foreign Affairs*, vol. 72, no. 3, Summer 1993.

Huxley, T., 'The tsunami and security: Asia's 9/11?', *Survival*, vol. 47, no. 1, Spring 2005.

Ikenberry, G. J., 'American grand strategy in the age of terror', *Survival*, vol. 43, no. 4, Winter 2001–2.

International Institute for Strategic Studies, *Military Balance 2006*, London: Routledge, 2006.

Jones, D.M. and Benvenuti, A., 'Tradition, myth and the dilemma of Australian foreign policy', *Australian Journal of International Affairs*, vol. 60, no. 1, March 2006.

Katzenstein, P.J. and Okawara, N., *Japan's National Security: Structures, Norms and Responses in a Changing World*, Ithaca, NY: Cornell University Press, 1993.

Keating, G., *Opportunities and Obstacles: Future Australian and New Zealand Cooperation on Defence and Security Issues*, working paper no. 391, Canberra: Strategic and Defence Studies Centre, Australian National University, 2004.

Keating, P., *Engagement: Australia Faces the Asia Pacific*, Sydney: Pan Macmillan, 2000.

Keith, K. (ed.) *Defence Perspectives: Papers Read at the 1972 Otago Foreign Policy School*, Wellington: Price Milburn, 1972.

Kelly, P., *Shipwrecked in Arcadia: The Australian Experiment*, Cambridge, MA: Harvard University Press, 2004.

Kelton, M., 'Perspectives on Australian foreign policy, 2005', *Australian Journal of International Affairs*, vol. 60, no. 2, June 2006.

Krepinevich, A.F., *Transforming America's Alliances*, Washington, DC: Centre for Strategic and Budgetary Assessments, February 2000.

Larkin, T.C. (ed.) *New Zealand's External Relations*, Wellington: New Zealand Institute of Public Administration, 1962.

Lee, K.Y., *From Third World to First: The Singapore Story: 1965–2000*, Singapore: Straits Times Press, 2000.

Liow, J.C.C. and Emmers, R. (eds) *Order and Security in Southeast Asia: Essays in Memory of Michael Leifer*, London: Routledge, 2006.

Liska, G., *Nations in Alliance: The Limits of Interdependence*, Baltimore, MD: Johns Hopkins University Press, 1962.

Lyon, R., *Alliance Unleashed: Australia and the US in a New Strategic Age*, Canberra: Australian Strategic Policy Institute, June 2005.

Lyon, R. and Tow, W.T., 'The future of the US–Australian security relationship', *Asian Security*, vol. 1, no. 1, January 2005.

Malik, M., 'Australia and the United States 2004–2005: all the way with the U.S.A.?', *Special Assessment Series*, Asia–Pacific Center for Security Studies, Hawaii, February 2005.

Manne, R. (ed.) *The Howard Years*, Melbourne: Black Inc, 2004.

McAllister, I., *Public and Elite Opinion in Australia Towards Defence Links with the United States*, Canberra: Australian National University, 2005.

McGibbon, R., *Pitfalls of Papua*, Lowy Institute paper 13, Sydney: Lowy Institute for International Policy, 2006.

Meaney, N., *The Search for Security in the Pacific 1901–14*, Sydney: Sydney University Press, 1976.

Mearsheimer, J., 'Why we will soon miss the Cold War,' *Atlantic Monthly*, vol. 266, no. 2, August 1990.

Menon, R., 'The end of alliances', *World Policy Journal*, vol. 20, no. 2, Summer 2003.

Metzemaekers, L., 'The Western New Guinea problem', *Pacific Affairs*, vol. 24, no. 2, June 1951.

Meyer, S.E., 'Carcass of dead policies: the irrelevance of NATO', *Parameters*, Winter 2003–4.

Mietzner, M., *The Politics of Military Reform in Post-Suharto Indonesia : Elite Conflict, Nationalism and Institutional Resistance*, Washington, DC: East West Center, 2006.

Monfries, J. (ed.) *Different Societies, Shared Futures: Australia, Indonesia and the Region*, Singapore: Institute of Southeast Asian Studies, 2006.

Norris, R.S. and Kristensen, H.M., 'India's nuclear forces, 2005', *Bulletin of the Atomic Scientists*, September/October 2005.

O'Callaghan, M., *Enemies Within: Papua New Guinea, Australia and the Sandline Crisis: The Inside Story*, Sydney and New York: Doubleday, 1999.

Patman, R.G., 'Globalisation and trans-Tasman relations: integration or divergence?', *Australian Journal of International Affairs*, vol. 55, no. 3, 2001.

Prins, G. (ed.) *Threats Without Enemies: Facing Environmental Insecurity*, London: Earthscan Publications, 1993.

Richardson, M., 'Australia–Southeast Asian relations and the East Asian Summit', *Australian Journal of International Affairs*, vol. 59, no. 3, September 2005.

Richelson, J.T. and Ball, D., *The Ties that Bind: Intelligence Cooperation between the UKUSA Countries*, London and Sydney: Allen & Unwin, 1985.

Riker, W.H., *The Theory of Political Coalitions*, New Haven, CT: Yale University Press, 1962.

Robinson, T.W. and Shambaugh, D. (eds) *Chinese Foreign Policy: Theory and Practice*, Oxford: Clarendon Press, 1994.

Rolfe, J., 'Australia–New Zealand relations: allies, friends, rivals', in Limaye, S. (ed.) *Asia's Bilateral Relations. Special Assessment October 2004*, Honolulu, HI: Asia–Pacific Center for Security Studies, 2004, pp. 8-1–8-8.

Rosecrance, R.N., *Australian Diplomacy and Japan, 1945–1951*, Melbourne: Melbourne University Press, 1962.

Rothstein, R.L., *Alliances and Small Powers*, New York: Columbia University Press, 1968.

Roy, D., 'The sources and limits of Sino–Japanese tensions', *Survival*, vol. 47, no. 2, Summer 2005.

Rubin, B. and Keaney, T. (eds) *US Allies in a Changing World*, London: Frank Cass, 2001.

Ryan, M. (ed.) *Advancing Australia: The Speeches of Paul Keating, Prime Minister*, Sydney: Big Picture Publications, 1995.

Sajima, N., *Japan and Australia: A New Security Partnership?*, working paper no. 292, Canberra: Strategic and Defence Studies Centre, Australian National University, 1996.

Shambaugh, D. (ed.) *Power Shift: China and Asia's New Dynamics*, Berkeley, CA: University of California Press, 2005.

Singh, B., *Arming the Singapore Armed Forces. Trends and Implications*, Canberra papers on strategy and defence no. 153, Canberra: Strategic and Defence Studies Centre, Australian National University, 2003.

——, *Defence Relations between Australia and Indonesia in the Post-Cold War era*, Westport, CT: Greenwood Press, 2002.

Snyder, G.H., 'Alliances, balance and stability', *International Organization*, vol. 45, no. 1, Winter 1991.

Spartalis, P., *The Diplomatic Battles of Billy Hughes*, Sydney: Hale & Iremonger, 1983.

Subianto, L.H., 'Transnational security threats', *The Indonesian Quarterly*, vol. 32, no. 3, 2004.

Tellis, A.J. and Wills, M. (eds) *Strategic Asia 2005–06: Military Modernization in an Era of Uncertainty*, Seattle and Washington, DC: National Bureau of Asian Research, 2005.

Tertrais, B., 'The changing nature of military alliances', *Washington Quarterly*, vol. 27, no 2, Spring 2004.

Thirlwell, M. and Bubalo, A., 'New rules for a new "great game": Northeast Asian energy insecurity and the G-20', Lowy Institute policy brief, Sydney: Lowy Institute for International Policy, November 2006.

Tow, W.T., 'Deputy sheriff or independent ally? Evolving Australian–American ties in an ambiguous world order', *Pacific Review*, vol. 17, no. 2, June 2004.

——, (ed.) *Australian–American Relations: Looking Towards the Next Century*, Melbourne: Macmillan, 1998.

Ungerer, C., 'Communication. Australia's policy responses to terrorism in Southeast Asia', *Global Change, Peace and Security*, vol. 18, no. 3, 2006.

United States Department of Defense, *Annual Report to Congress: Military Power of the People's Republic of China 2006*, Washington, DC: Department of Defense, 2006.

——, *Quadrennial Defense Review Report*, 6 February 2006.

Valencia, M.J., *The Proliferation Security Initiative: Making Waves in Asia*, Adelphi paper no. 376, Abingdon and New York: Routledge, 2005.

Wallander, C., 'Institutional assets and adaptability: NATO after the Cold War', *International Organization*, vol. 54, no. 4, October 2000.

Walt, S.M., 'Why alliances endure or collapse', *Survival*, vol. 39, no. 1, Spring 1997.

——, *The Origins of Alliances*, Ithaca, NY: Cornell University Press, 1987.

Weitsman, P., 'Intimate enemies: the politics of peacetime alliances', *Security Studies*, vol. 7, no. 1, Autumn 1997.

Wesley, M. and Warren, T., 'Wild colonial ploys: currents of thought in Australian foreign policy making', *Australian Journal of Political Science*, vol. 35, no. 1, April 2000.

White, H. and Wainwright, E., *Strengthening our Neighbour: Australia and the Future of Papua New Guinea*, Canberra: Australian Strategic Policy Institute, 2004.

Williams, B. and Newman, A. (eds) *Japan, Australia and Asia–Pacific Security*, London and New York: Routledge, 2006.

Woolcott, R., *The Hot Seat: Reflections on Diplomacy from Stalin's Death to the Bali Bombings*, Sydney: HarperCollins, 2003.

Index

For Product Safety Concerns and Information please contact our EU
representative GPSR@taylorandfrancis.com
Taylor & Francis Verlag GmbH, Kaufingerstraße 24, 80331 München, Germany

www.ingramcontent.com/pod-product-compliance
Lightning Source LLC
Chambersburg PA
CBHW050437280326
41932CB00013BA/2146